XHTML Essentials

Michael Sauers
R. Allen Wyke

Wiley Computer Publishing

John Wiley & Sons, Inc.

NEW YORK · CHICHESTER · WEINHEIM · BRISBANE · SINGAPORE · TORONTO

This book is dedicated to Shawna Ann, Julianne, Mitchell, and Dylan. The future is yours to command, make it bow to your will.

—Michael Sauers

I would like to dedicate this book to Chad and Marsha. They have both had to overcome incredible odds and deal with unnecessary distractions, but their willpower and dedication to do the right thing has kept their heads up, not only as respectable people, but as great parents as well.

—R. Allen Wyke

Published by John Wiley & Sons, Inc., New York

Published simultaneously in Canada.

Library of Congress Cataloging-in-Publication Data:

ISBN 0-471-41764-5

Printed in the United States of America.

10 9 8 7 6 5 4 3 2 1

Contents

About the Authors

Michael Sauers is the Internet Trainer for the Bibliographical Center for Research, a multistate nonprofit regional library consortium. Based in Aurora, Colorado, Michael travels extensively throughout 12 states for BCR training librarians and others how to use the Internet and its related technologies. His classes, offered live and online, range in topic from basic Internet use to Web design and accessible technology. Michael has given presentations at national conferences and has assisted the Library of Congress with the design of its Thomas Web site.

Prior to joining BCR in 1997, Michael was an independent consultant and trainer in Las Vegas, Nevada. He has also worked for the New York State Library and the New York State Assembly. He earned his Masters of Library Science from the University at Albany (SUNY) in 1995.

Michael has published three previous titles, *Mastering Microsoft Outlook 2000* (Quessing Courseware Corporation, 1999), *Microsoft FrontPage 2000 Advanced Topics* (Quessing Courseware Corporation, 2000) and *Using the Internet as a Reference Tool: A How-To-Do-It Manual for Librarians* (Neal-Schuman, Inc., 2001). His next project is *A Collector's Guide to Dean Koontz* for Cemetery Dance Publications.

R. Allen Wyke is Vice President of Research and Development at Engage, an e-marketing solutions company. where he works with product managers, product marketers, and engineerers to test, research, and prototype new products in both the online and offline worlds. He has also developed intranet Web pages for a leading telecommunications and networking company, and has worked on several Internet sites.

A resident of Durham, North Carolina, Allen is the author of roughly a dozen books on various Internet technologies, including Perl, JavaScript, PHP, and XML related standards. In the past, he has also written the monthly "Webmaster" column for *Unix Insider*, and a weekly column, "Integrating Windows and Unix," for ITworld.com.

Introduction

HTML is dead. Unfortunately, many Web designers don't know it yet. In 2000, HTML 4.01 was officially replaced with XHTML 1.0, a much more flexible, XML-based markup language for developing documents for publication on Web sites. With XHTML, gone are many of the problems that HTML developers have complained about over the years, regarding primarily the inability to develop a page that displays the same on all browsers.

By the time you finish this book, not only will you be prepared to write all of your new Web documents in XHTML, but you will also be able to quickly and easily convert your existing HTML document to XHTML, making them ready for future Web publishing technology advances.

Overview of the Book and Technology

XHTML offers many benefits over HTML: a better fit into an XML environment, increased separation of content from style,and the capability to have documents appear the same when displayed in different browsers on different platforms. XHTML does not come without a price, however; XHTML requires that you write clean and organized code. And though, as just stated, HTML has been replaced by XHTML, HTML will continue for some time to be a viable language for Web publishing, meaning you must learn how to transition from HTML to XHTML.

This book, then, is designed with two primary purposes: to introduce you to XHTML and to teach you how to make the transition from HTML to XHTML. To that end, the book details the workings of XHTML and compares it to HTML. Along the way, it explains the benefits of moving to an XHTML environment from an HTML environment. This book also takes a look at future developments, including XForms and the modularization of XHTML.

NOTE This book is based on a workshop that Michael offers to librarians in 12 states. However, it goes far beyond what that workshop covers; and, with the help of Allen's Web development experience, it explains the how and the why, and offers hands-on experience as well.

How This Book Is Organized

The first time through the book, we recommend that you read the chapters in the order they are given, because each chapter builds on the material and concepts presented in the previous chapters. You'll find examples and/or step-by-step exercises in each chapter, to help reinforce the topics covered. In Chapter 6, "Forms," a single exercise leads you through the development of a form ready for user input. In Chapter 4, "Converting and Validating XHTML," you'll be walked through the steps necessary for conversion. This is supplemented by a conversion exercise that illustrates not only the original document but also demonstrates the steps involved and the intended result.

In addition to the exercises and examples, this book details how to use the technology properly. Many, if not most, of the Web sites written in HTML are poorly coded and poorly designed, from a technology standpoint. In this book, when there is a "correct" method of doing something, we highlight it and explain why it is correct. Through this method, you'll learn how to write XHTML properly.

The chapters are structured as follows:

Chapter 1, "Setting the Stage," lays the groundwork for the book, providing overviews, definitions, and comparisons of XHTML to other popular scripting languages—in particular HTML. Comparisons are also made to SGML, the foundation language of HTML. This chapter stresses that XHTML combines the ease of HTML with the flexibility of XML.

You will also learn in Chapter 1 that HTML will slowly give way to XHTML, and that this trend will be motivated by the expansion of Web publishing to include platforms other than Web browsers on PCs, such as the Palm VII and WAP devices

Chapter 2, "Getting Started with XHTML," focuses on making the transition from HTML to XHTML, with special emphasis on the fact that "lazy" syntax is not tolerated in XHTML. You will learn that to write successful XHTML documents means writing them according to very strict syntax dictated by the XHTML 1.0 Recommendation. You will also learn in this chapter that there are actually three "official" versions of XHTML: Strict, Transitional, and Frameset, each available as an XML DTD.

Chapter 3, "Creating Documents," itemizes which browsers support XHTML today, and how to update your pages to be XHTML-compliant. Accessibility issues are explored, including font and color elements and their usage; the official W3C accessibility guidelines are listed as well. The parent-child relationship is described, with stress on how it affects the structure and function of an XHTML document. Also examined in this chapter are flow objects (including block flow objects and inline flow objects), document trees, nodes, parents, children, and siblings. Finally, to provide insight, the process by which an XHTML document is parsed by a Web browser is illustrated in various schematics and tables.

Chapter 4, "Converting and Validating XHTML," will involve you in hands-on exercises for creating, editing, and enhancing XHTML documents. You will take existing HTML files (provided on the bundled disc) and convert them to basic XHTML, testing their functionality in today's popular browsers. You will then enhance the sample XHTML document to take advantage of additional XHTML functionality.

You will then be ready to create XHTML documents from scratch, working completely within the framework of XHTML, with a focus on the tags (such as the XML and Doctype statements), attributes (xmlns), and syntactical conventions (strict adherence to the official 1.0 Recommendation) that are unique to XHTML. This material will then be contrasted to those same characteristics of HTML.

Chapter 4 also teaches the steps necessary to convert existing HTML documents into the new XHTML format. Though both manual and automatic processes will be discussed, the manual method is stressed since it is the best way to lean the new coding method and it does not require software to be loaded on the user's machine.

Chapter 4 also covers XHTML validation, specifically why validation is necessary in XHTML and wasn't in HTML. Rarely is any conversion from HTML to XHTML perfect on the first try, and validation is the best way to find mistakes. Both Web-based and local software methods are discussed, with stress on the Web-based method, as it does not require software to be loaded on the user's machine.

Chapter 5, "Tables," emphasizes the role and applicability of tables to common publishing issues, such as the presentation of tabular data and the logical and/or aesthetic layout of page content. Table functionality between HTML, XHTML, and CSS is explored, while you learn to create them, via explanations, examples, and exercises. The table examples explain how to develop rows and columns; add stylized structure to a table; manipulate borders and frames; use cell padding and cell spacing; implement CSS padding properties; and add background colors, cell colors, and captions.

Chapter 6, "Forms," introduces readers to the next generation of forms. It explains how forms have progressed in XHTML from their use in HTML. The chapter also includes a discussion of XForms, the future of forms in XHTML.

Chapter 6 also explores form automation, with a focus on input options and form field types. The ability to link form output to a CGI script running on a Web server is demonstrated and explained. Although a thorough knowledge of a language in which to write CGI scripts, typically Perl, is necessary to tap the power of forms in the real world, you will get the necessary hands-on experience to test client/server interaction.

Chapter 7, "Frames," compares the Frames DTD to the strict and transitional DTDs. Frames as implemented in HTML are contrasted with the new XML functionality afforded by XHTML 1.0. Because frames can be a complex and often confusing topic, a discussion on the concepts, both technical and programmatic, will be covered.

Chapter 8, "Cascading Style Sheets," gives detailed definitions and explanations of CSS and its elements. Comparisons are made between the Level 1 and Level 2 Recommendations, spotlighting the functionality new to CSS2. Positioning, linking, local styles, alternate fonts, inheritance, colors, hex codes, background textures, and images all are covered, including how to integrate these features into complete XHTML documents. In addition, local versus external style sheets are discussed and compared as a matter of style; and types of selectors, descendants, adjacent siblings (in the hierarchy model), and attributes are examined.

Classes and IDs, and their role in enabling programmers to create their own custom styles, are also explained, featuring a discussion of inline implementation of Class and ID, including <div> and <span>. Chapter 8 also addresses the nuances of popular browser support and offers some insight to CSS Level 3.

Chapter 9, "JavaScript," lays a foundation for the understanding of how JavaScript, a popular scripting language, interacts within Web pages. You'll be introduced to the important objects, methods, and properties that, you as a Web developer, should be concerned with.

Chapter 10, "Scripting XHTML Documents," walks you through the processes of accessing and controlling events in Web documents. Now that browsers support the

Document Object Model (DOM), you will see a shift in how dynamic HTML is coded. No longer will you see a combination of a poor document model, often referred to as DOM Level 0, and some hacked scripting methods. Scripting XHTML represents the combination of XHTML, DOM, and a scripting language such as JavaScript.

Chapter 11, "Metadata," explores the concepts and popular implementations of metadata on the Web. A mental model of "data about data" is provided to help you conceptualize the descriptive role of metadata—including the potential relationship between documents. We'll also explore the role of metadata in relation to popular search engines in the context of the <meta> element. This is followed by detailed discussions of namespaces and MIME types as they pertain to the XHTML language.

Chapter 12, "Events," explains what happens within a browser as it loads, interacts, and displays an XHTML document. We cover how these events can be captured and used; and we end the chapter with a discussion of XHTML Events, the next generation of XHTML document events.

Chapter 13, "XHTML Basic," describes a recently released standard that includes the minimal set of modules required to be an XHTML Host Language. It includes numerous modules—image, form, basic table, object, and others—that represent the basic items needed to publish many types of documents. Basic was designed for Web clients that do not intend to support the full set of XHTML features—for example mobile phones, PDAs, pagers, and set-top boxes. The document type is rich enough for content authoring.

Chapter 14, "Looking Ahead," predicts what the future will hold for XHTML, alerting you what you can expect next in the world of XHTML.

And because no XHTML book would be complete without a quick reference section. Appendix A, "XHTML Element Quick Reference," covers all of the elements in the 1.0 Recommendation, and contains a list of elements and attributes in an easy-to-access fashion.

Appendix B, "Resources," lists a multitude of XHTML resources, from specification details to design recommendations.

Who Should Read This Book

This book is designed for all Web authors who have a basic familiarity with HTML and its use in designing Web-based documents. Those with a limited knowledge of HTML, or who lack formal instruction in HTML, are encouraged to work through the book chapter by chapter, as the early part of the book introduces you to the underlying concepts of both XHTML and HTML. This will give you the background you need to get the most from the later chapters.

If you are more experienced in HTML, you may feel confident enough to skip the introductory chapters, but we recommend giving them at least a quick review, because though most self-educated Web developers know *how* things work, often they do not understand *why*. Moreover, over the past several years, the terminology has "warped" somewhat, and by reading the introductory chapters, you will be sure to be "on the same page" when it comes to the terminology used in the book and the reasons why certain topics are presented the way they are.

Tools You Will Need

You will need three tools to work through this book:

Standards-compliant browser. As of the writing of this book, the browser that meets most standards is Microsoft's Internet Explorer 5.5. As Netscape 6.x becomes more stable, it will become a viable alternative. Note, however, that in one chapter of the book, we use the Amaya browser from the W3C (www.w3.org/Amaya/). Although this browser is not required for the rest of the book, we do recommend that you install it, especially if you plan to do serious XHTML development.

Text editor. In most cases, a basic program such as Notepad (Windows) or Simple-Text (Mac) will do the job. However, for converting and validating, it would be a good idea to use something that numbers your lines of code. For this we use, and therefore recommend, HTML-Kit (www.chami.com/html-kit). This editor numbers lines, spell-checks, validates code , and offers many other wonderful features.

Internet connection. Most of the exercises in book can be done without connecting to the Internet: You can save your work on your local computer and view it offline in your browser. But when we convert and validate code, we use the W3C's HTML Validator; therefore you need to be connected to access it.

What's on the CD-ROM/Disk/Web Site

The CD contains all of the code examples in this book, including all of the sample files used in the HTML-to-XHTML conversion exercises. Although it is easy to just look at the code as printed in the book and/or copy it off the CD, we strongly recommend that you take the time to type it in yourself. This will give you the hands-on experience that will serve you well while learning XHTML.

Also on the CD is the Amaya browser from the W3C. Installation programs for both WinNT/2000 and Win95/98/Me are in the folder named "Amaya." If you need the installation files for other platforms, or need more detailed installation instructions, please go to www.w3.org/Amaya/.

The companion Web site contains links to additional online resources and reference documentation.

Up Next

Now that all the preliminaries are complete let's dive right into Chapter 1 and do some basic review.

Acknowledgments

I would like to thank the following individuals for their help and support: Allen for being in the right place at the right time, exactly when and where I needed him; Curt Robbins at Quessing Courseware Corp., for setting all this up in the first place; and Cary Sullivan and Christina Berry at Wiley for their eternal patience.

Last, a special thanks to my wife Denice who, despite all my quirks and faults, insists on loving me no matter what.

—*Michael Sauers*

On the publishing side, I would like to thank Bob Kern of TIPS Publishing and my co-author, Michael, for their professionalism, hard work, and overall support in the proposing and writing of this book. I would also like to thank Cary Sullivan, who has been nothing short of an absolutely fabulous acquisitions editor; and Christina Berry, who has done an excellent job developing the book and keeping us focused. Additionally, I would like to thank everyone at Wiley who worked on the book and helped make sure it was the best it could be.

Finally, I would like to thank the wonderful woman in my life, J, whose love and devotion make every day easy.

—*R. Allen Wyke*

Introduction to XHTML

Setting the Stage

Welcome to the eXtensible Hypertext Markup Language, XHTML, the next stage in Web page construction. This chapter sets the stage for our journey through XHTML. We start with a brief history of HTML, covering why it was developed, and the many stages it has gone through in the past decade. We then take a look at XML, a necessary component in the development of XHTML. Finally, we discuss why XHTML was developed and it's advantages over HTML.

A Brief History of HTML

The Hypertext Markup Language (HTML) was the brainchild of Tim Berners-Lee, a particle physicist at the Conseil Européen pour la Recherche Nucléaire (CERN) laboratories in Switzerland. At CERN in the late 1980s, Berners-Lee recognized that he needed to access a significant number of electronic documents on a regular basis; moreover, many of these documents referenced other documents.

Berners-Lee was familiar with the Standardized General Markup Language (SGML), a method for coding the structure of electronic documents, which had been around since the early 1980s, but knew that it was too complex for what he wanted to do: code and link his documents. He wanted a system that would allow for the simple coding of such documents, a way to transfer those documents through their networks, and the capability to link documents. Berners-Lee developed HTML to code the documents and the HyperText Transport Protocol (HTTP) for moving those documents. His system was launched by CERN in 1991.

HTML 1.0

The first version of HTML was actually quite limited. It established the method of tags, elements, and attributes that are used today. The elements included in HTML 1.0 were title, anchor, isindex, plaintext, listing, paragraph, headings, address, highlighting, definition lists, unordered lists, and menus. The following three symbols were also included: <, >, and &. Special characters (those you can't type on a keyboard) were not.

This first version did not even include images. It was designed purely for displaying and linking text-based documents in text-only browsers, as shown in the following code:

```
<TITLE>A sample HTML 1.0 document</TITLE>
<H1>Hello world!</H1>
<P>This is an example of a document written in HTML 1.0
<A href="next.html">next document</A>
```

As restricted as version 1.0 was, it was clear that HTML had great possibilities, and extensions for future HTML versions were quickly recommended. These included a body tag, document linking (not hyperlinks), dates, highlighting, base addresses, fixed-width text with anchors and indenting, ordered lists, link types, character entities (special characters), and comments. Many of these suggestions were addressed quickly. Others, like highlighting, would never appear in HTML (though they would later be implemented in cascading style sheets—CSS).

As the Web and the first version of HTML became popular methods for presenting and linking data on the Internet, it became clear that the development of HTML was too large a project for one man to handle. Thus, further development of HTML was handed over to the recently formed organization, the World Wide Web Consortium (W3C), an international group created specifically to recommend standards for all Web-related technologies.

HTML 2.0

It took four years for the next version of HTML to gain approval by the W3C. The release of version 2.0, in 1996, proved that significant steps had been taken to implement many of the recommendations made following the release of the first version; in addition, many other new ideas had been incorporated, including:

■ The text/HTML mime type was added.

■ HTML documents were specified as such with the <html> element, then divided into two sections by the <head> and <body> elements.

■ Support for base addresses with the base attribute, and linked documents with the <link> attribute, were added.

■ The capability to add descriptive information about the document through the <meta> element was added.

■ Physical markup elements were added, including <pre>, <blockquote>, <ol>, <dir>, <b>, <i>, and <u>.

■ Logical markup elements were added, including <cite>, <code>, <em>, <kbd>, <samp>, <strong>, and <var>.

■ Content could be broken up using the <br> and <hr> elements.

■ Using the <img> element, it became possible to insert graphic files into documents.

■ Forms were added so that authors could collect information from their users, then process the submitted data.

■ Character entities were added for inserting special characters into the content of a document.

In short, HTML 2.0 bore a close resemblance to the HTML we use today. Authors were given many more ways of formatting content visually, including the addition of images. This was important because graphical browsers such as NCSA Mosaic and Cello had started to come on the market. Clearly, now that browsers could render text in multiple ways, and display graphics, code was needed to take advantage of that software.

Following is a sample document written in HTML 2.0.

```
<html>
<head>
<TITLE>A sample HTML 2.0 document</TITLE>
</head>
<body>
<h1>Hello world!</h1>
<p>This is an example of a<br>
document written in HTML 2.0
<hr>
<pre>Here is some preformatted text.</pre>
<IMG src="Image.gif">
<a href="next.html">next document</a>
<p>&copy;1996, Michael Sauers
</body>
</html>
```

Still, authors wanted more from HTML; at the same time, browser makers decided that they didn't want to wait for another standard to be developed, so the major browser makers (Microsoft and Netscape) decided to extend HTML on their own. This led to elements and attributes that were supported in one browser but not another. This only helped to further frustrate authors.

HTML+/3.0

In 1993 and 1996, respectively, HTML+ and HTML 3.0 were both submitted to the W3C. Both were proposals to extend the current HTML 2.0 standard. Though neither was given final approval as a standard, they marked the earliest appearances of some of the future features included as part of the HTML standards. Some of these features became part of the next standard, such as tables; others did not, such as the <fig> element, implemented to create figures (images with captions).

During this time period (1993–1996), the "browser wars" heated up. Netscape's Navigator had become the dominant browser; based on NCSA's Mosaic, it would quickly replace its predecessor. Quick on Navigator's heels, Microsoft released Internet Explorer. In the effort by these two companies to capture market share, each began to offer newer and better features aimed at the HTML author. Each added support for features not in HTML 2.0; some of these worked in both browsers, others in only one or the other. The result was a no-win situation for both the browser makers and HTML authors; the latter became frustrated by the schism. Taking matters in their own hands, many started posting "best viewed with" or "designed for" messages on their sites.

Finally, the W3C decided the best approach was to regroup, take all the browser makers' "suggestions" into consideration, and incorporate them in the next version of HTML.

HTML 3.2

HTML 3.2 became an official W3C recommendation in January 1997. According to the specification, "HTML 3.2 aims to capture recommended practice as of early '96, and as such be used as a replacement for HTML 2.0." In other words, the W3C wanted to reclaim HTML as a standard, yet try to address all that the browser makers had been creating on their own.

The following features were added in HTML 3.2:

- <style> allows for the inclusion of style code in an HTML document. Usually cascading style sheets (CSS).

- <script> allows for the inclusion of scripting code in an HTML document. Usually JavaScript.

- Color (via the #nnnnnn format) allows for the specification of colors in a hexidecimal format.

- <div> allows the author to create a logical section of their document to which styles can be applied.

- <center> allows the author to center a section of the document.

- Tables are designed for the tabular presentation of data but also used to create a grid on the page with which page elements can be placed with better accuracy.

- <big>, <small>, <sub>, <sup> are inline elements that created bigger, smaller, subscripted, and superscripted text.

- <applet> allows for the inclusion of Java applications in the document.

- Imagemaps are single images that have hyperlinked hotspots. What happens when the user clicks on the image depends on where on the image the user clicked.

- <font> allows for font control such as the name, size, and color of the font to be displayed.

Version 3.2 incorporated many of the more advanced elements that authors use today, as shown here:

```
<html>
<head>
<TITLE>A sample HTML 3.2 document</TITLE>
</head>
<body>
<center>
<h1>Hello world!</h1>
<p><FONT face="arial">This is an example of a<br>
document written in HTML 3.2</font>
<hr>
<pre>Here is some preformatted text.</pre>
<IMG src="Image.gif">
<a href="next.html">next document</a>
<p><sup>&copy;</sup>1996, Michael Sauers
<center>
</body>
</html>
```

With the release of 3.2, the W3C had rescued HTML from becoming multiple proprietary versions supported by different browsers, but still there were differences, and more work was required to stabilize HTML.

HTML 4.0

Throughout 1997, the W3C worked hard to develop the next version of HTML. Their intention was twofold: to stabilize the propriety extensions added by the browser makers, and to anticipate what they would want and need in the future. This effort raised hopes that browsers would finally start to follow the standards, instead of creating their own. Finally, in December 1997, the HTML 4.0 recommendation was released.

This version added the following features:

- Internalization, allowing documents to be written in any language.

- The <!DOCTYPE> statement was added to allow the author to specify which version of HTML was being used.

- The <object> element standardized the proprietary <embed> element, both of which allowed the author to embed multimedia objects into their documents. For example, either of these elements could have been used to place a MPEG movie or sound file into the body of a document.

- Accessibility features, such as the <abbr> and <acronym> elements, along with the title and lang attributes, were added. These gave the author the ability to associate additional information in the document that might be used by software that assisted users with visual impairments or other accessibility issues.

- Support for style sheets was included to help in separating structure from style. In turn the <font> element was deprecated—that is, it was suggested that its use be limited if not stopped all together.

■ Additional table control was given, with the <colgroup>, <col>, <thead>, <tbody>, and <tfoot> elements. These gave the author the ability to apply style information to sections of tables.

In sum, version 4.0 added no significant features to HTML itself. In most cases, the new features were extensions of the current features or offered support for other resources, such as CSS. Here's an example of HTML 4.0's support of CSS:

```
<!DOCTYPE html PUBLIC "-//W3C/DTD HTML 4.0 Transitional//EN">
<html>
<head>
<TITLE>A sample HTML 4.0 document</TITLE>
<style>
<!--
p {font-family: arial}
-->
</style>
</head>
<body lang=en>
<center>
<h1>Hello world!</h1>
<pThis is an example of a<br>
document written in HTML 4.0
<hr>
<pre>Here is some preformatted text.</pre>
<IMG src="Image.gif">
<a href="next.html">next document</a>
<p><sup>&copy;</sup>1996, Michael Sauers
<center>
</body>
</html>
```

Unlike earlier new versions of HTML, 4.0 was not designed to change HTML, but to improve it by making it more flexible and accessible.

HTML 4.01: The Current Version

In December 1999, the latest version of HTML was released. Dubbed HTML 4.01, its numbering indicated it was not intended to be a significant overhaul of HTML as previous upgrades had been. In this version, the W3C wanted to address some leftover issues and correct some errors in HTML 4.0.

The updates to HTML 4.01 included removal of the mailto: action in forms, and use clarification of many attributes, including type, dir, and name. As such, HTML 4.01 could be likened to a patch released for software updates; and most authors were not affected by it.

The Rise of XML

In 1996, at the height of the browser wars, the W3C had also begun working on the eXtensible Markup Language (XML), a separate project from HTML, but one whose background is important to understanding XHTML, a combination of XML and HTML, and more importantly, the subject of this book.

When the XML project began, the aforementioned SGML, a complex method of structuring text for later processing, was being used primarily for very large projects—those involving millions of pages of documents. Recall that HTML at this time was a severely limited way of formatting documents for transport over the Internet and for display via a Web browser. The W3C's objective in developing XML was to create a markup language that had the power, but not the complexity, of SGML.

Defining XML

The following excerpt from "XML in 10 points" (located at www.w3.org/XML/1999/XML-in-10-points) defines the parameters of XML:

XML is a method for putting structured data in a text file.   For "structured data," think of such things as spreadsheets, address books, configuration parameters, financial transactions, technical drawings, etc. Programs that produce such data often also store it on disk, for which they can use either a binary format or a text format. The latter allows you, if necessary, to look at the data without the program that produced it. XML is a set of rules, guidelines, conventions, whatever you want to call them, for designing text formats for such data, in a way that produces files that are easy to generate and read (by a computer), that are unambiguous, and that avoid common pitfalls, such as lack of extensibility, lack of support for internationalization/localization, and platform-dependency.

XML looks a bit like HTML but isn't HTML.   Like HTML, XML makes use of tags (words bracketed by '<' and '>') and attributes (of the form name="value"), but while HTML specifies what each tag & attribute means (and often how the text between them will look in a browser), XML uses the tags only to delimit pieces of data, and leaves the interpretation of the data completely to the application that reads it. In other words, if you see "<p>" in an XML file, don't assume it is a paragraph. Depending on the context, it may be a price, a parameter, a person, a p... (b.t.w., who says it has to be a word with a "p"?)

XML is text, but isn't meant to be read.   XML files are text files, as I said above, but even less than HTML are they meant to be read by humans. They are text files, because that allows experts (such as programmers) to more easily debug applications; and in emergencies, they can use a simple text editor to fix a broken XML file. But the rules for XML files are much stricter than for HTML. A forgotten tag or a an attribute without quotes makes the file unusable, while in HTML such practice is often explicitly allowed, or at least tolerated. It is written in the official XML specification: applications are not allowed to try to second-guess the creator of a broken XML file; if the file is broken, an application has to stop right there and issue an error.

XML is a family of technologies.   There is XML 1.0, the specification that defines what "tags" and "attributes" are, but around XML 1.0, there is a growing set of optional modules that provide sets of tags & attributes, or guidelines for specific tasks. There is, e.g., Xlink (still in development as of November 1999), which describes a standard way to add hyperlinks to an XML file. XPointer & XFragments (also still being developed) are syntaxes for pointing to parts of an XML document. (An Xpointer is a bit like a URL, but instead of pointing to documents on the Web, it points to pieces of data inside an XML file.) CSS, the style sheet language, is applicable to XML as it is to HTML. XSL (autumn 1999) is the advanced language for expressing style sheets. It is based on XSLT, a transformation language that is often useful outside XSL as well, for rearranging, adding or deleting tags & attributes. The DOM is a standard set of function calls for manipulating XML (and HTML) files from a programming language. XML Namespaces is a specification that describes how you can associate a URL with every single tag and attribute in an XML document. What that URL is used for is up to the application that reads the URL, though. (RDF, W3C's standard for metadata, uses it to link every piece of metadata to a file defining the type of that data.) XML Schemas 1 and 2 help developers to precisely define their own XML-based formats. There are several more modules and tools available or under development. Keep an eye on W3C's technical reports page.

XML is verbose, but that is not a problem.   Since XML is a text format, and it uses tags to delimit the data, XML files are nearly always larger than comparable binary formats. That was a conscious decision by the XML developers. The advantages of a text format are evident, and the disadvantages can usually be compensated at a different level. Disk space isn't as expensive anymore as it used to be, and programs like zip and gzip can compress files very well and very fast. Those programs are available for nearly all platforms (and are usually free). In addition, communication protocols such as modem protocols and HTTP/1.1 (the core protocol of the Web) can compress data on the fly, thus saving bandwidth as effectively as a binary format.

Introducing XHTML

We now arrive at the topic of this book, XHTML, and raise the question, why XHTML? In 1999, with XML on the track to becoming a standard with practical applications, and HTML winding down, the W3C decided that the two should be merged, primarily to address the "increasing range of browser platforms." People today are surfing the Web not only on desktop and laptop computers, but with wireless devices such as PalmPilots, cell phones, televisions, and in many different locations.

Although these devices support HTML, HTML was designed for use on large displays with significant bandwidth. A new language was needed that had additional flexibility for viewing on multiple types of displays and the capability to easily incorporate new developments without the need to rewrite the standard, as was necessary with HTML.

The first specification under the XHTML name was released in January 2000. With this release, version 1.0, the W3C officially stopped supporting HTML as a standard, and shifted its focus to XHTML as the successor to HTML.

Advantages of XHTML

The advantages of XHTML over HTML are significant:

Structure is separated from style. HTML was intended to give documents structure, but it was quickly modified to include many stylistic elements such as font control, color, alignment, and images. Although these ideas worked well in principle, most authors agree that there are many problems associated with such style-based markup. For example, if the user's browser supports a lower number of colors than the computer the document was designed on, the page's presentation tends to deteriorate quickly. With XHTML, style has been mostly removed; structure is given the greatest importance. The presentation of the page is now handled by other technologies, such as CSS.

Additional elements can easily be added. Because XHTML is an XML language, it is easy for an author to create his or her own new elements for inclusion in a document. As long as the browser handles XHTML, the new element should be rendered as the author intended, regardless of the browser in use.

XHTML documents can take advantage of either the HTML or XML Document Object Models (DOM). This gives authors increased flexibility in creating interactive and dynamic documents.

Better support for multiple platforms is available. XHTML documents are focused on structure, so they can be moved from one platform to another without code editing, as was necessary for HTML. Using HTML, generally, different pages had to be written to accommodate different platforms, because the presentation of the document was built into the HTML code. By removing style from the document, no change is required to successfully move from one platform to another.

The XHTML Look

XHTML, for all its advantages over HTML, looks very similar to its predecessor, as the following example shows (it is our sample document rewritten in XHTML):

```
<?xml version="1.0" encoding="UTF-8"?>
<!DOCTYPE html PUBLIC "-//W3C/DTD XHTML 1.0 Transitional//EN"
"http://www.w3.org/TR/xhtml11/DTD/transitional.dtd">
<html xmlns="http://www.w3.org/1999/xhtml" lang="en" xml:lang="en">
<html>
<head>
<title>A sample HTML 1.0 document</title>
<style>
<!--
body {text-align: center}
p    {font-family: arial}
-->
</style>
</head>
<body>
<h1>Hello world!</h1>
<pThis is an example of a<br>
document written in XHTML</p>
<hr>
<pre>Here is some preformatted text.</pre>
<img src="Image.gif">
<a href="next.html">next document</a>
<p><sup>&copy;</sup>1996, Michael Sauers</p>
</body>
</html>
```

Summary

With an understanding of the roots of XHTML, we can move on to explore the details of its structure. We will demonstrate how exactly XHTML differs from HTML, and we can use it to create our documents.

Getting Started with XHTML

The brief introduction in Chapter 1 aside, it is in this chapter that we acquaint you with XHTML. We will discuss basic definitions, coding structure, and the differences between HTML and XHTML. We will also take a look at the basic elements and attributes available in XHTML.

NOTE Some of the material in this chapter will seem like a review to those already conversant in HTML, but as it sets the stage for the rest of the book, we recommend that you take the time to read the entire chapter.

Getting Started

To "get in shape" for working with XHTML, we need to go through a few exercises, to outline the semantics of the language and to point out some differences between XHTML and HTML. This section also addresses *user agents* and their role in rendering XHTML content.

Preparing to Use XHTML

Anyone familiar with coding Web documents in HTML will find XHTML to be very similar. Most of the existing elements and attributes from the HTML 4.01 specification are still available, and can be interpreted by browsers, as HTML authors would expect.

That said, many long-time HTML authors should be aware that certain functions of XHTML are not part of HTML 4.01. For example:

■ Elements must be enclosed within the familiar < and > tags.

■ Elements must always come first, followed by any and/or optional attributes.

Basic Definitions

The following is a brief list of some of the terms used throughout this book:

Tags. The symbols that separate the markup instructions from the document's content. In HTML and XHTML, those symbols are the greater-than (>) and less-than (<) characters. Anything enclosed within those tags will be considered instructions to be interpreted, as opposed to content to be displayed by the browser.

Element. The markup instruction given to the browser. Elements are contained within tags. Some elements are spelled out, such as blockquote; others are abbreviated such as p for paragraph. When it comes to elements, most people do not talk in strict terms. For example, most will say "You need to put a p tag there," when they mean that you need to insert the paragraph element enclosed in tags.

Attribute. Markup that modifies a related element. Attributes always follow the element, are preceded by a space, and are enclosed within the tags.

Displaying versus Parsing

In the heyday of HTML, browsers were designed specifically to display the results of HTML code that they were given. Those browsers displayed HTML through a set of hard-coded rules: for example, "at the appearance of <p>, skip a line and continue displaying the content." Rules such as these allowed HTML authors to take "legal" shortcuts—or, more accurately, to write plain, sloppy code. According to the rule just stated, there is no need to close a paragraph using </p> as long as the next one starts with <p>—the rule will work and the content will be displayed properly.

This is not the case with XML—and remember, XHTML is an XML language. XML documents are *parsed* before being displayed. Since XML languages can contain elements and attributes that the browser may not already be familiar with, all elements and attributes must be checked before being displayed. An XML parser does this checking; it checks to make sure that the document is well formed. (Later in this chapter we will cover all of the requirements of a well-formed document.) Usually, the first difference between XHTML and HTML that authors notice is that, in XHTML, all elements must be properly "closed." Thus, not only must you start each paragraph with <p>, but you must also end each paragraph with </p>. If you do not, the parser will emit an error and stop processing the document.

Parsing a document enforces good document structure. Think about an engineer designing a building. If the building is not structurally sound, there is no reason to build it, let alone live in it. Parsers ensure that documents are structurally sound before they are displayed to the user.

Flow

Another important aspect of XHTML documents is the *flow* (presentation of items appear in the browser in the order in which they occur in the XHTML code). This concept incorporates several theories and approaches, including:

Block-level elements. Block-level elements break the current flow of the document's content by inserting a blank line before continuing.

Inline elements. Inline elements position their content as specified by the element (and any relating style sheet information when available) without breaking the flow of other content.

Containment. Containment specifies where elements may be embedded within other elements. For example, when creating a table, contained within the <table>...</table> elements is one or more pair of table row elements—<tr>...</tr>s. Then, contained within a table row element pair may be one or more table data pairs—<td>...</td>s. In this example, certain element must be contained within others.

There are certain rules that an author must follow when placing block-level and inline elements in an XHTML document. Some of these are similar to those in HTML; others are not. Actually, all of these rules existed in HTML, but because most browsers were so loose in their implementation of the specifications, when these rules were broken, the browser made allowances. In XHTML, this flexibility does not exist.

In XHTML, elements may be embedded or nested within each other, but may not overlap. For example:

```
<h1><a href="link.html">content</h1></a>
```

illustrates an overlapping set of elements, whereas

```
<h1><a href="link.html">content</a></h1>
```

shows the correct way to write this code.

Trees, Nodes, and the Parent/Child Relationship

Again, the purpose of XHTML is to establish the document's structure, a structure that can be viewed in three different ways: as a tree, as nodes, or as a parent/child relationship.

All XHTML documents are created as trees, starting with the root element <html>. From there the tree branches out based upon the elements contained within the root element.

NOTE In some documentation you will see the term *node* used to describe a branch, thus making this view the same as the tree view.

The Amaya browser from the W3C allows us to view the tree structure of our document in a semigraphical way. First we see the root element <html> at the top of the page. From there extend two branches: <head> and <body>. Within the body are many sub-branches, including <h1>, <h2>, and <ol>. Within our ordered list are two more branches, each an <li>. Following is the code example:

```
<?xml version="1.0" encoding="UTF-8"?>
<!DOCTYPE html PUBLIC "-//W3C//DTD XHTML 1.0 Transitional//EN"
     "http://www.w3.org/TR/xhtml11/DTD/xhtml11-transitional.dtd">
<html xmlns="http://www.w3.org/1999/xhtml" xml:lang="en" lang="en-US">
<head>
<title>Editions and Printings</title>
</head>
<body>
<h1>Editions and Printings, How to Tell the Difference:<br />
a guide for book collectors<br />
by Michael Sauers</h1>
<hr />
<h2 id="toc">Table of Contents</h2>
<ol>
<li><a href="#intro">Introduction</a></li>
<li><a href="#def">Definitions</a></li>a
</ol>
<hr />
<h2 id="intro">1. Introduction</h2>
<p><span class="cap">I</span> have been collecting "modern firsts"
(there's a confusing term already but I'll get to that later) for over
15 years now (including as a bookseller and as a librarian) and have
come to think of myself as, not really an expert, but one with a good
eye for telling the difference between editions and printings.</p>
<p>Based on my more recent experiences with online auctions (eBay, Ama-
zon.com,
Yahoo, and their like) I find that many other collectors are not very
clear on just what "edition" means, how to tell a first, why a first is
significant, and the difference between an "edition" and a "print-
ing."</p>
<p>Through textual explaination and many visual examples, this document
is
designed to be a primer for the budding book collector, one looking to
take his or her collecting to the next level (usually meaning your
budget for a single book will have to increase from two-digit dollar
amounts to three- or even four-digit dollar amounts.)</p>
<p><a href="#toc">Table of contents</a></p>
<hr />
<h2 id="def">2. Definitions</h2>
<p><span class="cap">B</span>efore I go any further and get into the
core of this document--editions, printings and the ever-elusive
"first"--I'd like to get some terms and their definitions out of the
way. This will help you understand the rest of this document.</p>
<dl>
```

```
<dt>modern</dt>
<dd>The idea of a "modern" book has many varying time frames
depending on whom you ask. Some collectors view anything published
in the twentieth century and later as a "modern" book. Here I am going
to
take a significantly more narrow view on this term. For this
document, I will discuss books only from the 1970s onward. This
keeps me to a more limited set of circumstances for my later
examples. (I pick the 1970s because during that decade the ISBN was
established.) If your book was published prior to 1970s you can
still use this document, but the further back you go, the less my
comments will apply.</dd>
<dt>trade</dt>
<dd>A book published for sale by the bookselling trade. Typically,
books only found in bookstores.</dd>
<dt>mass-market</dt>
<dd>Books published to be sold anywhere. Most paperbacks are
mass-market, as they can be found not only in bookstores but in
grocery stores and department stores.</dd>
<dt>limited</dt>
<dd>Books published in severely limited quantities (usually in the
hundreds,) typically signed by the author and either numbered or
lettered. Usually only available for purchase directly through
the publisher; they are not generally available in bookstores</dd>
<dt>book club edition (BCE)</dt>
<dd>Version of a book offered specifically to members of a
particular subscription-based club. These books will be discussed
in their own section of this document.</dd>
</dl>
<p>More book-related definitions can be found at the abebooks.com
<a
href="http://www.abebooks.com/cgi/abe.exe/routera%5E_pr=glossary">Glos-
sary
of Terms.</a></p>
<p><a href="#toc">Table of contents</a></p>
<hr />
<p>&copy; MMI, Michael Sauers<br />
Last Updated: 17 January 2001
</p>
</body>
</h
```

Figure 2.1 shows this XHTML document as a tree via the Amaya browser.

I find looking at the structure of an XHTML document as a series of parent/child relationships to be the most convenient, since it works along with the concept of a family tree. Thus, in our previous example, <head> and <body> are both children of <html>; <head> has only one child, <title>. However, <body> has many children, including <h1>, <h2>, <ol>, and multiple <p>s. In turn, <ol> has two children, both <li>s, thereby making them grandchildren of <body>.

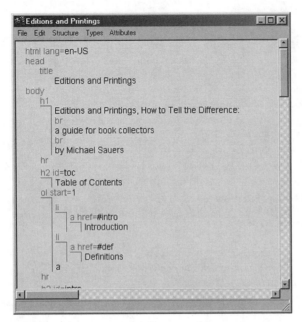

Figure 2.1   Our sample XHTML document shown as a tree via the Amaya browser.

Telling the Difference between HTML and XHTML

Although XHTML is very similar to HTML, it is important to keep in mind that XHTML is an XML derivative and therefore has significant differences. It's also important not to misconstrue these differences as minor, for they are at the heart of what an author needs to learn in order to take advantage of XHTML.

To begin this discussion, we introduce new elements that HTML authors may not be familiar with: <thead>, <tfoot>, <fieldset>, and <legend>. The first two deal with XHTML tables, the second two with XHTML forms. However, you will not get to know these elements in depth until later in the chapter, because we have something more important to explain first.

Learning the Five Major Changes

With the complete rewriting of the language came five major changes with which you, the HTML author, must familiarize yourself before attempting to write in XHTML. Failure to do so will cause your page to display incorrectly, if at all, for the parser will emit an error and stop displaying the document. Here are the rules:

- Elements must adhere to case-sensitivity.
- All elements must be closed properly.
- Empty elements must be closed.

■ Attribute values must be enclosed within quotation marks.

■ All attributes must be fully formed.

These changes were introduced to meet XML's requirement that documents be *well formed*. This requirement ensures that your documents can be displayed on the greatest number of platforms. But these changes were implemented to address a more far-reaching issue: to enable Web authors to produce documents that display the same in two different browsers. By enforcing such strict coding rules, it is hoped that authors will learn to write clean code as a matter of course, thus reducing the risk of different browsers displaying the same code in different ways.

Let's continue by addressing these five rules in turn.

Elements Must Adhere to Case-Sensitivity

In HTML, authors are free to type elements in upper- or lowercase—as long as they are spelled properly, they will work. For example, the following are three ways the body element can be written in HTML:

```
<body>
<BODY>
<bOdY>
```

But as a subset of XML, in XHTML, all elements are *case-sensitive*. Therefore, the preceding examples in XHTML would be three *different* elements. According to the XHTML Document Type Definition (DTD), all elements must be written in lowercase in order to achieve the same result that you would expect if you were writing an HTML document. Consequently, here, only the first example is a valid XHTML element.

All Elements Must Be Closed Properly

Many HTML authors, especially those self-taught using early versions of HTML, learned that many elements did not need to be closed in order for them to work properly. The two classic examples are the paragraph element <p> and the line item element <li>. HTML authors who hand-coded their documents used any and all shortcuts available to cut down on unnecessary typing, as shown here:

```
<p>This is a paragraph.
<p>This is another paragraph.
<ul>
<li>Item #1
<li>Item #2
<li>Item #3
</ul>
```

But as you know by now, for an XHTML document to be well formed, all elements must be closed. Therefore, </p> and </li> are no longer optional; they are now required. The following is the XHTML version of the preceding HTML code snippet:

```
<p>This is a paragraph.</p>
<p>This is another paragraph.</p>
<ul>
```

```
<li>Item #1</li>
<li>Item #2</li>
<li>Item #3</li>
</ul>
```

Empty Elements Must Be Closed

If all elements must be properly closed, how does an author deal with empty HTML elements, those that do not have matching close elements? The two most common examples of empty elements in HTML are <img> and <br>. XHTML requires that empty elements be closed by inserting a slash (/) after the element itself. Thus, in XHTML, the HTML <br> becomes <br />, and <img src="filename"> becomes <img src="filename" />. The following HTML code illustrates two empty elements:

```
<p>Within this paragraph there is a<br>
line break. Then there is an image.</p>
<img src="logo.gif">
```

Here is the XHTML version:

```
<p>Within this paragraph there is a<br />
line break. Then there is an image.</p>
<img src="logo.gif" />
```

Attribute Values Must Be Enclosed within Quotation Marks

HTML authors recognized that they could often get away with leaving out quotation marks from around attribute values. For example, in HTML <p align=center> would be accepted by most browsers. On the other hand, if the value were a number, or contained a space, many browsers would not accept the value unless it had been enclosed in quotation marks.

XML (and XHTML) settles the issue by requiring that all attribute values be enclosed within quotation. The following HTML code shows unquoted attribute values:

```
<p align=right>This is a right-justified paragraph.</p>
<table width=600>
```

Here is the XHTML version:

```
<p align="right">This is a right-justified paragraph.</p>
<table width="600">
```

All Attributes Must Be Fully Formed

Of the five new XHTML requirements, this is the one that most authors find the hardest to accept: *all* attributes must be fully formed.

In HTML, there are attributes that do not seem to have values. For example, the noshade attribute on horizontal rules:

```
<hr noshade>
```

tells the browser to display a horizontal rule on the screen, and to remove the 3D effect on the line and display it as a solid line. Here, the noshade attribute seems to have no value since it has no options. In actuality, there is a value for noshade—noshade. In HTML, the browser will assume, based on the absence of a stated value, that the value is the only available value, which in this case is the same as the attribute name.

XHTML does not allow for this assumption. Even if an attribute has only one possible value available, it must be explicitly stated. Therefore, the same code in XHTML must read as follows:

```
<hr noshade="noshade">
```

NOTE Don't forget, you must also quote the attribute's value.

Change Summary

At first, many of these rules will be quite an annoyance as you begin working with your first XHTML documents or converting your existing HTML documents to XHTML. As you become comfortable working with the new requirements, however, they will become second nature to you. In Chapter 4, "Converting and Validating XHTML," you will learn how to convert your documents and validate your XHTML code to ensure that it follows these new rules.

Supporting Agents

You may be wondering at this point, why bother to learn these new rules, since, as browser and Web history has shown, whenever a new language comes along, most browsers are slow at best to adapt and support the new language. Well, here is the good news that should make up for the annoyance of having to adhere to new rules: Because XHTML is just a reformulated version of the most recent HTML specification, if the browser supported your documents in HTML, it will support them in XHTML. So, if one of your pages worked as you designed it in its original HTML version, it will still work when you convert it to XHTML.

There is a caveat to the promise of conversion ease: It is dependent upon the browser's level of support for the elements and attributes in HTML (and related technologies such as style sheets and scripting). In many cases, this book will address the latest official code from the standards, and these elements and attributes may be new to you even if they are not new to XHTML. This is because of the lack of browser support for the standards. That means that if the browser did not support the HTML version of a particular element or attribute, it will not support the XHTML version of that element or attribute.

As of early 2001, the browsers listed here (with their Web addresses) offer the best support for the latest standards:

Microsoft Internet Explorer 5.x	www.microsoft.com/windows/ie/default.htm
Netscape Navigator 6.x	www.netscape.com/download/index.html
Opera 5	www.opera .com
Amaya 4.x	www.w3.org/Amaya/

GENERAL SYNTAX

Like HTML, XHTML was not designed to be a complex and complicated language. On the contrary, the language is meant to be relatively easy to learn. To make it so, we must follow up on certain basic syntactical rules that we have touched on earlier.

To that end, in the following list, we point out very specific rules that must be followed:

Element	Syntax
<element>content</element>	Syntax for an element with no attributes.
<p>*content*</p>	An element with no attributes
<element attribute="*value*">content</element>	Syntax for an element with an attribute
<p align="center">*content*</p>	An element with one attribute
<td valign="top" width="400">*content*</td>	An element with multiple attributes
<element />	Syntax for an empty element with no attributes
content *content*	An empty element with no attributes
<element attribute="value" />	Syntax for an empty element with one attribute
<img src="*filename.ext*" />	An empty element with one attribute
<hr noshade="noshade" width="50%" />	An empty element with multiple attributes

Basic Elements

This section offers a brief overview of the elements contained in XHTML, to include those that will be maintained for the foreseeable future. We have also included brief descriptions of the attributes unique to the particular element being presented.

NOTE Certain elements that have been deprecated—most of which are better dealt with in the context of CSS—are not included here.

Structural Markup

Structural markup includes the elements that establish the base-line structure of the document. These elements do not control the actual presentation of the document as the user sees it.

<html>...</html>

The <html> element is the root of all XHTML documents. It contains all other elements within the document, as shown here:

```
<html>
<head>
<title>document title</title>
</head>
<body>
document content...
</body>
</html>
```

`<head>...</head>`

The <head> element is typically the first after the root element in all XHTML documents. The <head> contains information about the document as a whole, including title and metadata information. The <head> element may also include style and scripting information. Most other elements, when included within the <head>, will be ignored. The following is an example of the <head> element:

```
<html>
<head>
<title>document title</title>
</head>
<body>
```

`<title>...</title>`

The <title> element appears only within the <head> of a document. The browser places the content of the <title> in its title bar at the top of the window. When creating a title, you should keep in mind the following points: The title should be descriptive of the document, shorter is generally better than longer; and the <title> content will be used as the text for a browser bookmark or "favorite." Here's an example <title> element:

```
<head>
<title>Introduction to XHTML</title>
</head>
```

`<meta />`

The <meta /> element contains information about the document for use in the indexing of the document by search engines, and for controlling how the browser may load the document. The <meta /> element must appear within the <head> of a document or it will be ignored. Note that <meta /> is an empty element and therefore requires the closing slash (/) within the tags. This element is covered in detail in Chapter 11, "Metadata," the following is an example:

```
<head>
<meta name="keywords" content="XHTML, HTML, XML" />
</head>
```

`<base />`

The <base /> element allows you to specify the location from which all other relative links or targets are to be determined. If this is not specified, then all relative links will be determined based upon the location of the current document. The <base /> element must appear within the <head> of a document. Like <meta /> just described, <base /> is an empty element and must therefore contain the closing slash. The <base /> element has the following attributes:

href="URL". Used in establishing a URL from which all other relative URLs in the document should be based, as shown here:

```
<head>
<base href="http://www.doamin.com/" />
</head>
```

target="framename". Used in establishing a default target when dealing with a frameset document. Following is an example (this is covered in more detail in Chapter 7, "Frames"):

```
<head>
<base target="right" />
</head>
```

<body>...</body>

The <body> element contains all of the content of the document to be displayed within the browser window. Thus, <body> is typically placed within the document after the </head> element and concludes before </html>, as shown here:

```
</head>
<body>
document content to be displayed in the browser window
</body>
</html>
```

<address>...</address>

The <address> element is typically used to contain information about the author and copyright of the document that should be displayed on the screen. As a block-level element similar to <p>, most browsers will display the content of <address> in italics. Any stylistic changes you may wish to make can be done through the use of CSS. Following is an example of the <address> element (see Figure 2.2 for the resulting browser display):

```
<address>
&copy;2001 Michael Sauers<br />
<ahref=http://www.webpan.com/msauers/">http://www.webpan.com/msauers/</a>
</address>
```

<blockquote>...</blockquote>

Typically in the publishing industry, when an author quotes a source and that content is more than three lines long, the quoted content is taken out of the main document content and indented on both sides. This is known as a *block quote* or *extract*. In XHTML,

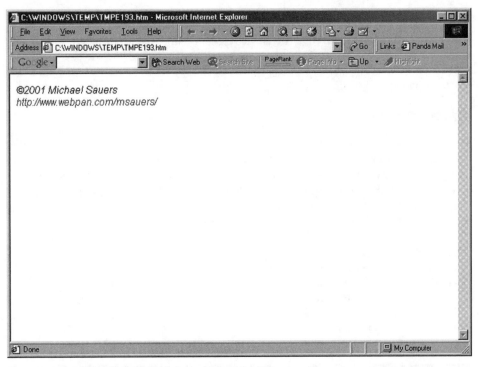

Figure 2.2 Browser display of the <address> element code.

<blockquote> is a block-level element similar to <p> but that indents the content on both the right and left sides. Following is an attribute of the <blockquote> element:

cite="content". Allows the author to add a citation to the blockquote. This citation can be textual or a URL. The XHTML standard does not include display instructions for this attribute, and current browsers will ignore it. The following is an example, with the resulting browser display shown in Figure 2.3:

```
<blockquote cite="William Shakespeare, Hamlet, Act III, Scene 1">
    To be, or not to be,--that is the question:--Whether 'tis nobler in the
mind to suffer the slings and arrows of outrageous fortune, or to take arms
against a sea of troubles, and by opposing end them?-- To die,--to sleep,--
No more; and by a sleep to say we end the heartache, and the thousand natu-
ral shocks that flesh is heir to,--'tis a consummation devoutly to be
wish'd. To die,--to sleep;--to sleep! perchance to dream:--ay, there's the
rub; for in that sleep of death what dreams may come, when we have shuffled
off this mortal coil, must give us pause: there's the respect that makes
calamity of so long life; for who would bear the whips and scorns of
time,the oppressor's wrong, the proud man's contumely, the pangs of despis'd
love, the law's delay,the insolence of office, and the spurns that patient
merit of the unworthy takes, when he himself might his quietus make with a
bare bodkin? Who would these fardels bear,to grunt and sweat under a weary
life, but that the dread of something after death,--the undiscover'd coun-
try, from whose bourn no traveller returns,--puzzles the will,and makes us
rather bear those ills we have than fly to others that we know not of? Thus
```

conscience does make cowards of us all; and thus the native hue of resolution is sicklied o'er with the pale cast of thought; and enterprises of
great pith and moment, with this regard, their currents turn awry, and lose
the name of action.--Soft you now! The fair Ophelia!--Nymph, in thy orisons
be all my sins remember'd.
    </blockquote>

<div>...</div>

The <div> is a generic block-level element to which styles can be applied. For example,
if a section of your document has multiple block-level elements to which you wish to
apply a certain style, you can do so by containing that section of your document within
a <div> pair, so that you only need to apply the style to that section, not to each individual element within the effected area. The following code shows how this was
accomplished before the <div> element was added:

```
<p>left-justified</p>
<p class="centered">centered</p>
<p class="centered">centered</p>
<p class="centered">centered</p>
<p class="centered">centered</p>
<p>left-justified</p>
```

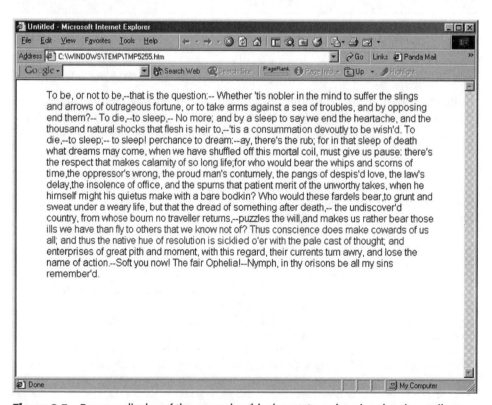

Figure 2.3 Browser display of the example <blockquote> code using the cite attribute.

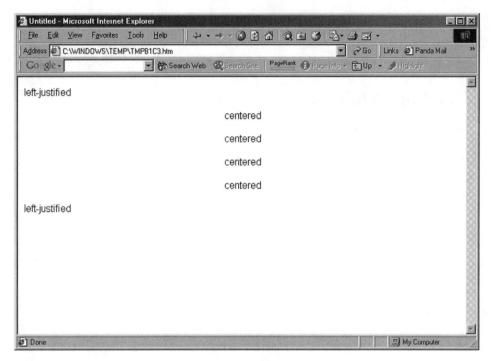

Figure 2.4 Browser display of the <div> element.

As you can see here, using the <div> element will accomplish the same results much more efficiently (Figure 2.4 shows the results on-screen):

```
<p>left-justified</p>
<div class="centered">
<p>centered</p>
<p>centered</p>
<p>centered</p>
<p>centered</p>
</div>
<p>left-justified</p>
```

<hn>...</hn>

XHTML has six built-in heading levels, numbered one through six. These headings are designed to specify sections and subsections of documents through their logical placement. Typically, however, they are placed in a document to establish visual formatting of the text. Today's browsers will, by default, boldface the header's content and change its font size depending on the header level: one is the largest, six the smallest. Through the application of CSS, you can completely control how the browser displays headings. Note that headings are block-level elements. Here are code examples of the six levels of headers, followed by the browser display in Figure 2.5:

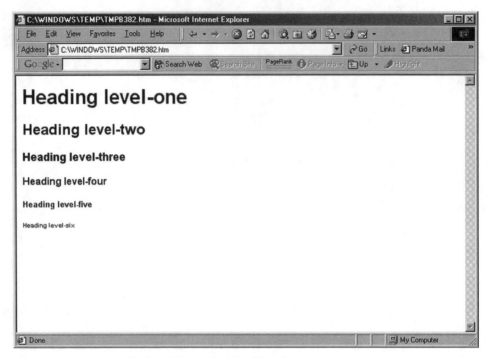

Figure 2.5 Browser display of the six levels of headers.

```
<h1>Heading level-one</h1>
<h2>Heading level-two</h2>
<h3>Heading level-three</h3>
<h4>Heading level-four</h4>
<h5>Heading level-five</h5>
<h6>Heading level-six</h6>
```

<hr />

The <hr /> element inserts a single line across the body of the document, as shown here (see Figure 2.6 for the resulting browser display):

```
<p>This is a paragraph.</p>
<hr />
<p>This is another paragraph.</p>
```

Note that <hr /> is an empty element and therefore cannot have any content. Also note that <hr /> acts as a block-level element and will therefore always be preceded by a blank line. Following are the attributes of the <hr /> element:

noshade="noshade". This is the single most counterintuitive attribute in all of XHTML. When applied to a horizontal rule, the line will be filled in, appearing as shaded to most viewers. In actuality, the shading is the 3D effect, which appears by default. Using this attribute will create a solid line.

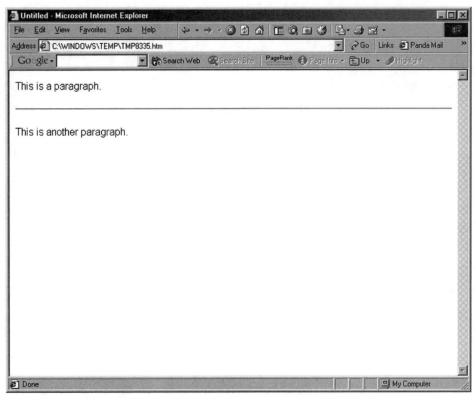

Figure 2.6 Browser display of <hr /> with no attributes.

size="n". This attribute controls the line thickness, measured in pixels.The default value for this attribute is 2.

width="n | n%". This attribute specifies the width of the line in either pixels (n) or as a percentage of the available window width (n%). The default value for this attribute is 100%.

The following code shows the <hr /> element attributes in use, followed by the browser display in Figure 2.7:

```
<p>This is a paragraph.</p>
<hr noshade="noshade" size="10" width="50%" />
<p>This is another paragraph.</p>
```

*
*

The
 (commonly known as a *line break*) is an inline element that directs the browser to stop whatever it is displaying on the screen and to continue the content on the immediate next line. The following are <br /> attributes:

clear="left | right". Used to specify that the browser should insert a line break but not continue with content display until it can do so on a line that would reach

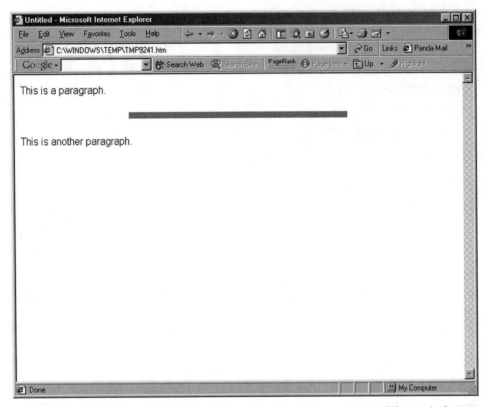

Figure 2.7 Browser display of the <hr /> element attributes for a solid, 10-pixel, 50% width horizontal rule.

the left or right margin accordingly. This attribute is typically used to end text that is along one side of an image and to continue the text beneath the image. The following is an example of using the <br /> element to split content over two lines (see Figure 2.8 for the resulting browser display):

```
<p>This is a pararaph that has text<br />
on two different lines</p>
```

In this example we have a large image with some text to the right of it in a paragraph. By adding clear="left" to the line break we force the next paragraph to start below the image, as shown in Figure 2.9.

```
<img src="largeimage.jpg" align="left" />
<p>This content is to the right of the image. This content is to the
right of the image. This content is to the right of the image. This con-
tent is to the right of the image. This content is to the right of the
image. This content is to the right of the image.</p>
<br clear="left" />
<p>This content is beneath the image.</p>
```

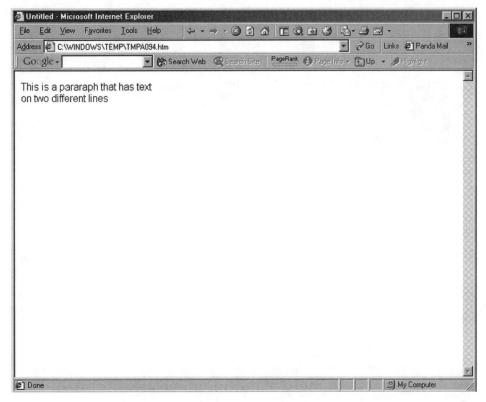

Figure 2.8   Browser display of the example <br /> code, used to split content over two lines.

<p>...</p>

This is the paragraph element, the most commonly used element in text-oriented documents. It establishes a section of text. It is a block-level element, hence all paragraphs will be preceded by a blank line. Following is a code example of the <p> element (Figure 2.10 has the resulting browser display):

```
<p>Paragraph one.</p>
<p>Paragraph two.</p>
```

<pre>...</pre>

The <pre> element instructs the browser to treat the content as preformatted text. This forces the browser to recognize all spacing and hard returns contained within the content of the element. Current browsers will render this text in a monospaced font, typically a variant of Courier. For this reason, it is generally recommended that this element only be used for presentation of computer code that must be spaced properly, as shown in this example and in Figure 2.11:

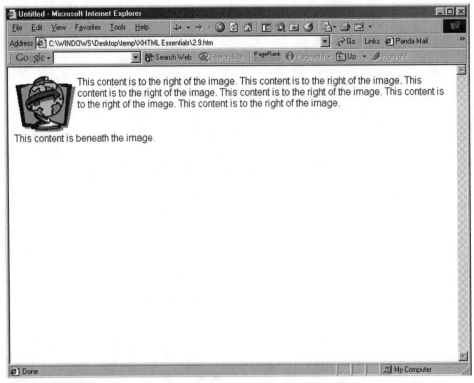

Figure 2.9 Browser display of the example `<br clear="left" />` code.

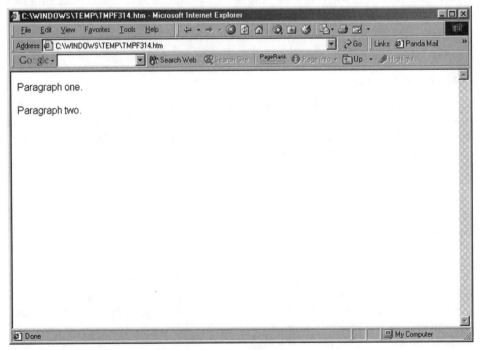

Figure 2.10 Browser display of the example `<p>` element code.

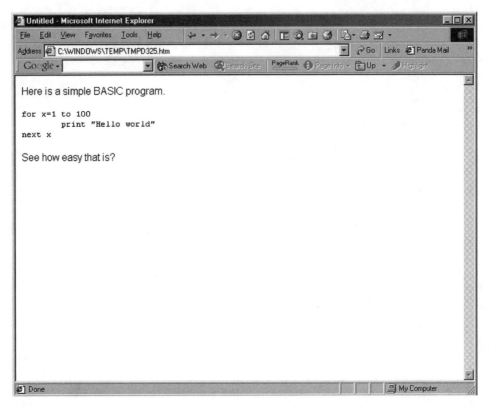

Figure 2.11   Browser display of the example <pre> element code.

```
<p>Here is a simple BASIC program.</p>
<pre>
for x=1 to 100
     print "Hello world"
next x
</pre>
<p>See how easy that is?</p>
```

<dl>...</dl>

The <dl> is a container element for a definition list. This element should always contain the <dt> and <dd> elements, explained immediately following. Here is an example of <dl>:

```
<dl>
...
</dl>
```

<dt>...</dt>

The <dt> element appears within <dl>, and specifies the term being defined. A <dl> may contain multiple <dt>s. The following is an example of <dt>:

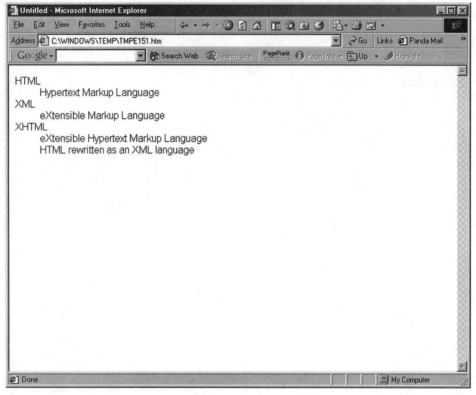

Figure 2.12 Browser display of the example code using <dl>, <dt>, and <dd> to create a definition list.

```
<dl>
<dt>HTML</dt>
</dl>
```

<dd>...</dd>

The <dd> element, which stands for definition data, appears within <dl> and after a <dt>, and specifies the definition for the <dt>. Following is an example of <dd>:

```
<dt>HTML</dt>
     <dd>Hypertext Markup Language</dd>
```

The code here shows how to use <dl>, <dt>, and <dd> to create a definition list; note that multiple <dd>s may accompany each <dt>. Figure 2.12 shows the resulting browser display.

```
<dl>
<dt>HTML</dt>
     <dd>Hypertext Markup Language</dd>
<dt>XML</dt>
     <dd>eXtensible Markup Language</dd>
```

```
<dt>XHTML</dt>
    <dd>eXtensible Hypertext Markup Language</dd>
    <dd>HTML rewritten as an XML language</dd>
</dl>
```

<ol>...</ol>

The <ol> element is a containing element for an ordered (or numbered) list (see Figures 2.13 through 2.15). The content of an <ol> should be one or more <li> elements and/or embedded <ol>s or <ul>s. Each embedded <li> will be sequentially ordered based upon the value of the type attribute. Following are <ol> attributes:

type="1 | A | a | I | i". Specifies the type of label for the enclosed <li> elements: 1 is the default; uppercase A specifies capital letters; lowercase a specifies lowercase letters; capital I specifies uppercase Roman numerals; and lowercase i specifies lowercase Roman numerals.

This code is for an ordered list (see Figure 2.13 for the resulting browser display):

```
<ol>
<li>Item</li>
<li>Item</li>
<li>Item</li>
</ol>
```

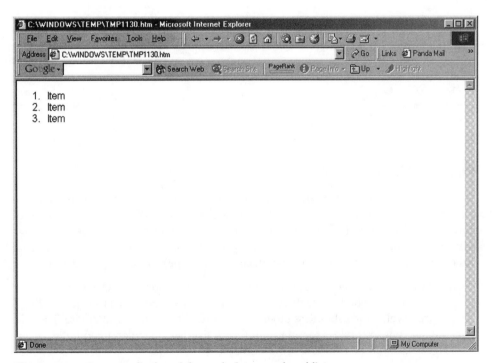

Figure 2.13 Browser display of the code for an ordered list.

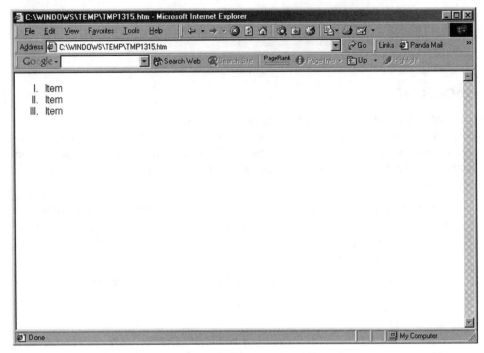

Figure 2.14 Browser display of the code for an ordered list using Roman numerals.

Here's the code for an ordered list using Roman numerals (see Figure 2.14 for the resulting browser display):

```
<ol type="I">
<li>Item</li>
<li>Item</li>
<li>Item</li>
</ol>
```

<ul>...</ul>

The <ul> element is the containing element for an unnumbered or bulleted list. The content of a <ul> should be one or more <li> elements and/or embedded <ol>s or <ul>s. By default, a first-level <ul> will have solid, circular bullets. Embedded <ul>s will have so-called empty circular bullets, and third-level <ul>s will have filled square bullets. These may be changed through the use of the type attribute, defined as follows:

type="disc | circle | square". Specifies the type of bullet for the enclosed <li> elements. As described, these three choices will be used as the defaults depending on the level of the list, unless otherwise specified through this attribute. The following code example is for an unnumbered list using circular, filled bullets (see Figure 2.15 for the resulting browser display):

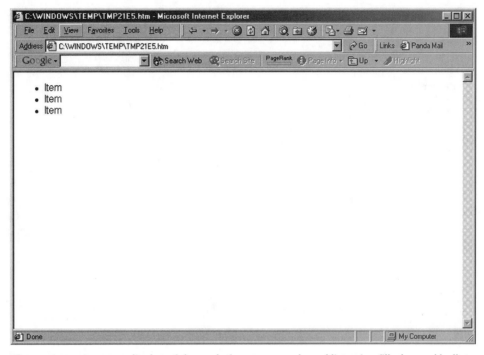

Figure 2.15 Browser display of the code for an unnumbered list using filled round bullets.

```
<ul>
<li>Item</li>
<li>Item</li>
<li>Item</li>
</ul>
```

Here's the code for an unnumbered list using filled square bullets (see Figure 2.16 for the resulting browser display):

```
<ul type="square">
<li>Item</li>
<li>Item</li>
<li>Item</li>
</ul>
```

This code is an example of an ordered list with an embedded unnumbered list using empty circular bullets (see Figure 2.17 for the browser display):

```
<ol>
<li>Item</li>
<ul>
<li>Item</li>
<li>Item</li>
<li>Item</li>
```

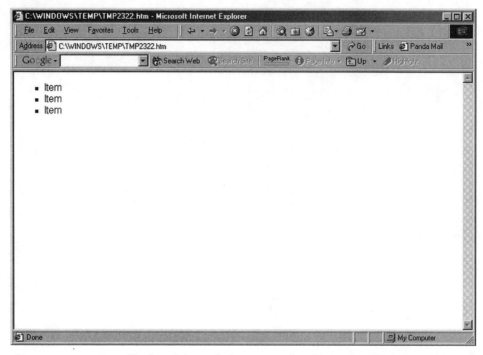

Figure 2.16 Browser display of the code for an unordered list using filled square bullets.

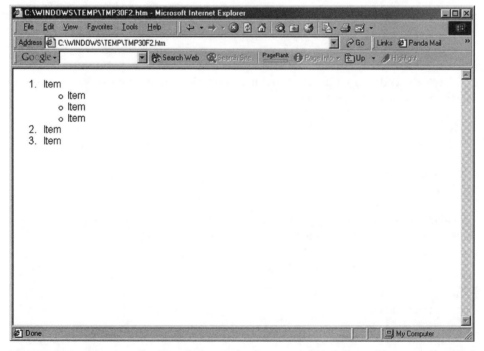

Figure 2.17 Browser display of the code for an ordered list with an embedded unnumbered list.

```
</ul>
<li>Item</li>
<li>Item</li>
</ol>
```

<li>...</li>

The <li> element contains the content of list items. The bullet or label preceding the content will be determined based upon the containing list element and its attribute, if present.

Physical Markup

If you take a look at the XHTML specifications as set by the W3C, most of the following physical markup elements have been deprecated for replacement with CSS code. But because many users are still using browsers that do not support CSS, these elements are included here. We do recommend, however, to implement CSS code whenever possible instead of these XHTML elements.

Note that all these are inline elements and will not cause the natural flow of content to be interrupted.

<b>...</b>

As shown here and in Figure 2.18, content enclosed within the <b> element should be displayed in boldface type:

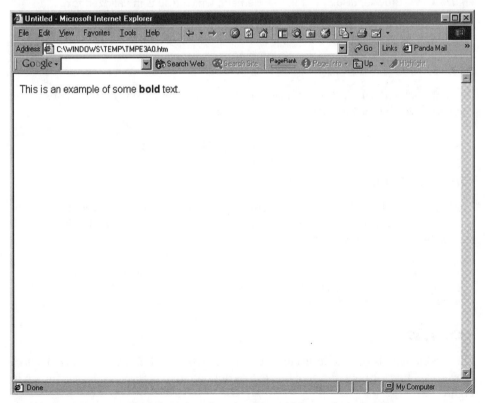

Figure 2.18 Browser display of the <b> element, which results in boldface text.

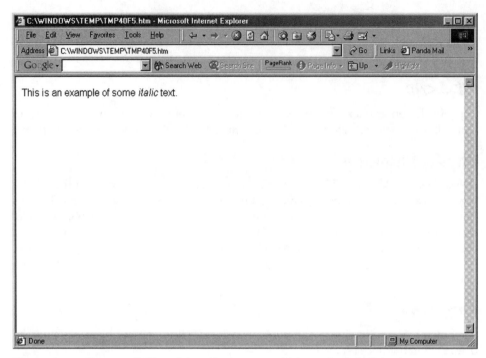

Figure 2.19   Browser display of the <i> element, which results in italicized text.

```
<p>This is an example of some <b>bold</b> text.</p>
```

<i>...</i>

Content enclosed within the <i> element displays as italicized. Here's the example code, followed by the browser display in Figure 2.19:

```
<p>This is an example of some <i>italic</i> text.</p>
```

<nobr>...</nobr>

Content enclosed within the <nobr> element precludes a line break, even upon reaching the right-hand margin. The example code shows the markup, and Figure 2.20 shows the resulting browser display:

```
<p><nobr>This paragraph is a long one. Even if the text of this para-
graph reaches the opposite margin, it will not wrap to the next line
since it also includeed the nobreak element.</nobr></p>
```

<s>...</s>

The <s> element is used to indicate text that has been struck through, that is, deleted. A one-pixel line is drawn through the text, as defined in the sample code and shown in Figure 2.21:

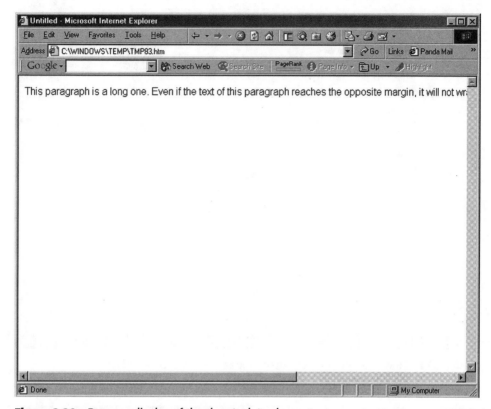

Figure 2.20 Browser display of the the <nobr> element.

```
<p>This paragraph contains <s>struck</s> text.</p>
```

<small>...</small>

Any text enclosed within the <small> element will display one size smaller than the default font size of the document. This is an element where using CSS gives you much greater control, as a point-size difference can vary significantly in various browsers. Here's the markup of <small>, followed by its display in Figure 2.22:

```
<p>Some of this text is <small>a little smaller</small> than the rest of
the paragraph.</p>
```

<big>...</big>

The direct opposite of the <small> element is <big>, which displays any text enclosed within it one size larger than the default font size of the document. Likewise, using CSS with <big> will give you much greater control, for the same reason just described for <small>. Here's an example of <big>, with its accompanying display in Figure 2.23:

```
<p>Some of this text is <big>a little larger</big> than the rest of the
paragraph.</p>
```

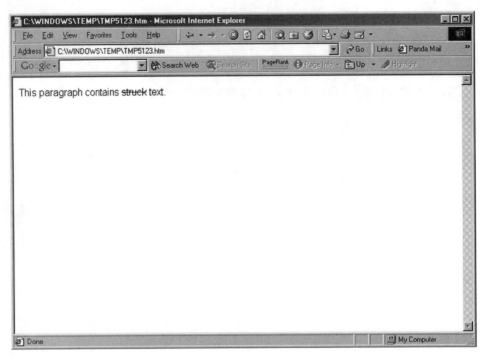

Figure 2.21 How use of the <s> element appears in the browser display.

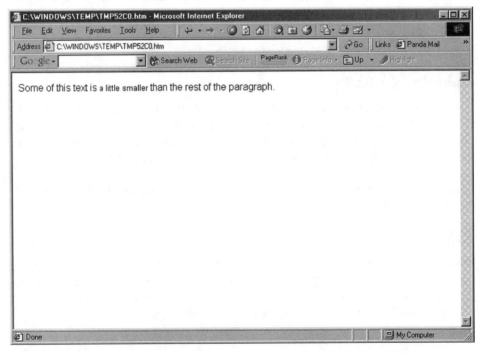

Figure 2.22 How code including the <small> element displays in the browser.

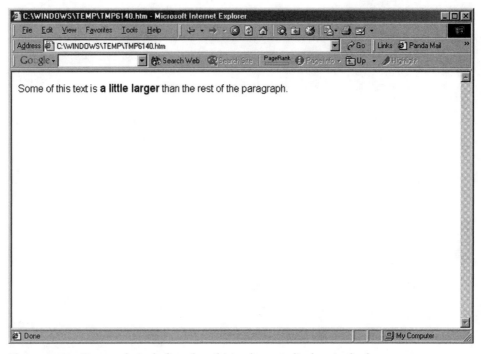

Figure 2.23   How code including the <big> element displays in the browser.

<span>...</span>

The <span> element is a generic inline container that allows you to add style code to a subsection of a block-level element. This element is similar to <div> but is much more specific, as shown in this example code and in Figure 2.24:

```
<p>Some of this paragraph has a <span class="red">CSS class</span>
applied to it, and the rest does not.</p>
```

_{...}

The <sub> element is used to display content in a subscript font, as shown in this example code and in Figure 2.25:

```
<p>This paragraph contains <sub>subscripted</sub> text.</p>
```

^{...}

Conversely, the <sup> element is used to display content in a superscript font, as given in this example code and in Figure 2.26:

```
<p>This paragraph contains superscripted<sup>1</sup> text. It can be
useful for creating footnote links.</p>
```

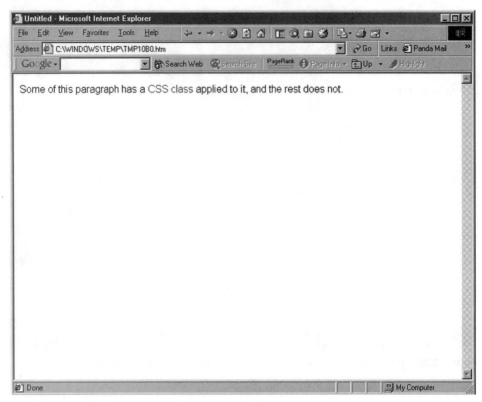

Figure 2.24 Browser display of the example code for the <span> element.

<tt>...</tt>

Content enclosed within the <tt> element will be displayed in a teletype font, typically a monospaced font such as Courier (commonly use to represent computer code). This element is similar to the block-level element <pre>, but works inline and therefore ignores additional spacing or hard returns. Here's an example of <tt> markup, followed by its browser display in Figure 2.27:

```
<p>At the prompt type <tt>cd...</tt> and then press <tt>enter</tt>.</p>
```

<u>...</u>

When you enclose any content within the <u> element, it will display underlined, as shown in this example code and in Figure 2.28:

```
<p>This paragraph contains <u>underlined</u> text.</p>
```

> **NOTE** It is strongly recommended that you resist using the <u> element as a text highlight, as most browsers automatically treat underlined text as hyperlinks; moreover, users by now are familiar with this use of underlined text, hence may become confused. Consider using italics instead to emphasize text.

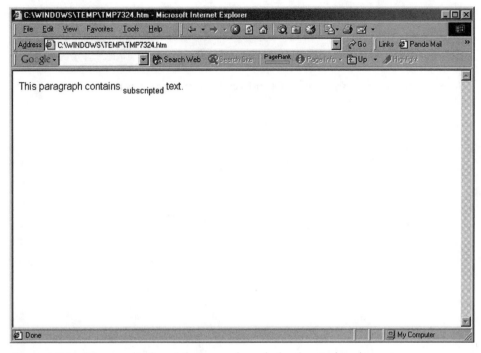

Figure 2.25 Browser display of the example code for the <sub> element.

<bdo>...</bdo>

The final physical markup element we will describe is <bdo>, which allows you to override the default direction of the current text. In European languages, readers go from left to right, top to bottom. To display languages that should be rendered right to left, such as Hebrew, use this element to enclose that text. Following are <bdo> attributes:

lang="languagecode". Specifies the language of the enclosed text.

dir="ltr | rtl". Specifies the direction of the enclosed text. Left to right is the default.

Here's example code using <bdo>, followed by its display in Figure 2.29:

```
<bdo lang="he" dir="rtl">Hebrew text</bdo>
```

Logical Markup

Logical markup elements allow you to specify such details as when text has been inserted or deleted, when it has emphasis, or when it is computer code. How current browsers display such content varies significantly, and the details of those variations are beyond the scope of this text; just be aware that, for best results, each of these elements should be used in conjunction with a CSS to enable you to specify how you want such text to appear to the user. For example, you could use CSS to specify that <del> text should be in red, and struck through, while <ins> text be underlined and in green.

Figure 2.26   Browser display of the example code for the <sup> element.

The following subsections define the logical markup elements with which you should familiarize yourself.

<abbr>...<abbr>

Text enclosed within the <abbr> element indicates an abbreviation. The following is an attribute of the <abbr> element:

title="text". When the title attribute is added, the abbreviation's definition can be included. Here's an example:

```
<p>The standards can be found at the <abbr title="World Wide Web Con-
sortium">W3C</abbr> Web site.</p>
```

<acronym>...<acronym>

Text enclosed within the <acronym> element is an acronym. As with <abbr>, the title attribute can be used to spell out the acronym, as shown here:

```
<p>The <acronym title="American Library Association">ALA</acronym> is
sponsoring this event.</p>
```

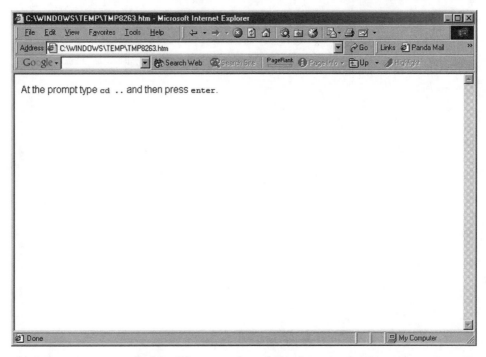

Figure 2.27   Browser display of the example code for the <tt> element.

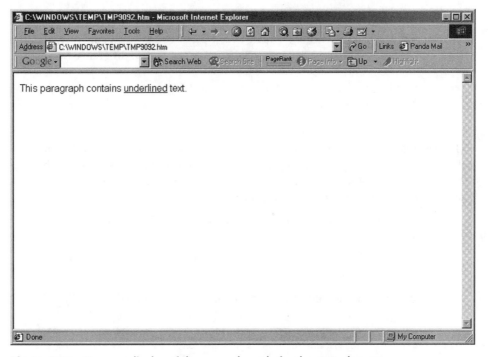

Figure 2.28   Browser display of the example code for the <u> element.

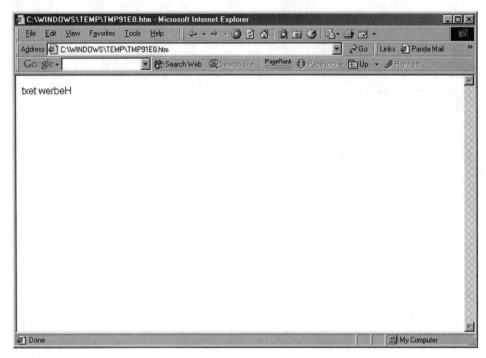

Figure 2.29 Browser display of the example code for <bdo> element attributes.

<code>...</code>

Text enclosed within the <code> element is computer code. This element works the same as <tt>. Here's an example of <code>, showing the logical difference from <tt>:

```
<p>At the prompt type <code>cd...</code> and then press
<tt>enter</tt>.</p>
<del>...</del>
```

Text enclosed within the <del> element will be deleted, meaning that the browser will not display this content unless you specify that it should be displayed to the user via CSS code. For example, you could specify, using CSS, that <del> text should be displayed with a strikethrough. Following are <del> attributes:

cite="URL". Allows you to point to a document that explains why the text was deleted.

datetime="YYYY-MM-DDThh:mm:ssTZD". Allows you to specify a date and time that the text was deleted.

The following is an example of <del> element attributes in use:

```
<p>The author will <del cite="explainations.html" datetime="2001-03-
11T10:50:01MDT">not</del> deliver the book on time.</p>
```

<dfn>...</dfn>

Text enclosed within the <dfn> element indicates a defined term. Typically, this is used at the first appearance of a term in a document, as shown here:

```
<p>A <dfn>parser</dfn> is what the code must pass through before it is
displayed on the screen.</p>
```

<em>...</em>

Text enclosed within the <em> element will be emphasized, typically in italics, as shown in the following sample:

```
<p>This book <em>must</em> be done on time!</p>
```

<ins>...</ins>

As you might expect, text enclosed within the <ins> element will be inserted. Following are <ins> element attributes:

cite="URL". Allows you to point to a document that explains why the text was inserted.

datetime="YYYY-MM-DDThh:mm:ssTZD". Allows you to specify a date and time that the text was inserted.

The following is an example of <ins> element attributes in use:

```
<p>The author will <ins cite="explainations.html" datetime="2001-03-
11T10:50:01MDT">not</ins> deliver the book on time.</p>
```

<q>...</q>

The <q> element is an inline element used to specify that the content enclosed within is a quotation. However, note that at the time of this writing, no browser displays this content differently from regular content, though authors anticipate they will eventually do so as the standards receive better browser support. Following is a <q> element attribute:

cite="content". Allows you to add a citation to the blockquote. This citation can be textual or a URL. However, currently, the XHTML standard does not include display instructions for this attribute, and current browsers will ignore it. Here's a sample of this <q> attribute in use:

```
<p>Hamlet said <q>"To be or not to be"<q>.</p>
```

<samp>...</samp>

You use the <samp> element to indicate that text enclosed within it is a sample of computer input or output. Similar to <code> and <tt>, it is really up to you which to use as long as you are consistent. Here's an example of <samp>:

```
<p><samp>javascript:history.back();</samp> when used in place of a URL as
the value of href will simulate the click of the browser's back button.</p>
```

<strong>...</strong>

Text enclosed within the <strong> element should have additional emphasis above what <em> offers, usually bold, as shown here:

```
<p>This book <strong>really must</strong> be done on time!</p>
```

<var>...</var>

The <var> element is used to indicate a variable—that is, a placeholder for input the individual users will supply. Here's an example of <var>:

```
<p>At the prompt enter <var>your age</var>.</p>
```

Hypertext

Only one element is discussed in this section—<a>...</a>, the anchor element—but it is the single most complex element in XHTML. It has many different attributes you can choose from, depending on the type of link you're creating. First we present the element itself, and then work our way through the relevant attributes.

Anchor Element

The anchor element is at the base of all hyperlinks. It specifies where in the document the link is. Through its various attributes we can describe the type of link we want and where the user will be sent when he or she clicks the link. Following are attributes of the <a> element:

href="URL". This is the hypertext reference of the anchor. Typically, the value of this attribute is the URL (either absolute or relative—which we'll define in a moment) of the linked document. This value may also be a location internal to the current document (preceded by the pound symbol [#]) as specified in the name attribute.

Following is an example of an absolute link. In this case, we're linking to a document on another server, and are instructing the browser to retrieve it via the HTTP protocol:

```
<a href="http://www.domain.com/filename.html">link</a>
```

To ask the browser to fetch another document on the same server, we'd use the following code:

```
<a href="file.html">link</a>
```

The browser would know to look on the same server because we have not specified a server name nor a protocol. This, then, is a *relative link*.

An internal link is generally a relative link but points to a location within the current document. Here is an example:

```
<a href="#top">link</a>
```

The pound symbol that precedes the word "top" indicates to the browser that it is to look for a point in the current document labeled "top."

name="*text*". This attribute is used as a replacement for href when specifying a location in a document as the destination of an internal link. Although technically an anchor, due to the use of the <a> element, this is the destination of a link, not the starting point. Be aware that the value of this attribute is case-sensitive and must not contain spaces. The following is an example of the name attribute using the location pointed to in the internal link example:

```
<a name="top"><h1>This is the first line of the document</h1></a>
```

id="top". Although the name attribute is valid XHTML, it has been supplemented by the id attribute. The use of the id attribute allows for much more efficient coding since there is less code to type. Unfortunately, many older browsers do not support the id attribute so authors must fall back on the use of the name attribute. Here's an example of using the id attribute instead of the name attribute:

```
<h1 id="top">This is the first line of the document</h1>
```

rel="linktype". This attribute specifies the type of document being linked to and its relation to the current document. Though the XHTML specification does not define a list of available values, those from HTML 4.0 are:

alternate. An alternative version of the document.

start. The first document in the group.

next. The next document in the group.

prev. The previous document in the group.

contents. The table of contents for the group.

index. The index for this document.

glossary. The glossary for this document.

copyright. The document that offers copyright information.

chapter. The chapter for this group.

section. The section for this group.

subsection. A subsection of this group.

appendix. An appendix for this group.

help. A document giving helpful information.

bookmark. A key related document.

The rel attribute defines the relationship of the linked document to the current document, as shown here:

```
<a href="chapter1.html" rel="next">link</a>
<a href="chapter2.html" rel="chapter">link</a>
<a href="chapter3.html" rel="chapter">link</a>
<a href="index.html" rel="index">link</a>
<a href="glossary.html" rel="index">link</a>
```

rev="linktype". The rev attribute is similar to the rel attribute in that it defines the relationship between the current document and the linked document; but where rel specifies the relationship of the linked document to the current document, rev specifies the relationship of the current document to the linked document, as shown in this example, where the code specifies that this is the table of contents for chapter1.html:

```
<a href="chapter1.html" rev="next">link</a>
```

accesskey="*character*". The accesskey attribute is used to improve the accessibility of documents for users who have motor impairments. By setting this attribute you specify an Alt-key combination that will simulate a mouse-click on the link, thereby activating the link. The specified character must be in uppercase. (Note: Be careful not to use key-character combinations already reserved by browser software companies, for accessing menus, such as Alt-F to access the File menu.) Following is an example using the accesskey attribute; here, the user can press Alt-D on his or her keyboard to activate the link:

```
<a href="http://www.domain.com/" accesskey="D">link</a>
```

tabindex="*n*". By default, users may use the Tab key to move from link to link within a document based on the order in which the links appear in the XHTML code. By numbering the links using the tabindex attribute, you may override the default. Be careful using this, however, as users will expect to tab to the next logical link (left to right, top-down, in most cases) and may become confused.

The following code is an example of using the tabindex attribute to override the default tab order between links:

```
<a href="http://www.domain.com/" tabindex="1">link</a>
<a href="http://www.domain.com/" tabindex="4">link</a>
<a href="http://www.domain.com/" tabindex="2">link</a>
<a href="http://www.domain.com/" tabindex="3">link</a>
```

charset="*encodingtype*". The charset attribute denotes the character set used in the linked document. In the following charset attribute example, the linked document uses the SHIFT_JIS character set:

```
<a href="http://www.domain.com/" charset="SHIFT_JIS">link</a>
```

Use this attribute only when you are linking to a document with a different character set from that of the document containing the link.

NOTE A complete list of character sets can be found at ftp://ftp.isi.edu/in-notes/iana/assignments/character-sets.

type="mediatype". When linking, the browser assumes that you will be connecting to another XHTML or HTML document. But, in fact, you can link to any type of computer file, and you use this attribute to specify the type of the linked file. The following is an example of the type attribute; here, the linked file is an Apple Quicktime file:

```
<a href="http://www.domain.com/" type="video/quicktime">link</a>
```

When you implement this attribute, essentially, it gives the browser a heads-up as to what type of file it will be retrieving, ensuring that it will be handled properly. If the browser does not know what to do with that file, it will typically ask the user.

NOTE For a complete list of media types, go to ftp://ftp.isi.edu/in-notes/iana/assignments/media-types/.

hreflang="*language*". The hreflang attribute denotes the language used in the document that will be retrieved when the link is clicked. This example of the hreflang attribute specifies that the linked document is in German—the "de" is an abbreviation for Deutsche:

```
<a href="http://www.domain.com/" hreflang="de">link</a>
```

Note that current browsers do not implement this attribute in any special way and they have not indicated that they will do so in the near future.

target="*framename*". The target attribute, used in the context of frameset documents, allows you to specify a particular frame in which the resulting document will appear. In this example, the document will appear in the right-hand frame:

```
<a href="http://www.domain.com/" target="right">link</a>
```

NOTE We cover frames in detail in Chapter 7.

Advanced Elements

This section is intended only as a brief introduction to XHTML elements used in tables, forms, objects, applets, and scripts. Later chapters address each of these areas in greater detail.

Tables

Tables allow you to present tabular data to the user, such as a spreadsheet does. Many authors also use tables to establish a grid on their screen for the purpose of laying out a document's content. We will discuss the difference between these uses in more detail in Chapter 5, "Tables." Here are the attributes you can use with tables:

<table>...</table>. Indicates the start and end of a table. All other elements in a table should always be enclosed within this element.

<tr>...</tr>. Indicates the start and end of a table row. A row contains one or more cells.

<td>...</td>. Indicates the start and end of a table cell. Contains the content, or data, that appears in the cell.

<th>...</th>. Indicates the start and end of a table header cell. Similar to <td>, but browsers usually center and bold the content within this element.

<caption>...</caption>. Establishes a caption for the table. Should be included within the table, before the first row.

<colgroup>...</colgroup>. Establishes a group of columns to which a single set of styles can be applied.

<col />. Establishes a column within a <colgroup>.

<tbody>...</tbody>. When used in conjunction with <thead> and <tfoot>, described next, allows the author to divide the table into three logical areas. The <tbody> element is the middle of those three sections, and contains one or more table rows.

<thead>...</thead>. Establishes the top three sections of the table. The <thead> typically contains only one table row.

<tfoot>...</tfoot>. Establishes the bottom three sections of the table. The <tfoot> typically contains only one table row.

Frames

Frames give you the ability to divide the browser window into multiple independent areas in which different documents can be displayed. Through the use of the target attribute on <a>, the anchor element, you can make an action in one frame affect the contents of another.

<frameset>...</frameset>. Establishes the start and end of a frameset. This is used in place of <body>. A <frameset> contains one or more <frame />s.

<frame />. Contained within a <frameset>, <frame /> establishes the size and contents of a window area.

<noframes>...</noframes>. Contains alternate content to be displayed when the user's browser does not have the capability to display <frameset> content.

Objects and Applets

Objects and applets refer specifically to elements that allow Web developers to embed external programs within their XHTML documents. Although the <applet> element has been deprecated in favor of the <object> element, you will still find it heavily used on Web sites today. To stay current, however, you should begin using the <object> element for all Java applet inclusions.

In addition to these two elements, there is also an optional element, <param/>, that can be used to pass parameters into the object. Table 2.1 contains a list of the attributes of these three elements.

Table 2.1 Attributes of the <object>, <applet>, and <param> Elements

ATTRIBUTE	APPLIES TO	DESCRIPTION
align	<object> and <applet>	Allows you to specify alignment.
alt	<applet>	Allows you to specify alternate text.
archive	<object> and <applet>	Comma-separated list of URIs containing classes and other resources that should be preloaded.
border	<object>	Specifies the amount, if any, of border you want around the item.
class	<object> and <applet>	References a class defined in a style sheet.
classid	<object>	Used to specify the URI of the object's implementation.
code	<applet>	Specifies the name of the Java class that should be loaded.
codebase	<object> and <applet>	Specifies the base URI for the code.
codetype	<object>	Specifies the content-type of the classid object being downloaded.
data	<object>	Used to specify the location of the object's data.
declare	<object>	Boolean attribute that makes the current <object> a declaration only.
height	<object> and <applet>	Specifies the initial height of the item.
hspace	<object> and <applet>	Specifies the amount of white space inserted to the right and left of the item.
id	<object> and <applet>	Assigns an identifier to the item.
lang	<object>	Specifies the language used.
name	<object>,<applet>, and <param>	Specifies a name of the instance or parameter.
object	<applet>	Names a resource containing a serialized representation of an applet's state.
standby	<object>	Specifies a message the user agent can display while loading.

continues

Table 2.1   Attributes of the \<object>, \<applet>, and \<param> Elements *(Continued)*

ATTRIBUTE	APPLIES TO	DESCRIPTION
style	\<object> and \<applet>	Provides the capability to apply a style sheet.
tabindex	\<object>	Specifies the indexed position of the element in tabbing order.
title	\<object> and \<applet>	Provides a means to include a more descriptive title.
type	\<object> and \<param>	Specifies the content type of the value of the data (\<object>) or value (\<param>) attribute being downloaded.
usemap	\<object>	Specifies the name of a client-side image map.
value	\<param>	Specifies the value of the attribute defined in the name attribute.
valuetype	\<param>	Specifies the type of value of the value attribute.
vspace	\<object> and \<applet>	Specifies the amount of white space inserted above and below the item.
width	\<object> and \<applet>	Specifies the initial width of the item.
onclick ondblclick onmousedown onmouseup onmouseover onmousemove onmouseout onkeypress onkeydown onkeyup	\<object>	Identifies intrinsic events. See Chapter 12 for more information on these.

Scripts

The scripting elements are the last we cover in this chapter. There are only two elements, and both are covered in detail in Chapter 9, "JavaScript." For that reason, here we include only a brief description of both:

\<script>...\</script>. Establishes the start and end of an embedded script. Through the use of the type attribute, you can set the language used for the code within these elements..

<noscript>...</noscript>. Contains alternate content to be displayed when the user's browser does not have the capability to display <script> content.

Summary

This chapter delved into the differences between HTML and XHTML, most of which stem from the fact that XHTML is an XML-based language, dictating that documents created in XHTML be well-formed. The chapter also presented an overview of the majority of XHTML elements and their attributes. Based on this knowledge, in the next chapter, we begin to create a document from scratch in XHTML, highlighting additional differences from HTML.

Creating Documents

As we begin this chapter, keep in mind that XHTML, as an XML derivative, requires that a document be well formed, meaning that without the <html>, <head>, and <body> elements, and a few others we'll discuss shortly, no document will display properly, and the browser may even report an error. This, as noted previously, is in stark contrast to using HTML: If you left out any of these elements when designing an HTML document, it would, in most cases, still display properly in the user's browser. This was possible simply because most browsers assumed that any document it received would be in HTML, as that was what the browsers were designed to handle.

Meeting XHTML's Minimal Requirements

XHTML is not nearly as forgiving as its predecessor; in short, as well as the elements just mentioned, a significant amount of additional information is required to produce a well-formed document. This additional information includes an XML statement, the XML encoding scheme, a doctype element, and the root element, along with at least one XML namespace and the language specifications of both the document itself and of the code being used. As you can see, the requirements for producing a minimal XHTML document are more complex than for developing a minimal HTML document.

Comparing XHTML with HTML

To make this important point more clearly, let's examine some actual code from the two markup languages. To begin, the following shows an HTML document minimally coded, as needed by today's browsers:

```
<p>content
<p>more content
```

As you see, there's not much to it. Again, this is because an HTML browser assumes that you are sending it an HTML document and therefore follows the hard-coded rules it has been given for display.

If we were to follow to the letter the standards as of HTML 3.2 (which many authors are still doing) our minimal document might look like this:

```
<html>
<head>
</head>
<body>
      content
</body>
</html>
```

So far, this code adheres to the new rules that we must follow in XHTML: lowercase elements, followed by their proper closing. (The issues of fully formed attributes and quoted attribute values are not relevant in this situation.)

With the advent of HTML 4.0, many editors started preceding the <html> element with the DOCTYPE statement to specify the version of HTML being used. The following code shows our minimal document with such a statement:

```
<!DOCTYPE html PUBLIC "-//W3C/DTD HTML 4.0 Transitional//EN">
<html>
<head>
</head>
<body>
      content
</body>
</html>
```

NOTE We examine the !DOCTYPE element in more detail a little later in this chapter.

Learning the Additional Requirements of XHTML

As an XML language, XHTML will be parsed before being displayed. With HTML we relied on our browser to know what to do with our code. In contrast, the parser takes direction from us as to how to handle the code and content we are sending it. This means that the parser will not assume, as a browser does, that what we are sending it is an

HTML document; nor will it assume that it is an XML document. We must specify this information or the parser will emit an error and stop the document from displaying.

With that in mind, let's look at the additional elements and attributes XHTML requires before a document can be considered well formed. They are:

- The XML statement
- A !DOCTYPE statement
- A namespace statement

Because parsers do not make assumptions about our documents as browsers do, XML-based documents require that certain information appear prior to the root element of the document, <html> in our case. This information includes the XML statement, to specify that this is an XML-based document, the XML encoding scheme, which lets the parser know which character set is being used to code this document, and a !DOCTYPE statement, to alert the parser as to which version of XHTML we are using. The following subsections examine each of these important elements in greater detail.

The XML Statement

This element does not exist in HTML; and just from its name we can see that it indicates that XHTML is based on XML.

The following code shows the default XML version statement:

```
<?xml version="1.0"?>
```

The version attribute states which version of XML is being used—in this case version 1.0—and the encoding scheme being used.

> **NOTE** XML statements do not have a closing element; that is, <?/xml> does not exist. The last element in any XML-based document should always be the close of your root element, in our case, </html>.

XML Encoding Schemes

With the creation of XML, many developers started to recognize the Web as a global medium, and that, like all global environments, its users speak different languages with different character sets. The ASCII character set, with which most Web authors are familiar, was developed based on Latin languages, specifically with English, in mind. But as more documents came to be coded in other languages, using multiple character sets, a way had to be found to encode the XML itself so that it could be identified by all computers, whichever languages their users spoke.

The scheme being used in your documents is specified through the encoding attribute on the XML statement. Here's the complete XML statement:

```
<?xml version="1.0" encoding="UTF-8"?>
```

When stating your document's encoding scheme, as shown here, you must use Latin-based characters. The default encoding scheme is UTF-8, which includes the direct representation of English characters (which many of us are used to from ASCII), but which also supports multibyte encoding for other characters.

Currently, XML requires that parsers support the following encoding schemes: UTF-8, UCS-2, and UTF-16. Table 3.1 lists the encoding schemes recommended for support in the XML standard.

Table 3.1 Common XML Encoding Schemes

ENCODING SCHEME	NUMBER OF BITS	NOTES
UCS-2	16	Unicode character set
UCS-4	32	Unicode character set in 32-bits
UTF-8	8	Unicode Transformation
UTF-7	7	Unicode Transformation (for mail and news)
UTF-16	16, 32	Unicode that escapes 32-bit characters
ISO-8859-1	8	Latin alphabet (Western Europe and Latin America)
ISO-8859-2	8	Latin alphabet (Central and Eastern Europe)
ISO-8859-3	8	Latin alphabet (Southeastern Europe and miscellaneous countries)
ISO-8859-4	8	Latin alphabet (Scandinavia and Baltic States)
ISO-8859-5	8	Latin/Cyrillic
ISO-8859-6	8	Latin/Arabic
ISO-8859-7	8	Latin/Greek
ISO-8859-8	8	Latin/Hebrew
ISO-8859-9	8	Latin/Turkish
ISO-8859-10	8	Latin/Lappish/Nordic/Eskimo
ISO 10646	32	32-bit extended set (includes Unicode as a subset)
EUC-JP	8	Japanese, using multibyte encoding
Shift_JIS	8	Japanese, using multibyte encoding
ISO-2022-JP	7	Japanese, using multibyte encoding for mail and news

The !DOCTYPE Element

Though the !DOCTYPE element exists in HTML, it is considered optional. In XHTML, you must include it. The !DOCTYPE element tells the parser which language the document is written in, hence the rules for being well formed. Though, as noted repeatedly, most of today's browsers will assume that a document is written in HTML, and will display the document appropriately, now that we are creating documents in another language, we must specifically tell the browser that, so it will apply the appropriate display rules to our page.

Three different !DOCTYPE elements are available to you in XHTML. They are:

- Strict:
  ```
  <!DOCTYPE html PUBLIC "-//W3C//DTD XHTML 1.0 Strict//EN"
  "http://www.w3.org/TR/xhtml1/DTD/strict.dtd">
  ```
- Transitional:
  ```
  <!DOCTYPE html PUBLIC "-//W3C//DTD XHTML 1.0 Transitional//EN"
  "http://www.w3.org/TR/xhtml1/DTD/transitional.dtd">
  ```
- Frameset:
  ```
  <!DOCTYPE html PUBLIC "-//W3C//DTD XHTML 1.0 Frameset//EN"
  "http://www.w3.org/TR/xhtml1/DTD/frameset.dtd">
  ```

Though as you no doubt noticed, all three are very similar in structure and content. Nevertheless, let's take a moment to deconstruct the code because it is much more complicated than typical XHTML code.

!DOCTYPE. The public text identifier, indicating that the document conforms to a particular Document Type Definition (DTD). The content within the first set of quotation marks is the formal public identifier, specifying the specific DTD being used.

html. Indicates the top-level element used in the DTD, in this case <html>.

PUBLIC. Specifies the availability of the DTD. PUBLIC indicates that you are using a publicly accessible DTD, as opposed to a local one, in which case you would use SYSTEM.

"-. Indicates whether the originating organization is registered with the International Standards Organization (ISO): A minus sign means it is not; a plus sign means it is. The W3C is not, so a minus is used.

//. In all occurrences, indicates the keyword field delimiter.

W3C. The owner ID for the originating organization for the DTD.

DTD. The public text class, that is, the type of document being referenced. In this case, we are referencing a DTD.

XHTML 1.0 type. The public text description, or the name of the specific DTD being referenced.

EN". The public text language, that is, the language used in the creation of the document being referenced. Choices are from the ISO 639 list of two-letter uppercase language codes.

"**URL**". The location of the DTD should the browser need to fetch it for instructions.

Now we're prepared to delve into the three !DOCTYPE elements.

Strict

The use of the strict DTD indicates that the browser is to adhere to the official standards (rules) of the language without variation (see Figure 3.1). As an author, you may find this to be quite restrictive; on the other hand, it can be a great way to make sure your code meets the published standard 100 percent.

Transitional

The transitional DTD is the most commonly used of the three versions, as it gives authors much greater flexibility in their code, and allows the browser to be somewhat forgiving in its interpretation of the XHTML code (see Figure 3.2).

Frameset

The frameset DTD is used in one, and only one, situation: when you are creating a frameset document (see Figure 3.3). If you do not use this DTD for a frameset document, the browser may not display the frames appropriately, if at all.

Choosing the Right !DOCTYPE

Choosing which !DOCTYPE to use is one part easy, one part more complex. The easy part is deciding when to use the frameset DTD. As just stated, you use it when you are creating a frameset document. If you are not using frames in your document, don't use it.

NOTE The transitional DTD does, however, include frame elements that are available in the frameset DTD.

If you have ruled out the frameset DTD, your choice is narrowed to the strict or transitional DTD. Here, the decision is a little more complicated. The graphical representations of the DTDs in Figures 3.1 to 3.3 show you that there are a significantly different number of elements available to you depending on the !DOCTYPE you use.

NOTE Because of space limitations, in these graphical representations, not all of the branches have been expanded—specifically in the <head> element. Also note that the anchor element is not shown in the strict DTD image, though it is in the DTD.

Table 3.2 lists those elements that are in the transitional DTD, but not in the strict DTD. If your document uses any of these elements, you must either use the transitional DTD or remove them. If you are converting a lot of documents from HTML to XHTML in a short period of time, you way wish to use only the transitional DTD to get everything up and running quickly. Later, you can go back, update your code, and change to the strict DTD.

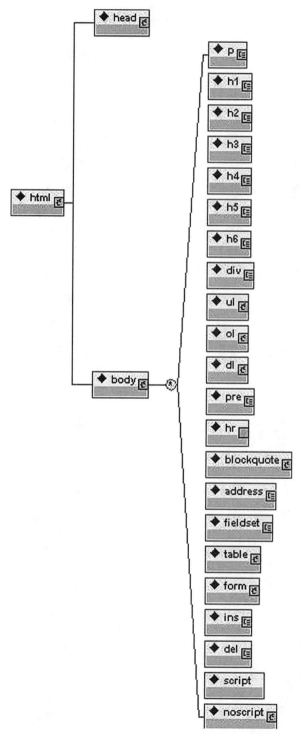

Figure 3.1 Graphical representation of the strict DTD.

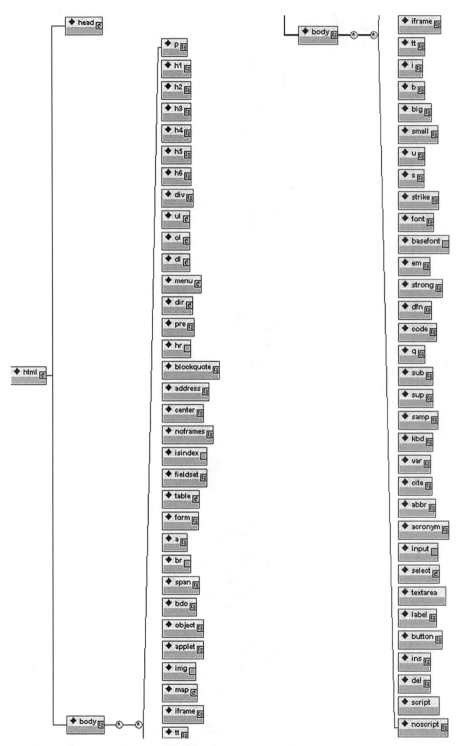

Figure 3.2 Graphical representation of the transitional DTD.

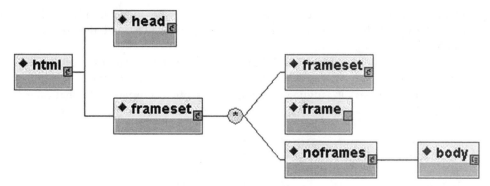

Figure 3.3 Graphical representation of the frameset DTD.

Specifying an XML Namespace

The root (first) element in an XHTML document must be <html>, just as in HTML documents. But XHTML also requires that you specify certain attributes before the parser will accept the input as valid. These attributes specify the default XML namespace (xmlns) and the language being used both for the code (xml:lang) and the document content (lang). The namespace attribute tells the parser that the document is using XHTML, a subset of XML.

The following code shows the root element for an XHTML document with an XML namespace:

```
<html xmlns="http://www.w3.org/1999/xhtml">
```

Table 3.2 Elements Not in the Strict DTD

ELEMENT	DESCRIPTION
<applet>	Java applet
<basefont>	Default font
<center>	Centered block
<dir>	Directory list
<font>	Font
<iframe>	Inline frame
<isindex>	Input prompt
<menu>	Menu list
<s>	Strike-through text
<strike>	Strike-through text
<u>	Underlined text

By now in our document, we will have specified that the document is an XHTML document through both the !DOCTYPE element (not shown) and the namespace attribute.

The core power of namespaces in XML comes from being able to use multiple subsets in a single document. For example, let's say we have a document written in MathML, the math markup language used for representing complex mathematical formulas (see Figure 3.4 for the resulting screen in the Amaya browser):

```
<?xml version="1.0" encoding="UTF-8"?>
<!DOCTYPE math PUBLIC "-//W3C//DTD MathML 2.0//EN"
"http://www.w3.org/TR/MathML2/dtd/mathml2.dtd">
<mml xmlns="http://www.w3.org/1998/Math/MathML">
      <munderover>
        <mo>&Sum;</mo>
        <mrow>
          <mi>i</mi>
          <mo>=</mo>
          <mn>1</mn>
        </mrow>
        <mi>n</mi>
      </munderover>
</mml>
```

In MathML, <mml> is the root element. On that root element, we are specifying the default namespace as being MathML. This enables the browser to access the namespace and to interpret the code for the rest of the document.

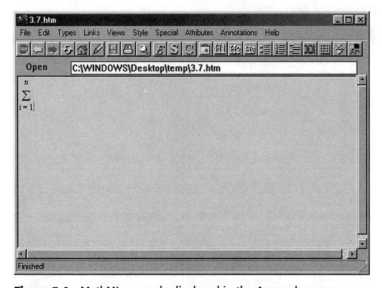

Figure 3.4   MathML example displayed in the Amaya browser.

Language Attributes

In addition to the namespace attribute, you must also include the lang and xml:lang attributes to indicate the language being used in the code and the document itself.

NOTE We recommend you include both the xml:lang and lang attributes, although both serve the same purpose—to create a consistent way to identify the language being used within elements. And because we are writing in XHTML, an XML-based language, technically, the xml:lang attribute is the appropriate one to use; but since most browsers do not yet support the xml:lang attribute, play it safe and include lang as well.

The following code identifies English ("en") as the default language being used within elements (note that the two-letter language codes are from the ISO 639 standard):

```
<html xmlns="http://www.w3.org/1999/xhtml" xml:lang="en" lang="en">
```

Both lang and xml:lang may be used on any element within the document. If, for example, you had a <blockquote> in Latin within your English document, you could do the following:

```
<p>Then the priest said <span xml:lang="la" lang="la">de mortuis nil
nisi bonum</span>.</p>
```

When you use the language attributes, other capabilities become possible. For example, a voice browser may then be able to switch pronunciation styles, or even voice, when it finds text in another language. If a user has translation software, these attributes make it possible to react to the change in language within a document.

You can also extend the value for either language attribute by following the two-letter language code with a hyphen and a two-letter country code. For example, to specify English spoken specifically in the United States, you could use the value "en-US". To specify English spoken in the United Kingdom, you would use "en-UK". Note: Unlike other XML values, these are not case-sensitive.

Basic Structure

The rest of XHTML is very similar to the HTML you are familiar with—but there is one caveat: you must follow the new rules set out earlier. The only other required elements for a well-formed XHTML document are <head>...</head> and <body>...</body> (unless you are creating a frameset document, then you would use <frameset> ...</frameset> instead of body).

Here, we'll briefly present pertinent additional rules regarding what can and should go into each part of an HTML and XHTML document.

<head>

The head of a document may contain only certain types of information. This information should apply to the document as a whole; it must not be document content. Included in the head is:

Title. Though not required, all documents should have a title that is descriptive of the content of the document. Keep in mind that, generally, search engines treat a title as more important than the body of the document; it is the text that becomes a bookmark for a page.

Metadata. Also known as *metatags*, this is data that describes your document. This topic will be covered in more detail in Chapter 11, "Metadata."

Scripts. Generally placed in the head of a document to ensure that they are loaded before the rest of the document. This enables the user to access the script's functionality before the entire document has loaded. This topic will be covered in more detail in Chapter 9, "JavaScript."

Style Sheets. Contain style information. In this book, cascading style sheets (CSS) can be linked to the document if contained in a separate file. If the style information is included in the document, it should go in the head to ensure that the style information is loaded prior to the document's content. This topic will be covered in more detail in Chapter 8, "Formatting with Style Sheets."

<body>

As it's name implies, the body contains the content of the document—what the user sees in the browser's main window. The body can include:

Block-level elements. Elements treated as a block, and preceded by a blank line in the browser display. Paragraphs, headings, and lists are all block-level elements.

Inline elements. Elements that can be contained within block-level elements; they are not preceded by a blank line. Breaks, hyperlinks, and images are all inline elements.

Style information. Attributes such as italics, boldfacing, and inline CSSs can be included in the body. When using XHTML, it is preferable to use cascading style sheets; therefore, we recommend that CSS information be included as a separate file, or in the head of the document. Chapter 8 covers styling in greater detail.

Scripting. JavaScript or other scripting language commands that add interactivity to the document through such means as capturing mouse movement or activating a function in the head of the document. Chapter 9 covers scripting in greater detail.

Hyperlinks. Links to other, external, documents or to locations within the current document.

Images. Graphics that add to the presentational value of the information.

Multimedia. Typically, audio and video files, but also includes any other non-HTML file types such as PDF documents and MS Excel spreadsheets.

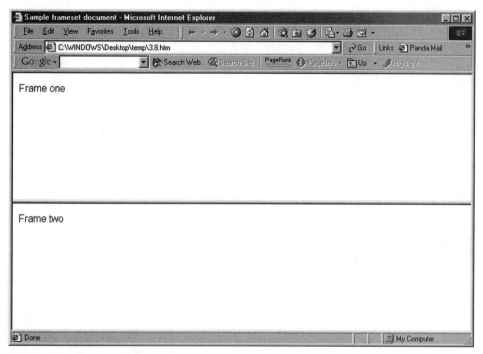

Figure 3.5 Browser display of frameset code.

<frameset>

Documents that establish the layout of frames in the browser window are called frameset documents. As noted earlier, these documents do not use the <body> element; instead, they use <frameset>.

Framesets may include only <frame> and <noframe> elements. The following code shows a simple frameset document (see Figure 3.5 for the resulting browser display). You will quickly notice that this code is significantly different from your typical XHTML document. Though the document starts out the same way as strict and transitional documents, with only the minor change of specifying the frameset DTD, but once we get past the document's <head>, things start to change significantly.

```
<?xml version="1.0" encoding="UTF-8"?>
<!DOCTYPE html PUBLIC "-//W3C/DTD XHTML 1.0 Frameset//EN"
English")>"http://www.w3.org/TR/xhtml1/DTD/frameset.dtd">
<html xmlns="http://www.w3.org/1999/xhtml" xml:lang="en" lang="en">
<head>
<title>Sample frameset document</title>
<frameset rows="50%,50%">
     <frame src="frame1.html" name="one" />
     <frame src="frame2.html" name="two" />
</frame>
<noframes>
     <body>
```

```
        <p>Sorry, your browser does not support frames.</p>
        </body>
    </noframes>
</html>
```

In this example, the frameset element specifies that the browser's window should be divided in half, horizontally. The top frame contains the document one.html, the bottom, two.html. We have also given the browser the capability to display alternate material from the <noframes> element if it does not support frames. Note that this section does contain a body, but it is nested within the <noframes> element and therefore is not a required component of a minimal document.

NOTE Frameset documents are given more coverage in Chapter 7, "Frames."

A Complete Minimal XHTML Document

The following code lays out a complete minimal XHTML document (not a frameset document):

```
1.  <?xml version="1.0" encoding="UTF-8"?>
2.  <!DOCTYPE html PUBLIC "-//W3C/DTD XHTML 1.0 Transitional//EN"
        "http://www.w3.org/TR/xhtml1/DTD/transitional.dtd">
3.  <html xmlns="http://www.w3.org/1999/xhtml" xml:lang="en" lang="en">
4.  <head>
5.  <title>Though not required all documents should have a title</title>
6.  </head>
7.  <body>
8.   Document content appears here.
9.  </body>
10. </html>
```

Sequentially, our minimal XHTML document contains:

1. The XML statement, specifying the XML encoding scheme.

2. The !DOCTYPE statement, indicating that we are using the public XHTML 1.0 transitional DTD and the address where that DTD is located.

3. The root element, specifying the default XML namespace, the XML language, and the document content language.

4. The start of the document head.

5. The title of the document.

6. The end of the document head.

7. The start of the document body.

8. The document content (optional).

9. The end of the document body.

10. The end of the document.

Including Other XML Languages in Your Document

Earlier in the chapter we showed you how to specify the XML language being used: specifically, the primary example indicated how to specify XHTML; the secondary used MathML. Each of these languages was indicated through the use of the xmlns attribute on the root element. But you also need to learn what to do if you had an XHTML document in which you needed to include some MathML language. The problem is twofold: First, once you have established the document as being written in XHTML, the browser will not understand MathML elements and attributes; second, XML does not allow for multiple !DOCTYPE statements.

The solution is to establish multiple namespaces. Take a look at the following code. Here we establish the default namespace as XHTML; a secondary namespace (math) is established as MathML.

```
<html xmlns="http://www.w3.org/1999/xhtml"
      xmlns:math="http://www.w3.org/1998/Math/MathML">
```

To tell the browser when we are using MathML, all we need to do is precede the MathML element with the namespace indicator math. Following is our composite XHTML/MathML document, including MathML code:

```
<?xml version="1.0" encoding="UTF-8"?>
<!DOCTYPE html PUBLIC "-//W3C/DTD XHTML 1.0 Transitional//EN"
"http://www.w3.org/TR/xhtml1/DTD/transitional.dtd">
<html xmlns="http://www.w3.org/1999/xhtml"
      xmlns:math="http://www.w3.org/1998/Math/MathML">
<head>
<title>Mixing XHTML and MathML</title>
</head>
<body>
<h1>Here is an example of a mathematical formula rendered using
MathML.</h1>
        <math:munderover>
          <math:mo>&Sum;</math:mo>
          <math:mrow>
            <math:mi>i</math:mi>
            <math:mo>=</math:mo>
            <math:mn>1</math:mn>
          </math:mrow>
          <math:mi>n</math:mi>
        </math:munderover>
</body>
</html>
```

Note that in this example, because we are actually using more MathML markup than XHTML markup, it may have made more sense to set MathML as the default namespace and set up XHTML as the secondary namespace. But for the purposes of

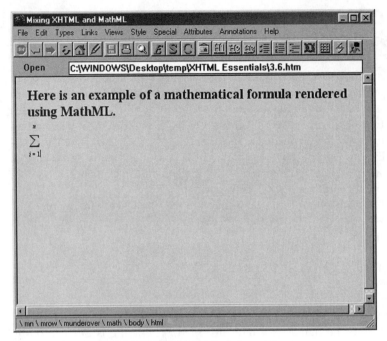

Figure 3.6 Our hybrid XHTML/MathML document.

this book, whose main topic is XHTML, we did it the other way. Also note that we assume here that the browser through which the document will be viewed supports MathML. Figure 3.6 shows our hybrid XHTML/MathML document as it is rendered in the Amaya browser.

Another important point to keep in mind is that multiple namespaces can also be embedded into the document. The MathML code could also be written as shown here:

```
<?xml version="1.0" encoding="UTF-8"?>
<!DOCTYPE html PUBLIC "-//W3C/DTD XHTML 1.0 Transitional//EN"
"http://www.w3.org/TR/xhtml1/DTD/transitional.dtd">
<html xmlns="http://www.w3.org/1999/xhtml">
<head>
<title>Another way to mix XHTML and MathML</title>
</head>
<body>
<h1>Here is an example of a mathematical formula rendered using
MathML./h1>
<!-- Start a new namespace -->
<math xmlns="http://www.w3.org/1998/Math/MathML">
    <munderover>
      <mo>&Sum;</mo>
      <mrow>
        <mi>i</mi>
        <mo>=</mo>
        <mn>1</mn>
```

```
            </mrow>
            <mi>n</mi>
         </munderover>
</math>
<!-- Back to the default namesapce -->
</body>
</html>
```

In the previous examples, we showed you how to mix two XML languages (XHTML and MathML) within the same document. We used these languages specifically because they do *not* have any similar elements. Now let's take it one step further. Let's say we have two XML languages that *share element names*. For example, suppose we want to use XHTML, and include information using NAML, the Name and Address Markup Language. Like XHTML, NAML uses the <title> element, but in a different context. Following is the code for a document using both XHTML and NAML:

NOTE Details on NAML language can be found at www.ozemail.com.au/~sakthi/dtd/dtd.html.

```
<title>Best Employees</title>
...
<p>Here are our best employees.<p>
<hr />
<naml>
  <record>
  <person_details>
     <title>Mr</title>
     <first_name>Michael</first_name>
     <last_name>Sauers</last_name>
  </person_details>
  <address_lines address_type="billing">
     <address_line1>BCR</address_line1>
     <address_line2>14394 E Evans Ave</address_line2>
     <address_line3>Aurora CO 80014</address_line3>
     <address_line4>USA</address_line4>
  </address_lines>
  <address_details address_type="postal">
     <postal_details postal_type="POBox">
            <postal_number>123</postal_number>
     </postal_details>
     <locality>Aurora</locality>
     <state>CO</state>
     <postalcode>80014</postalcode>
     <country>USA</country>
  </address_details>
  <other_data>Phone: 303-555-9787</other_data>
  </record>
 <hr />
 ...
```

In XHTML, <title> specifies the title of the document; in NAML, <title> specifies the employee's job title. How do browsers or other processing software handle this? Do they treat the content of the element as the document title or as the employee's job title? This is where specifying namespaces comes into play. We could set up XHTML as the default namespace, and HRML (Human Resources Markup Language) as a secondary namespace. Then, through the modification of our code, we would have <title> and <hrml:title>, two distinctly different elements, as shown here:

```
<html xmlns="http://www.w3.org/1999/xhtml"
      xmlns:hrml="namespaceURL">
<head>
<title>Best Employees</title>
</head>
...
<p>Here are our best employees.
<hr />
<naml>
  <hrml:record>
  <hrml:person_details>
     <hrml:title>Mr</hrml:title>
     <hrml:first_name>Michael<hrml:/first_name>
     <hrml:last_name>Sauers</hrml:last_name>
  </hrml:person_details>
  <hrml:address_lines address_type="billing">
     <hrml:address_line1>BCR<hrml:address_line1>
     <hrml:address_line2>14394 E Evans Ave</hrml:address_line2>
     <hrml:address_line3>Aurora CO 80014</hrml:address_line3>
     <hrml:address_line4>USA</hrml:address_line4>
  </hrml:address_lines>
  <hrml:address_details address_type="postal">
     <hrml:postal_details postal_type="POBox">
            <hrml:postal_number>123</hrml:postal_number>
     </hrml:postal_details>
     <hrml:locality>Aurora</hrml:locality>
     <hrml:state>CO</hrml:state>
     <hrml:postalcode>80014</hrml:postalcode>
     <hrml:country>USA</hrml:country>
     </hrml:address_details>
     <hrml:other_data>Phone: 303-555-9787</hrml:other_data>
  </hrml:record>
 <hr />
 ...
```

We'll take this one step further still, by creating a document that contains three different XML languages: XHTML, Math Markup Language (MML), and Chemical Markup Language (CML), such as the following:

```
<?xml version="1.0" encoding="UTF-8"?>
<!DOCTYPE html PUBLIC "-//W3C/DTD XHTML 1.0 Transitional//EN"
```

```
"http://www.w3.org/TR/xhtml1/DTD/transitional.dtd">
<html xmlns="http://www.w3.org/1999/xhtml" xml:lang="en" lang="en"
      xmlns:math="http://www.w3.org/1998/Math/MathML">
<head>
<title>Example of a document containing three XML languages</title>
</head>
<body>
<!-- XHTML -->
<h1 align="center">This document contains XHTML, MML, and CML.</h1>
<hr width="50%" />
<p>Here is an example of MML (MathML)</p>
<!-- CML -->
<molecule xmlns="http://www.xml-cml.org/xmlns/cml10" convention="MDLMol"
id="acetate" title="ACETATE">
  <date day="23" month="11" year="1995">
  </date>
  <atomArray>
    <atom id="a1">
      <string builtin="elementType">C</string>
      <float builtin="x2">0.27</float>
      <float builtin="y2">0.1217</float>
    </atom>
    <atom id="a2">
      <string builtin="elementType">C</string>
      <float builtin="x2">-1.27</float>
      <float builtin="y2">0.1246</float>
    </atom>
    <atom id="a3">
      <string builtin="elementType">O</string>
      <float builtin="x2">1.0623</float>
      <float builtin="y2">-1.2937</float>
    </atom>
    <atom id="a4">
      <string builtin="elementType">O</string>
      <float builtin="x2">1.1008</float>
      <float builtin="y2">1.4332</float>
    </atom>
  </atomArray>
  <bondArray>
    <bond id="b1">
      <string builtin="atomRef">a1</string>
      <string builtin="atomRef">a2</string>
      <string builtin="order">1</string>
    </bond>
    <bond id="b2">
      <string builtin="atomRef">a1</string>
      <string builtin="atomRef">a3</string>
      <string builtin="order">1</string>
    </bond>
    <bond id="b3">
```

```
            <string builtin="atomRef">a1</string>
            <string builtin="atomRef">a4</string>
            <string builtin="order">2</string>
        </bond>
    </bondArray>
</molecule>
<!-- XHTML -->
<hr width="50%" />
<p>Here is an example of CML (ChemicalML)</p>
<!-- MML -->
        <math:munderover>
          <math:mo>&Sum;</math:mo>
          <math:mrow>
            <math:mi>i</math:mi>
            <math:mo>=</math:mo>
            <math:mn>1</math:mn>
          </math:mrow>
          <math:mi>n</math:mi>
        </math:munderover>
<!-- XHTML -->
</body>
</html>
```

> **NOTE** We could not include a screenshot of this code's display, because at the time of this writing there was no single browser that supported XHTML, MML, and CML. Details about CML (including the Jumbo CML browser) can be found at www.xml-cml.org.

Here's how this example breaks out:

- The document has a default namespace of XHTML, which we established through the xmlns attribute on the root (<html>) element.

- We included two other languages, MML and CML, using two different methods to specify their namespaces. For MML, we added a secondary namespace on the root element. In this case, we specified that elements preceded with math: should use the MML namespace.

- For the CML section of the document, we specified the namespace on the <molecule> element. This instructs the parser to use the CML namespace until it reaches the </molecule> element.

This example was included to demonstrate the various methods available to you as an XHTML author. But we recommend that when actually working with multiple XML languages you choose one method or the other, and be consistent throughout the whole document.

Summary

This chapter defined exactly what you must include in a well-formed XHTML document at the most basic level: specifically, an XML statement, a !DOCTYPE statement, a root element establishing the default namespace and languages, and the document head, title, and body. Without this information, the XML parser will emit an error, and stop the display of your document.

The next step is to place content into the document. In the rest of this book, you'll learn how to describe the document and make it interactive to the user.

Converting to
and Validating XHTML

Once you have finished reading this book, you will know how to create your own XHTML documents from scratch. But what about your existing HTML documents? Chances are you already have many of those, and the last thing you want to have to do is rewrite them. Well, you don't have to. In this chapter, you'll learn the skills necessary to quickly and easily convert your documents from HTML to XHTML, either manually or automatically.

NOTE In this chapter, we will focus on the manual process of converting HTML to XHTML documents, because performing this process on documents you are already familiar with will help you better learn XHTML.

Throughout this book, we've been stressing that the key to writing a Web document in XHTML is making sure the document is well formed. Fortunately, in addition to learning the rules for developing well-formed XHTML documents, a tool is available to help you make sure you have accomplished your task. Called the *XHTML validator,* this tool is important when you are writing from scratch, but it is essential to use when you are converting a document from HTML to XHTML, as it will catch any mistakes you've made or changes you've neglected to implement.

Converting from HTML to XHTML

As you know by now, HTML is very similar to XHTML, so converting from the former to the latter is not difficult: most of the work is already done. But before we begin to delve into what exactly is involved in converting HTML to XHTML, let's review the differences between them. In contrast to HTML, in XHTML:

- All elements must be closed properly.
- Elements are case-sensitive.
- Attribute values must be enclosed within quotation marks.
- Empty elements must be closed.
- All attributes must be fully formed.

Manual Conversion

The first instruction for converting a document manually from HTML to XHTML may seem daunting at first: You must go through your HTML document line by line to ensure that it follows the five rules of XHTML. But rest assured, "manually" does not mean you cannot use your computer editor's find and replace function. By manually, we mean you will not be using a software program that processes your document all at once. That would be what we define as an *automatic* process.

Furthermore, there are steps you can take to make the manual conversion process easier still:

1. There are only two empty elements that most people use in HTML documents, <br> and <hr>. Use the find and replace feature of your editor to replace these with <br /> and <hr />, respectively. (Note, however, this will not fix any of those elements that have attributes.)

2. If you were in the habit of using uppercase elements, again use find and replace to find and fix these occurrences. For example, find <P and replace it with <p, find <TD and replace it with <td. (Note: Do not include the greater-than symbol or you will miss paragraph elements with attributes.)

3. Find the common attributes that did not need values in HTML and replace them with the fully formed versions. For example, find noshade and replace it with noshade="noshade".

Once you have completed these steps, you'll see that a significant amount of the work has been done. Depending on your coding style, here's what's left:

1. Go through your document and make sure all elements are properly closed. The most common element to overlook is </p>. (If you are already in the habit of using </p>, then you can skip this step.)

2. Verify that all of your attribute values are enclosed within quotation marks.

3. Add the XML and !DOCTYPE statements to the beginning of the document.

4. Add the xmlns, xml:lang, and lang attributes to the <html> element.

Take a look at the following example of a simple HTML document:

```
<HTML>
<HEAD>
<TITLE>Simple HTML document to be converted to XHTML</TITLE>
```

```
</HEAD>
<BODY>
<P>This is a paragraph with<BR>
two lines of text.
<P>Here is another paragraph.
</BODY>
</HTML>
```

To convert this document to XHTML, follow these steps:

1. Change all of the elements to lowercase.
2. Close the line breaks.
3. Close all paragraph elements.
4. Add the XML statement.
5. Add the !DOCTYPE statement.
6. Add the namespace and language attributes.

After performing these steps, you should end up with the following:

```
<?xml version="1.0" encoding="UTF-8"?>
<!DOCTYPE html PUBLIC "-//W3C//DTD XHTML 1.0 Transitional//EN"
"http://www.w3.org/TR/xhtml11/DTD/xhtml1-transitional.dtd">
<html xmlns="http://www.w3.org/1999/xhtml" xml:lang="en" lang="en">
<head>
<title>Simple html document to be converted to xhtml</title>
</head>
<body>
<p>This is a paragraph with<br />
two lines of text.</p>
<p>Here is another paragraph.</p>
</body>
</html>
```

Once you have gone through all of these steps, and believe that you have done all that is needed, you can move on to the validation process to check your work.

NOTE **At the end of this chapter is an exercise section that includes a larger HTML file with which you can practice your conversion skills.**

Automatic Conversion

Initially, as we said, we recommend—especially to new authors—the manual process of conversion, as a means of learning how XHTML works and understanding how to integrate its new rules; but once you are comfortable with the differences between the two markup languages, you'll want to move ahead more quickly, at which point you'll no doubt want to use the automatic conversion process.

The automatic conversion process involves using a software program designed specifically for the purpose. We'll focus on one, called HTML Tidy, to explain how it works.

Table 4.1 HTML Tidy Conversion Options

add-xml-decl:yes	Adds the XML declaration to the output file.
output-xhtml:yes	Outputs the !DOCTYPE statement as the XHTML version appropriate to the document.
drop-font-tags:yes	Removes all font elements and their associated attributes.

HTML Tidy

HTML Tidy accepts an HTML file as input, and can either output the converted document as a new file or overwrite the original file. HTML Tidy has many features to assist you in cleaning up your code, but we'll focus on just those necessary to convert from HTML to XHTML. Table 4.1 lists some of the options you will need to use to convert from HTML to XHTML. All of HTML Tidy's other features, including how to run the program against your files, are fully described at its Web site.

NOTE HTML Tidy can be found at the W3C Web site at www.w3.org/People/Raggett/tidy/. At the time of this writing, HTML Tidy is available only in a command-line interface.

Note that the output-xhtml:yes option will preserve the case of your elements even though XHTML requires lowercase elements. If you used uppercase elements in your HTML document, you may want to run HTML Tidy once just to convert your elements to lowercase before using these options to convert to XHTML.

Validating XHTML Documents

Once you have created an XHTML document, whether through the conversion of an existing HTML document or from scratch, you must validate that document. Doing so will ensure that you have followed the five rules for producing a well-formed XHTML document, thereby ensuring that it will display in the browser as you intended.

NOTE Because HTML was so flexible, too many authors developed their own style for coding documents—some used </p> all the time, others never did; some put quotation marks around all attribute values, others only when it was necessary to make the attribute work. It was this individualistic approach to HTML coding that led to the development of XHTML. As a result, browsers had to be flexible to accommodate the various coding techniques. Consequently, as all Web authors know, even when our code is correct, browsers still may not always respond as we expect. We believe that only through following correct standards for coding can we demonstrate to browser makers that we want and expect identical and predictable behavior from all browsers.

Though HTML code validators have been around for years, the majority of HTML authors did not use them—they didn't have to, because HTML and browser flexibility meant that as long as a document looked fine in the browser window, authors did not have to care what the corresponding code looked like.

XHTML, as you know by now, requires Web authors to conform their coding styles and idiosyncrasies to the five rules of XHTML if they hope to produce browser-displayable documents. To help with that mind-set transformation, we recommend that all authors use code validators.

How to Validate

You can validate using either a software program that is loaded on your computer (usually as part of an editing program) or through a Web-based service. We encourage you to use the Web-based validator offered by the World Wide Web Consortium (W3C), http://validator.w3.org/.

NOTE The rest of this section explains the validation process using the W3C HTML Validation Service. Other validators may have different options than the ones discussed here.

Validator Options

You may tell the validator which document to validate through two methods, URI (URL) or upload:

URI (URL). This method allows you to put in the address of the document you wish to validate (see Figure 4.1). If your document is on a remote Web server, this is the choice for you.

Upload. If your document is on the same computer from which you are accessing the validator, you can use the upload feature (see Figure 4.2). This option allows you to browse your computer system for the file and then send it directly to the validation system.

Once you have chosen your input method, there are four output options that you can choose from (see Figure 4.3):

Show source input. Reports the results of the validation and provides a line-numbered copy of the original code. This output can assist you in two ways: First, if you are not using an editor that uses line numbers, it is easier to figure out to which line the validator is referring; and, second, it allows you to generate a complete printout of your source code and validation results for future reference.

Show an outline of the document. Reports back any validation errors, along with an outline of your document, based on any included headings. This can be helpful in determining whether you're using headings properly.

Show parse tree. Reports back any validation errors, along with all of your code. The validator reports on each line, whether correct or incorrect.

Exclude attributes from the parse tree. Works as the "show parse tree" option does but does not report on attributes as part of the parse tree.

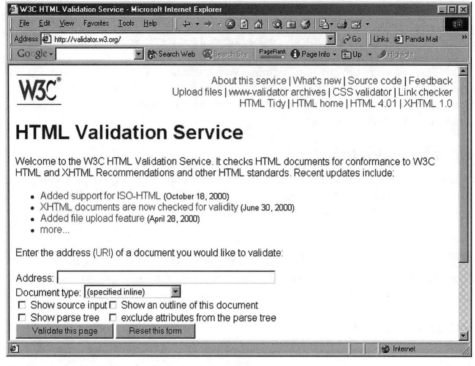

Figure 4.1   The URI input method of validation.

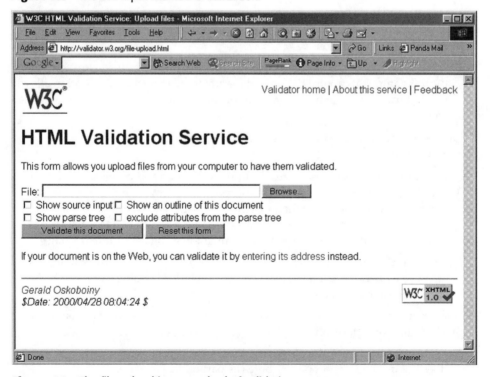

Figure 4.2   The file upload input method of validation.

The Validation Process

In this section, we'll validate the document we converted earlier in the chapter, using the upload input option to send the file to the validator. Note that none of the output options are necessary for this exercise, but you can use them if you wish to see how they work. Once you have input the filename and your output options, click the "Validate this page" button, which you can see in Figure 4.3. The result is shown in Figure 4.4.

Now let's take a look at that document again but this time assume we made an error—we'll assume we forgot to close the line break. In this case, our code would look like this:

```
1.    <?xml version="1.0" encoding="UTF-8"?>
2.    <!DOCTYPE html PUBLIC "-//W3C//DTD XHTML 1.0 Transitional//EN"
3.    "http://www.w3.org/TR/xhtml11/DTD/xhtml1-transitional.dtd">
4.    <html xmlns="http://www.w3.org/1999/xhtml" xml:lang="en" lang="en">
5.    <head>
6,    <title>Simple html document to be converted to xhtml</title>
7.    </head>
8.    <body>
9.    <p>This is a paragraph with<br>
10.   two lines of text.</p>
11.   <p>Here is another paragraph.</p>
12.   </body>
13.   </html>
```

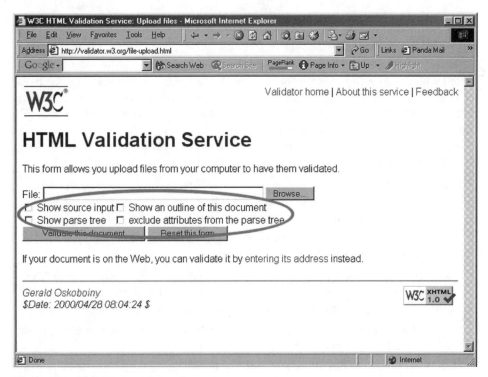

Figure 4.3 Validator output options.

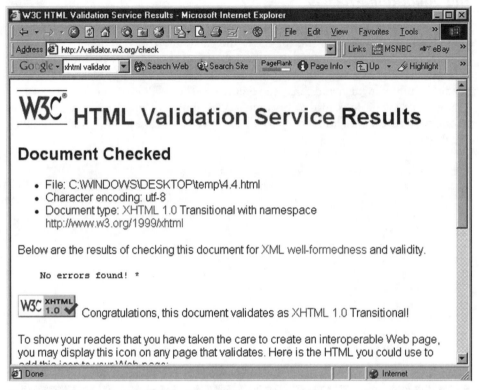

Figure 4.4 A successfully validated XHTML document.

When we submit this file to the validator, as you can see in Figure 4.5, we are presented with the error "end tag for "br" omitted." The second error, "start tag was here" tells us where the start of the tag for the earlier error is. In this case, of course, it seems pointless since this is an empty element, but if this error were to occur on a paragraph, this would point out where the start of the paragraph was.

Now we must find that line break element in line 9 and close it properly. Upon doing so and revalidating the document, we will receive the result shown in Figure 4.6.

End tag for "X" omitted. Occurs when you have started an element but have not ended it. Common examples include forgetting the close paragraph element (</p>) and slashes from empty elements, such as <br> and <hr>.

There is no attribute "X". Occurs when you use an attribute that does not exist in the DTD you have specified.

Element "X" undefined. Occurs when you use an element that is not valid XHTML. This may happen when you use an element that is proprietary to a particular company's browser or when you have failed to type the element in lowercase.

Required attribute "X" not specified. Occurs when you have used an element but have left out a required attribute.

Document type does not allow element "X" here. Occurs when you illegally place an element; for example, a paragraph embedded within another paragraph.

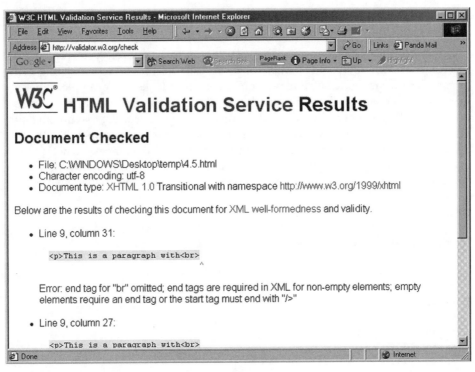

Figure 4.5   An XHTML document with an error.

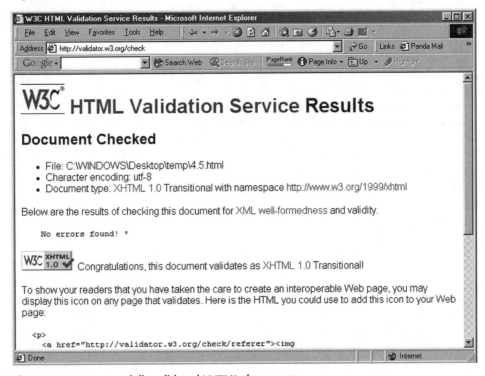

Figure 4.6   A successfully validated XHTML document.

End tag for element "X" that is not open. Occurs when you have ended an element but not properly opened it, if at all.

Before you have the conversion process "down to a science," you may initially receive what seems like a large number of errors, especially if you are validating a long or complex document. Relax; it may not be as bad as it looks. For example, a missing quotation mark early in the document may lead the validator to report that there are other errors that do not really exist, but are merely a consequence of that missing quotation mark. But if, in fact, your document does have numerous errors to fix, the best approach is to tackle a few at a time and then revalidate the document. Do not try to fix everything all at once. Frequently, you will find that fixing one real error may make several others disappear. To illustrate this point, try validating the following code:

```
<?xml version="1.0" encoding="UTF-8"?>
<!DOCTYPE html PUBLIC "-//W3C//DTD XHTML 1.0 Transitional//EN"
"http://www.w3.org/TR/xhtml11/DTD/xhtml1-transitional.dtd">
<html xmlns="http://www.w3.org/1999/xhtml" xml:lang="en" lang="en">
<head>
<title>Simple html document to be converted to xhtml</title>
</head>
<body>
<p>Paragraph 1
<p>Paragraph 2</p>
<p>Paragraph 3</p>
<p>Paragraph 4</p>
<p>Paragraph 5</p>
<p>Paragraph 6</p>
<p>Paragraph 7</p>
</body>
</html>
```

Figure 4.7 shows the validation results.

According to the validator, there are eight problems in this document. But most of these problems stem from one mistake: not properly closing paragraph 1. This error caused the validator to "see" the other six paragraphs as embedded within the first one, and one of the paragraphs left open.

If we fix the "real" problem, we solve all of the consequent problems, as shown in the repaired code:

```
<?xml version="1.0" encoding="UTF-8"?>
<!DOCTYPE html PUBLIC "-//W3C//DTD XHTML 1.0 Transitional//EN"
"http://www.w3.org/TR/xhtml11/DTD/xhtml1-transitional.dtd">
<html xmlns="http://www.w3.org/1999/xhtml" xml:lang="en" lang="en">
<head>
<title>Simple html document to be converted to xhtml</title>
</head>
<body>
<p>Paragraph 1</p>
<p>Paragraph 2</p>
<p>Paragraph 3</p>
```

```
<p>Paragraph 4</p>
<p>Paragraph 5</p>
<p>Paragraph 6</p>
<p>Paragraph 7</p>
</body>
</html>
```

After revalidating the document, we receive the approved validation report, as shown in Figure 4.8.

A Conversion and Validation Exercise

Let's test what we've learned by working on a much longer document. The following code shows a multipage HTML document. Go through the conversion and validation process on your own and see if you can produce a well-formed and validated XHTML document. Later in this section is a version of the code that has gone through this process. Here are some helpful hints:

■ All elements need to be closed—(<p>).

■ All elements need to be in lowercase—(<meta> and <h1>).

■■ Attribute values need to be enclosed within quotation marks—(right and center).

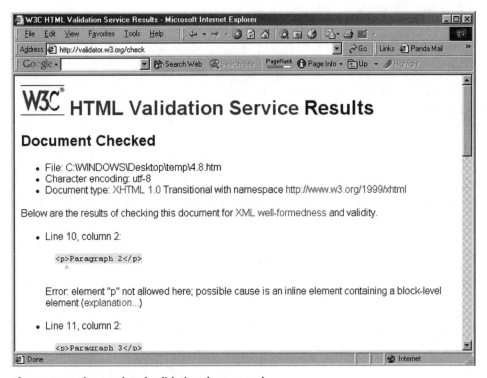

Figure 4.7 The results of validating the test code.

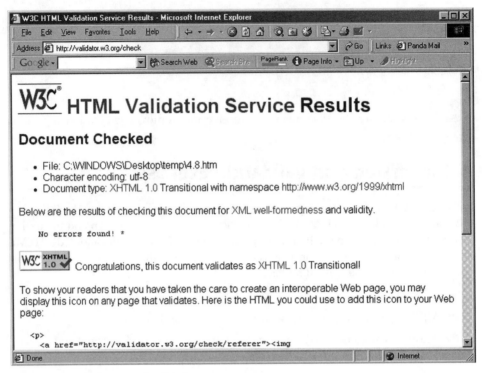

Figure 4.8 The approved validation report.

- Empty elements need to be closed—(
 and <hr>).
- The alt attribute needs to be added to the image.
- The !DOCTYPE statement must be added.
- The namespace and language attributes must be added to the <html> element.

```
<html>
<head>
<title>BCR - Mission</title>
<META name="description" content ="BCR Mission">
<META name="keywords" content="Bibliographical Center for
Research,BCR,library services, mission">
</head>
<body>
<table width="600" align="center">
<tr>
<td>
<img src="logo.gif" width="592" height="114" border="0">
</td>
</tr>
<tr>
<td>
<b>BCR Board of Trustees</b>
```

```
<H1>BCR's Mission Statement and Goals</H1>
<p>
The Bibliographical Center for Research, (BCR) is organized
as a not-for-profit corporation to assist in the effective
and economical delivery of high-quality library and
information services. BCR operations serve the membership by
helping the library community to share information
resources, by providing access to information services, by
developing and promoting new technologies for information
organization and delivery and by carrying out training and
technical assistance in the use of information services. BCR
encourages and assists communication among the members and
serves as their advocate on regional and national library
and information issues.
<p>
BCR will be governed by a Board of Trustees, which
includes representatives of the broad interests of the
members, provides a forum for the resolution of
organizational issues, and is open to and encouraging of the
expression of the concerns of the membership.
<p>
BCR will encourage the participation of individuals
from its member institutions in its organizational
activities.
<p>
BCR will maintain its not-for-profit status.
<p>
BCR will maintain a financial condition that will
allow the lowest possible pricing for products and services
to its members while maintaining its ability to respond to
future needs.
<p>
BCR will promote communication, cooperation, and
resource sharing among its members, as well as with other
library and information service institutions and
organizations.
<p>
BCR will seek new members to enhance its base for
cooperation and resource sharing.
<p>
BCR will market itself and its products and services
to current and potential members.
<p>
BCR will offer products and services that will
promote the effectiveness and efficiency of library and
information organizations.
<p>
BCR will diversify its products and services in
response to the changing needs of members, while maintaining
high standards of quality and performance.
<p>
```

```
BCR will provide resources and a working environment
that will support the development of staff.
<hr width="25%">
<p align=center>
<a href="aboutbcr.html">About BCR</a> |
<A HREF="botdir.html">Board of Trustees </A>
</p>
<p align=right>
December 05, 2000<br>
Copyright &copy; 2000 BCR
</td>
</tr>
</table>
</body>
</html>
```

Here is the converted and validated XHTML code:

```
<!DOCTYPE html PUBLIC "-//W3C//DTD XHTML 1.0 Transitional//EN"
@Code:"DTD/xhtml1-transitional.dtd">
<html xmlns="http://www.w3.org/1999/xhtml" xml:lang="en" lang="en">
<head>
<title>BCR - Mission</title>
<meta name="description" content="BCR Mission" />
<meta name="keywords" content="Bibliographical Center for
Research,BCR,library services, mission" />
</head>
<body>
<table width="600" align="center">
<tr>
<td>
<img src="logo.gif" width="592" height="114" border="0" alt="BCR Logo" />
</td>
</tr>
<tr>
<td>
<b>BCR Board of Trustees</b>
<h1>BCR's Mission Statement and Goals</h1>
<p>The Bibliographical Center for Research, (BCR) is organized as
a not-for-profit corporation to assist in the effective and
economical delivery of high-quality library and information
services. BCR operations serve the membership by helping the
library community to share information resources, by providing
access to information services, by developing and promoting new
technologies for information organization and delivery, and by
carrying out training and technical assistance in the use of
information services. BCR encourages and assists communication
among the members and serves as their advocate on regional and
national library and information issues.</p>
<p>BCR will be governed by a Board of Trustees, which includes
representatives of the broad interests of the members, provides a
```

```
forum for the resolution of organizational issues, and is open to
and encouraging of the expression of the concerns of the
membership.</p>
<p>BCR will encourage the participation of individuals from its
member institutions in its organizational activities.</p>
<p>BCR will maintain its not-for-profit status.</p>
<p>BCR will maintain a financial condition that will allow the
lowest possible pricing for products and services to its members
while maintaining its ability to respond to future needs.</p>
<p>BCR will promote communication, cooperation, and resource
sharing among its members, as well as with other library and
information service institutions and organizations.</p>
<p>BCR will seek new members to enhance its base for cooperation
and resource sharing.</p>
<p>BCR will market itself and its products and services to
current and potential members.</p>
<p>BCR will offer products and services that will promote the
effectiveness and efficiency of library and information
organizations.</p>
<p>BCR will diversify its products and services in response to
the changing needs of members, while maintaining high standards
of quality and performance.</p>
<p>BCR will provide resources and a working environment that will
support the development of staff.</p>
<hr width="25%" />
<p align="center">
<a href="aboutbcr.html">About BCR</a> |
<a href="botdir.html">Board of Trustees</a>
</p>
<p align="right">
December 05, 2000<br />
Copyright &copy; 2000 BCR
</p>
</td>
</tr>
</table>
</body>
</html>
```

Summary

In this chapter, we walked you through the two methods for creating an XHTML document: from scratch and through converting existing HTML documents. We recommended that, at least initially, you do the conversion process manually, as opposed to using automatic aids, to help you learn what's necessary to produce well-formed XHTML documents. Only after you have a solid grasp of XHTML should you implement automated conversion tools, such as HTML Tidy.

Tables

Since version 2.0, HTML has given authors the capability to include tables in their documents. With the release of HTML 4.0 and XHTML, their ability to control tables has increased. Previously, authors were forced to think exclusively in rows. Now with such new elements as <thead>, <tfoot>, <tbody>, <colgroup>, and <col> it is possible to design in columns as well. The purpose of this chapter then is twofold: first, to serve as a review of the traditional table design methods, and, second, to introduce readers to the new elements and attributes available to them.

Using Tables

Traditionally, tables used in HTML documents had two purposes: to *present tabular data* and for *layout purposes*.

Present tabular data. Tables were specifically designed to present information displayed in rows and columns, as on a spreadsheet. Following is a simply-coded XHTML document and the data it presents:

```
<table border="1">
<caption>Cups of coffee sold this weekend</caption>
<tr>
    <td> </td>
    <td>Saturday</td>
    <td>Sunday</td>
```

```
      </tr>
      <tr>
         <td>Regular</td>
         <td>30</td>
         <td>20</td>
      </tr>
      <tr>
         <td>Decaf</td>
         <td>12</td>
         <td>10</td>
      </tr>
      </table>
```

The browser display for this sample is shown in Figure 5.1.

Layout. HTML authors quickly discovered that through the subtle manipulation of table code, they could lay out their document in more innovative ways, using columns. For example, an author might create a two-column layout by first generating a table with a single row and two cells, then fill the cells with content, and, finally, turn off the table's borders. Here is the code for this design, followed by the browser display in Figure 5.2:

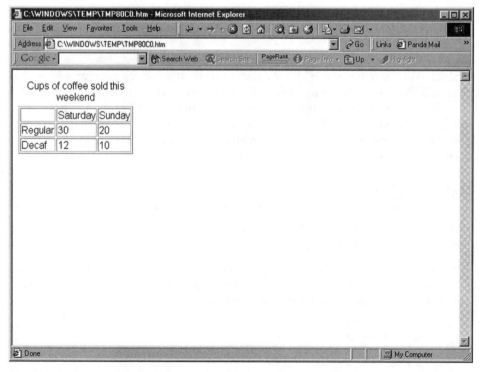

Figure 5.1   Browser display of a simple table in XHTML.

```
<table border="0">
<tr>
   <td>Column One Column One Column One Column One Column One Column
One Column One Column One Column One Column One Column One Column One
Column One Column One Column One Column One Column One Column One Col-
umn One Column One Column One Column One Column One Column One Column
One Column One Column One Column One Column One Column One Column One
Column One Column One Column One Column One Column One Column One Col-
umn One Column One Column One Column One Column One Column One Column
One</td>
   <td>Column Two Column Two Column Two Column Two Column Two Column
Two Column Two Column Two Column Two Column Two Column Two Column Two
Column Two Column Two Column Two Column Two Column Two Column Two Col-
umn Two Column Two Column Two Column Two Column Two Column Two Column
Two Column Two Column Two Column Two Column Two Column Two Column Two
Column Two Column Two Column Two Column Two Column Two Column Two Col-
umn Two Column Two Column Two Column Two Column Two Column Two Column
Two</td>
</tr>
</table>
```

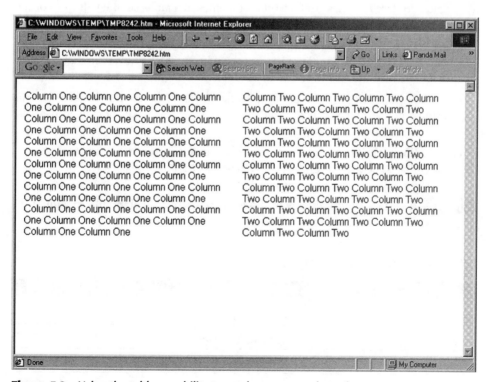

Figure 5.2   Using the table capability to produce a two-column layout.

NOTE The creators of the HTML did not intend the table capability to be used for layout purposes, therefore the rest of the examples in this chapter are used to present tabular data. In Chapter 8, "Formatting with Style Sheets," we explain how to implement the positioning aspects of CSS, level 2, as an alternative to using tables for layout purposes.

HTML Table Coding Review

An author using HTML to create a table had to master a minimum of three elements: <table>, <tr>, and <td>. Two others, <th> and <caption>, allowed an author to customize his or her table a little further. Table 5.1 shows these elements and their related attributes.

The following subsections define each of these elements more fully.

<table>...</table>

The <table> element specifies the start and end of a table. Its related attributes are:

border. Specifies, in number of pixels, the thickness of the border of the table. The outside border of the table is given a beveled appearance, which is more noticeable with larger values. To turn off all the lines in a table, set the value of border to zero (border= "0").

align. Specifies the horizontal alignment of the entire table on the page. The three available values are left (default), center, and right. Note, however, that setting the align attribute on the table will not affect the alignment of any cell content.

cellspacing. Specifies the amount of space, in pixels, between individual cells. This value will affect all cells within the table. (A word of caution: Don't confuse this attribute with cellpadding, defined next.)

cellpadding. Specifies the amount of space, in pixels, between the inside edge of the cell and the content of the cell. This value will affect all cells within the table.

NOTE A table may contain any of the other table-related elements, including another table.

Table 5.1 HTML Table Elements and Attributes

ELEMENT	ATTRIBUTES
table	border, align, width
tr	height, width, align
td	height, width, align, colspan, rowspan
th	height, width, align, colspan, rowspan
caption	align

The next example is of a table that is centered, and has a thin border, a 5-pixel gutter between cells, and a 3-pixel cellpad:

```
<table align="center" border="1" cellspacing="5" cellpadding="3">
...
</table>
```

<tr>...</tr>

The <tr> element specifies the start and end of a table row. This element is central to a HTML-based table, because, as you'll recall, HTML does not allow the author to work in columns.

A related attribute to <tr> is align. But in contrast to its use on the <table> element to set the alignment of the table itself, when used with <tr>, this attribute sets the alignment of the content of all the cells in the row. Available values are left (default), center, right, and justify.

Table rows may contain data and headings. This example shows a table row with all cell content right-justified:

```
<table align="center" border="1" cellspacing="5" cellpadding="3">
<tr>
...
</tr>
</table>
```

<td>...</td>

The table data (<td>) element can be thought of as an individual cell in a row; that is, the content that the author wishes to appear in a particular cell. This element's related attributes are:

align. When used on a cell, sets the alignment of the content of only that cell. The available values are left (default), center, right, and justify. Setting the align attribute on a particular cell will override any align value set on the row that contains the cell. It will not override any other cell in the row.

> **NOTE** If the align attribute has been set on a row, all cells in that row will automatically inherit that value. Thus, if the row has the align attribute set to right, the default justification for all cells in that row will be right, not left.

width. Enables you to set the width of a particular cell. Values can be set as pixels (width="n") or as a percentage of the whole table (width="n%"). Setting the width attribute overrides the default width of that cell (based upon the width of the actual content). Setting the width attribute also overrides the default width of the column containing that cell (based upon the width of the widest content within that column).

height. Allows you to specify the height of a particular cell. Values can be set as pixels (height="n") or as a percentage of the whole table (height="n%"). Setting the height attribute overrides the default height of that row (based upon the height of the actual content). Setting the height attribute also overrides the default height of the row containing that cell (based upon the greatest height within that row).

colspan. Enables you to specify that the cell extend beyond its established columnar boundaries into the area set aside for additional columns. This makes it possible to have a different number of cells in one row than in others. The number of columns spanned, plus the number of single columns, should equal the total number of cells in the row with the most cells.

rowspan. Lets you specify that the cell extend beyond the established row boundaries into the area set aside for additional rows in that column. This means you can include a different number of cells in one column than in others. The number of rows spanned, plus the number of single cells in that column, should equal the total number of rows in the column with the most cells.

Table data may include any other valid element and must be enclosed within a table row (see Figure 5.3 for the resulting browser display):

```
<table align="center" border="1" cellspacing="5" cellpadding="3">
<tr>
      <td>Cell one</td>
      <td>Cell two</td>
      <td>Cell three</td>
</tr>
</table>
```

For our next example, we'll modify the alignment of two of the cells (see Figure 5.4 for the resulting browser display):

```
<table align="center" border="1" cellspacing="5" cellpadding="3">
<tr>
      <td>Cell one</td>
      <td align="center">Cell two</td>
      <td align="right">Cell three</td>
</tr>
</table>
```

Since currently the table's width is being determined by the content of the three cells, our alignment changes are not visible. Shortly we'll extend the width of our table and our alignments will become visually evident.

Now we'll add a second row, composed of only one cell, with its content centered across the whole table (see Figure 5.5 for the resulting browser display):

```
<table align="center" border="1" cellspacing="5" cellpadding="3">
<tr>
      <td>Cell one</td>
      <td align="center">Cell two</td>
      <td align="right">Cell three</td>
</tr>
```

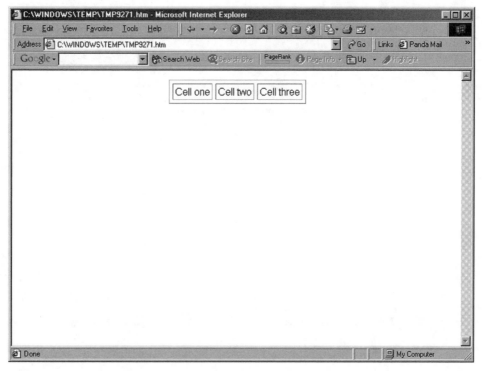

Figure 5.3 Browser display of the <td> element.

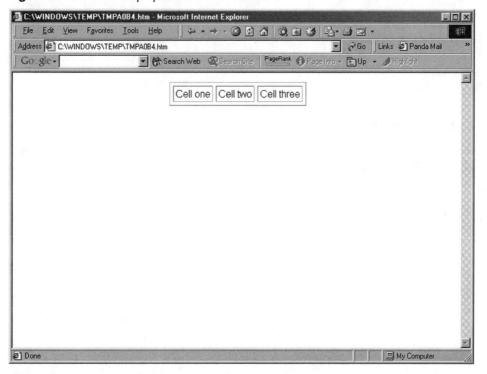

Figure 5.4 Modifying cell alignment.

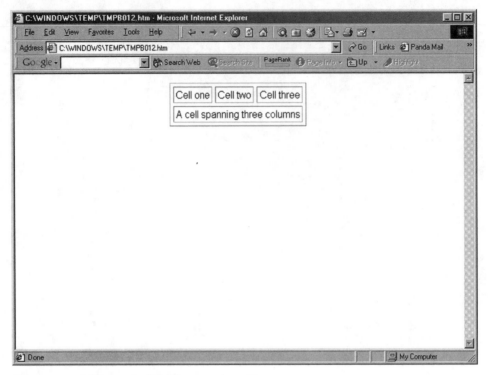

Figure 5.5 Adding a single-cell row to the table.

```
<tr>
    <td colspan="3" align="center">A cell spanning three columns</td>
</tr>
</table>
```

Creating an Empty Cell

An empty cell is as its name implies: a cell that contains no data. To add an empty cell, all you need to do is include nothing between the start and end elements, as shown here:

```
<table align="center" border="1" cellspacing="5" cellpadding="3">
<tr>
    <td>Cell one</td>
    <td align="center"></td>
    <td align="right">Cell three</td>
</tr>
<tr>
    <td colspan="3" align="center">A cell spanning three columns</td>
</tr>
</table>
```

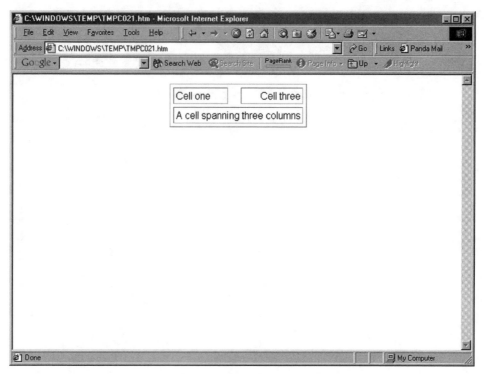

Figure 5.6 Attempting to establish an empty cell.

But in the browser display (see Figure 5.6), you can see a problem: rather than look-ing like a cell with no content, it looks like a blank area. As it turns out, for the browser to display the inside border of a cell, the cell must have content. So how can we give the cell content that doesn't display to the user?

Over the years, many solutions to this question have been attempted; and many work in most browsers—but not all. Other solutions involve graphics, a process that requires more time, effort, and code. Fortunately, there is one solution that will work in all browsers with a minimal amount of effort: You can simply include a nonbreaking space within the cell, as shown in the code here and in Figure 5.7:

```
<table align="center" border="1" cellspacing="5" cellpadding="3">
<tr>
     <td>Cell one</td>
     <td align="center"> </td>
     <td align="right">Cell three</td>
</tr>
<tr>
     <td colspan="3" align="center">A cell spanning three columns</td>
</tr>
</table>
```

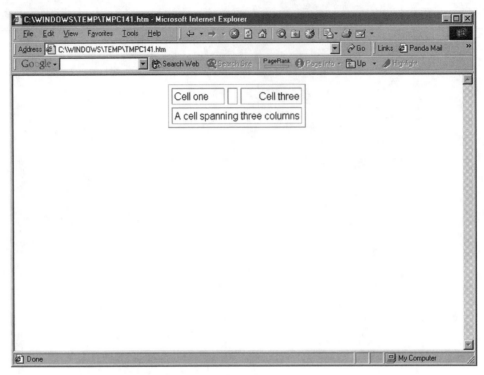

Figure 5.7 Solving the empty cell dilemma.

<th>...</th>

Table headers, <th>, commonly appearing only in the first row of a table, are used to describe the data in the column beneath this cell. In most browsers, table headers are displayed in boldface and centered. The same attributes used for table data can be used with headers; and headers may include any other valid element.

> **NOTE** Chapter 8, "Formatting with Style Sheets," will show you how to change the style of table headers to the style of your choosing.

This example adds a header row to our table:

```
<table align="center" border="1" cellspacing="5" cellpadding="3">
<tr>
    <th>Column 1</th>
    <th>Column 2</th>
    <th>Column 3</th>
</tr>
<tr>
    <td>Cell one</td>
    <td align="center"> </td>
    <td align="right">Cell three</td>
```

```
    </tr>
    <tr>
        <td colspan="3" align="center">A cell spanning three columns</td>
    </tr>
    </table>
```

<caption>...</caption>

The <caption> element is used to give a title to a table, and may include any other pre-sentational elements. In most browsers, this is set above the table and centered. In addition to serving as a descriptive label for a table, the caption becomes part of the table, meaning that if the table is moved, the caption goes with it.

The following code adds a caption to our table (see Figure 5.8 for the resulting browser display):

```
<table align="center" border="1" cellspacing="5" cellpadding="3">
<caption> Sample XHTML Table</caption>
<tr>
    <th>Column 1</th>
    <th>Column 2</th>
    <th>Column 3</th>
</tr>
```

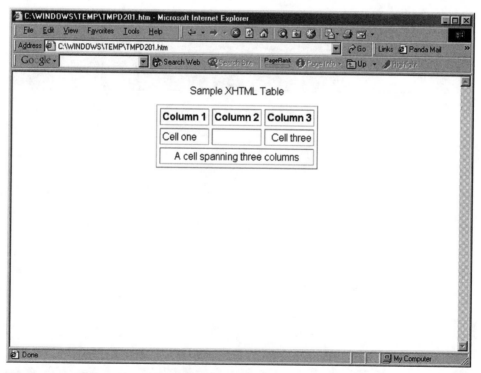

Figure 5.8 Adding a caption to a table.

```
<tr>
     <td>Cell one</td>
     <td align="center"> </td>
     <td align="right">Cell three</td>
</tr>
<tr>
     <td colspan="3" align="center">A cell spanning three columns</td>
</tr>
</table>
```

By adding the align element with its various attributes, we can modify the location of the caption in relation to the table, in these ways:

■ align="top" (the default), as shown in Figure 5.8.

■ align="bottom", as shown in Figure 5.9.

■ align="left", as shown in Figure 5.10.

■ align="right", as shown in Figure 5.11.

As our table stands, the width is being determined by the width of the content, giving it a somewhat cramped appearance. We can improve upon that by adding a width attributes in some key places, thereby making the table much more readable (see Figure 5.12 for the resulting browser display):

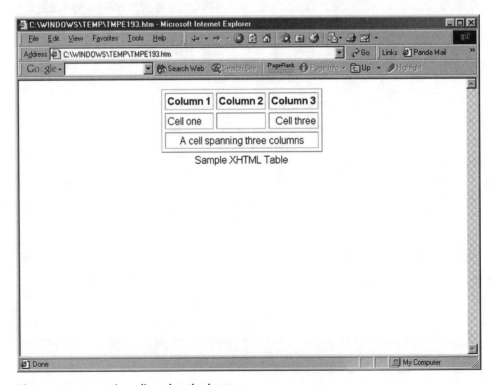

Figure 5.9   A caption aligned at the bottom.

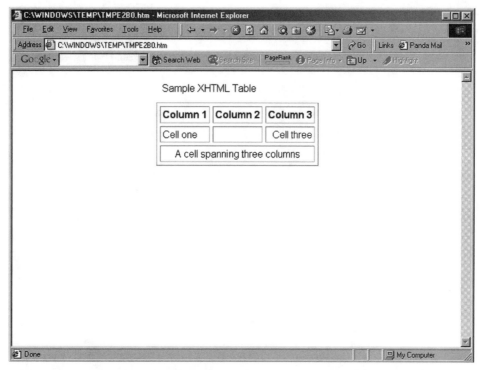

Figure 5.10 A caption aligned left.

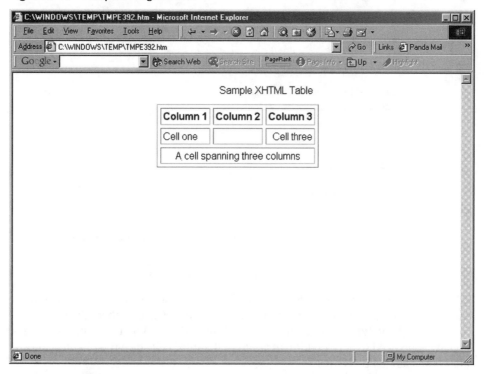

Figure 5.11 A caption aligned right.

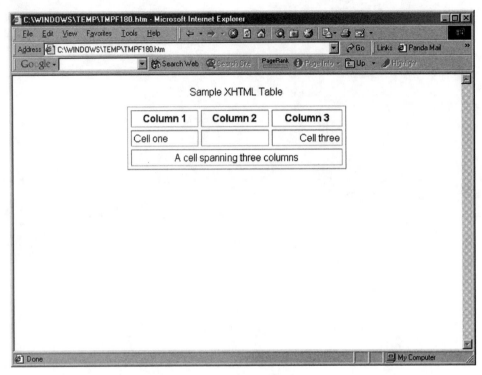

Figure 5.12   Spacing out the table for better readability.

```
<table align="center" border="1" cellspacing="5" cellpadding="3"
width="50%">
<caption> Sample XHTML Table</caption>
<tr>
     <th width="33%">Column 1</th>
     <th width="33%">Column 2</th>
     <th>Column 3</th>
</tr>
<tr>
     <td>Cell one</td>
     <td align="center"> </td>
     <td align="right">Cell three</td>
</tr>
<tr>
     <td colspan="3" align="center">A cell spanning three columns</td>
</tr>
</table>
```

By adding the width attribute to the table element, we have established that the table must take up 50 percent of the available window. We have then given each column (approximately) the same width by adding width="33%" to the first two cells. There was no need to add a width attribute to the third cell since it will automatically take what's left (34 percent).

Table 5.2 XHTML Table Formatting Elements and Attributes

ELEMENT	ATTRIBUTES
Table	frame, rules
Thead	*none*
Tfoot	*none*
Tbody	*none*
Colgroup	span, width
Col	width

XHTML Table Formatting Tools

XHTML give you, the author, additional table elements, meaning greater flexibility for table design. Table 5.2 shows these new formatting elements, along with their attributes, if applicable.

NOTE Again, these new elements are not intended for layout purposes.

Each of these elements is described fully in the subsequent subsections.

<thead>, <tfoot>, and <tbody>

Though the <thead>, <tfoot>, and <tbody> elements were added to the HTML 4.0 specification in 1998, browser manufacturers took their time in supporting them. Fortunately, current browsers support XHTML coding, thus, these elements.

There are a couple of rules you must follow when implementing these three elements:

- Though you don't have to use all three of these elements in any particular table, if you use either <thead> or <tfoot>, you must also use <tbody>.

- If you use all three, to be processed correctly, they must follow this order: <head>, <foot>, <body>. Although this may seem illogical (head, body, foot being the assumed sequence), this is the order in which your table must be coded to ensure that it displays correctly.

The following code introduces a new sample table, one that shows the number of widgets sold in a year, broken down by week (see Figure 5.13 for the resulting browser display):

```
<table border="1" width="75%" align="center">
<caption>Widgets sold this year</caption>
<tr>
    <td> </td>
    <th>Monday</th>
```

```
        <th>Tuesday</th>
        <th>Wednesday</th>
        <th>Thurday</th>
        <th>Friday</th>
        <th>Saturday</th>
        <th>Sunday</th>
    </tr>
    <tr>
        <td>Week 1</td>
        <td>200</td>
        <td>200</td>
        <td>200</td>
        <td>200</td>
        <td>200</td>
        <td>200</td>
        <td>200</td>
    </tr>
    <tr>
        <td>Week 2</td>
        <td>200</td>
        <td>200</td>
        <td>200</td>
        <td>200</td>
        <td>200</td>
        <td>200</td>
        <td>200</td>
    </tr>
    <tr>
        <td> </td>
        <th>Monday</th>
        <th>Tuesday</th>
        <th>Wednesday</th>
        <th>Thurday</th>
        <th>Friday</th>
        <th>Saturday</th>
        <th>Sunday</th>
    </tr>
    </table>
```

In this example, we are only two weeks into the year, so the table is not difficult to use. But consider that by the time we get to the end of the year, this table will have a total of 53 rows (one for each week plus the heading row), and will no doubt scroll off the screen. We can overcome this problem by using a combination XHTML's three new elements. Here's how:

1. Rearrange the rows so that the last row is the second row listed.

2. Embed the first row between <thead> and </thead>.

3. Embed the second row between <tfoot> and </tfoot>.

4. Embed the remaining rows between <tbody> and </tbody>.

Here's how the code looks now:

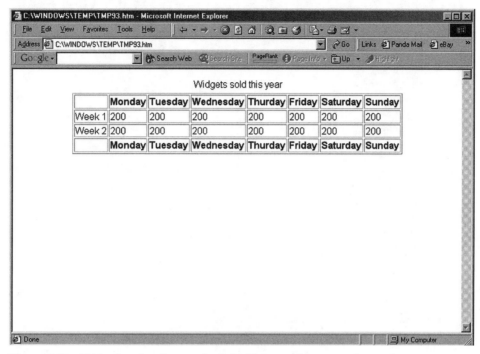

Figure 5.13   Table showing the number of widgets sold in a year, by week.

```
<table border="1" width="75%" align="center">
<caption>Widgets sold this year</caption>
<thead>
<tr>
     <td> </td>
     <th>Monday</th>
     <th>Tuesday</th>
     <th>Wednesday</th>
     <th>Thurday</th>
     <th>Friday</th>
     <th>Saturday</th>
     <th>Sunday</th>
</tr>
</thead>
<tfoot>
<tr>
     <td> </td>
     <th>Monday</th>
     <th>Tuesday</th>
     <th>Wednesday</th>
     <th>Thurday</th>
     <th>Friday</th>
     <th>Saturday</th>
     <th>Sunday</th>
</tr>
</tfoot>
```

```
<tbody>
<tr>
      <td>Week 1</td>
      <td>200</td>
      <td>200</td>
      <td>200</td>
      <td>200</td>
      <td>200</td>
      <td>200</td>
      <td>200</td>
</tr>
<tr>
      <td>Week 2</td>
      <td>200</td>
      <td>200</td>
      <td>200</td>
      <td>200</td>
      <td>200</td>
      <td>200</td>
      <td>200</td>
</tr>
...rows four through 53 go here...
</tbody>
</table>
```

Figure 5.14 shows how this looks in the browser.

NOTE Current browser support for these three elements is pretty good. The current versions of both Netscape Navigator and Internet Explorer support them.

Future Developments

A future development to be on the lookout for in regard to the use of these elements is browser capability to "lock" the table to a size no larger than that of the browser window. That would mean, if the height of the table was greater than that of the browser window, the head and foot rows would appear at the top and bottom of the window with as many of the rows that would fit. The rest of the rows would be accessible via a scroll bar. With this lock feature in place, the user will always be able to see the headers and footers on the table columns.

Moreover, this feature gives authors the ability to simulate frames, by having a locked top and bottom, without having to code a frameset document and create three separate content documents.

\<colgroup\> and \<col /\>

As stated in the beginning of this chapter, many early versions of HTML precluded the use of designing columns; only rows were possible. With visual editors, it was possible to view columns and adjust them accordingly. In these versions of HTML, by default, the width of a particular column in a table was determined by the cell containing the data of the greatest width. To specify the width of a column, the author typically had to set the width attribute on one cell (usually the first one to get the job done and out

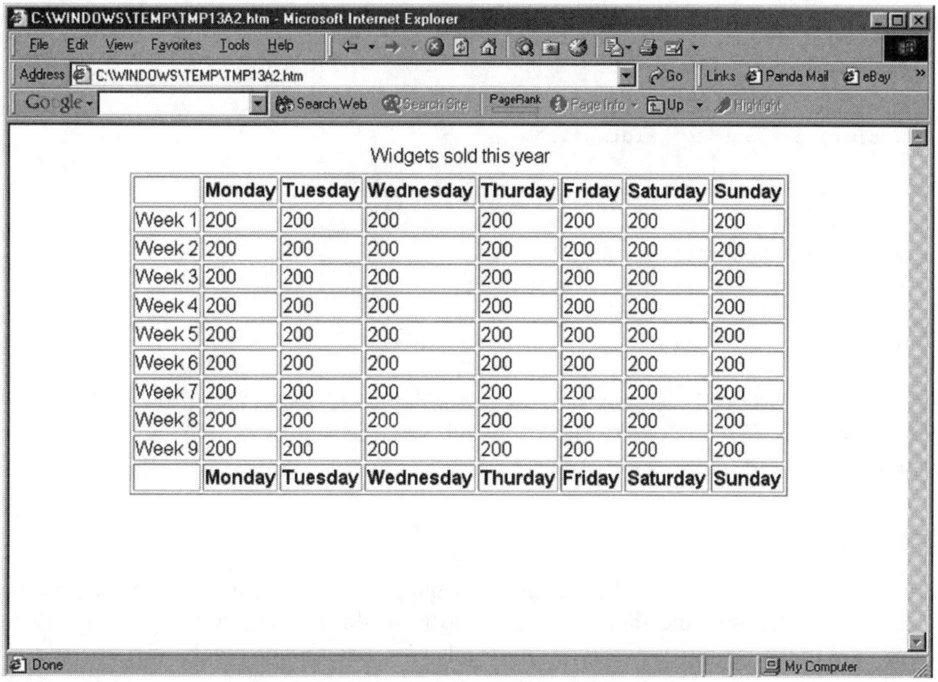

Figure 5.14   The table after adding <thead>, <tfoot>, and <tbody>.

of the way) in that column. But some visual editors would take this to the extreme, and set the width attribute in every cell in that column. Thus, if you had a table with 100 rows, for example, there would be so much redundant code that document would load more slowly on lower-powered Internet connections.

Fortunately, with the advent of HTML 4.0 and, now, XHTML, it is possible to set the widths of columns with the <colgroup> and <col> elements.

<colgroup>...</colgroup>

The <colgroup> element allows you to specify a group of columns that you want to treat in a certain way. This element has only two attributes, span and width.

The span attribute is used to specify the number of columns to be applied to the column group. For example, the following code will set a table with 25 columns, divided into three groups of 10, 5, and 10, left to right:

```
<table>
<colgroup span="10">
</colgroup>
<colgroup span="5">
</colgroup>
<colgroup span="10">
</colgroup>
...
</table>
```

From there we can then add the width element to specify the width, in pixels (width="n"), of each cell in the groups, as shown here:

```
<table>
<colgroup span="10" width="25">
</colgroup>
<colgroup span="5" width="10">
</colgroup>
<colgroup span="10" width="25">
</colgroup>
. . .
</table>
```

In addition to pixels, as shown in the preceding code, the value of the width attribute can be specified as a percentage of the whole table (width="n%") and as a relative value (width="n*").

<col />

Instead of assigning the number of columns in a group using the span attribute on the <colgroup> element, and then using the width attribute to assign the same width to every cell in that group, you can use the <col> element, and be much more specific.

The <col> element is an empty element, and therefore requires the closing slash within the tags. It is also a child element of <colgroup> and therefore must be contained within that element. Here's an example of code that establishes our table as having 10 columns in three groups of 3, 5, and 2 cells, respectively:

```
<table>
<colgroup>
     <col />
     <col />
     <col />
</colgroup>
<colgroup>
     <col />
     <col />
     <col />
     <col />
     <col />
</colgroup>
<colgroup>
     <col />
     <col />
</colgroup>
. . .
</table>
```

Certainly, the preceding code could have been written more succinctly by using the span attribute on the <colgroup> elements, but doing so would not allow us to set different widths to cells within the same column group, as shown in the following code:

```
<table>
<colgroup>
        <col width="0*" />
        <col width="20" />
        <col width="20" />
</colgroup>
<colgroup>
        <col width="15%" />
        <col width="5%" />
        <col width="15%" />
        <col width="5%" />
        <col width="15%" />
</colgroup>
<colgroup>
        <col width="1*" />
        <col width="3*" />
</colgroup>
. . .
</table>
```

Let's examine this code in more detail:

- The first column group has three columns. Column 1 is allowed to use the default amount of space it needs; columns 2 and 3 use 20 pixels each.

- The second column group has five columns, with columns 1, 3, and 5 each using 15 percent of the whole table, and columns 2 and 4 each using 5 percent of the whole table.

- The second column group takes up the middle 55 percent of the table.

- There are two columns in the third column group.

- The remaining table space is divided into four equal parts (1+3=4), one of which will be used by column 1, and the remaining three going to column 2.

NOTE The examples given in this chapter for using <colgroup> and <col> do little more than illustrate an alternative method for specifying the widths of columns. In Chapter 8, you'll learn to use style sheets to apply styles to your groups. As a preview, let's say you wanted all of the columns in the first group to have a blue background, those in the middle group to have a green background, and those in the last group to have a red background. Using style sheets, you could create the appropriate styles as classes and then apply them to each group on the <colgroup> element.

The Frame and Rules Attributes

Traditionally, in HTML the only way to modify the lines around a table was to use the border attribute. You could turn the border off by using border="0" or you could make the border thicker by using a larger number. Now you have the frame and rules attributes with which you can modify that border even further.

Table 5.3   Frame Attribute Values

box	Box appears around the table, similar to the border attribute.
void	No box appears. Same as border="0".
above	Border appears along top edge of table.
below	Border appears along bottom edge of table.
rhs	Border appears along right edge of table.
lhs	Border appears along left edge of table.
hsides	Border appears along right and left edges of table.
vsides	Border appears along top and bottom edges of table.

frame. Replaces the border attribute, allowing you to modify the effect of the border around a table. The available values are presented in Table 5.3.

rules. Allows you to specify the thickness of lines between cells. The available attributes are listed in Table 5.4.

The following code snippets demonstrate how the frame and rules attributes can be used to establish or remove the lines from around the cells in a table. To give a table an outside border, but no internal table lines, use:

```
<table frame="box" rules="none">
```

To create the opposite effect, displaying internal lines, but no outside border, use:

```
<table frame="void" rules="all">
```

Table 5.4   Rules Attribute Values

all	Default choice.
groups	Establishes thicker lines between row and column groups as directed by the <thead>, <tfoot> <tbody>, <colgroup>, and <col> elements.
rows	Places lines only between rows.
cols	Places lines only between columns.
none	Displays no lines inside the table.

Summary

Although most authors working in HTML use tables to create a grid-based layout system for their pages, this chapter focused on the original purpose for tables: to present tabular data. This was done for a reason: as you'll learn in Chapter 8, there is now a better way to position items in your document: using style sheets. Moreover, XHTML includes additional elements and attributes that allow for better control and presentation of tables.

Forms

Web sites, as you know, are great for presenting static documents and hyperlinks. But when you, as the author of a Web site, want to involve your users, you need to use forms. In many different scenarios, you will want to collect information from your users, information that you can parlay into improving your site. As you will learn in this chapter, you can collect data in three different formats: textual input, mutually exclusive choices (yes or no), and option selection. After users fill out the form, the data is passed along to a program that processes and distributes it according to your direction: you may save the data to a file, run it as a database query, or email it to someone.

We begin this chapter by describing how forms are used and how the Common Gateway Interface (CGI) is often implemented to process the collected data. Next we will design our form in XHTML and introduce you to form elements that are new with XHTML. You will also be given guidelines for good form design.

Understanding How Forms Are Used

It's probably safe to say that everyone, in his or her Web travels, has filled in a form. If you have accessed an Internet search engine such as Google or AltaVista, typed in a few keywords, and then clicked a search button, you have filled out a form—albeit a very simple one—and had the site process your information. Perhaps you ordered a copy of this book online through Borders.com or Amazon.com, in which case you filled out several much more complex forms. First, you had to find the book you were looking for; next, you may have registered with the site by providing such information as your name and address; last, you filled in one or more forms describing your method of payment and the address to which you wanted the book shipped.

In both of these situations—the first simple, the second more complex—you (the user, in this case) were required to supply information to the site and then click a button issuing the command for the site to process your input based on a set of prewritten instructions. Those instructions are known as a Common Gateway Interface (CGI) script.

The Common Gateway Interface

The CGI is the interface between the client and the server. In most cases, the client computer (the user) is running a different operating system and using different hardware from that of the server (the computer housing the form). The CGI application (script) to which you send your data enables a smooth transition of that data from client to server. CGI scripts are also flexible; they can be written in any of a number of computer languages, including C, Visual Basic, and Perl.

NOTE To learn how to write your own scripts, check out some of the many books available on this topic. In this book, we will be working with a prewritten script that is available free of charge on the Web.

Most data is transferred between the client browser and a Web server in *headers*. These headers take the form of *name=value*, or name-value pairs. Two of the more common headers include HTTP_USER_AGENT=*"browser name and version number"* and REMOTE_HOST=*"IP number of your computer"*.

When the form collects the data from the user, it is transmitted to the script as headers in name-value pairs. These name-value pairs are in addition to those that your browser normally transmits to the server. In most cases, the name is preprogrammed into the form by you, the form's author. In some cases, the value is input by the user or selected by the user from a list of prearranged choices. For example, if you create a field named firstname, and the user inputs the text "Michael," then the name-value pair will be sent to the script as firstname=Michael.

When the script on the server receives the name-value pairs, it takes over and follows its preprogrammed instructions for processing that data. Once the data has been processed, the server sends back a response to the user's browser for display. This response is controlled by the script that processed the data. Depending on the purpose of the script, the response may be the result of a database search or an XHTML document confirming the data that the user sent.

Creating Forms in XHTML

The first step in creating a form in XHTML is to design the form as the user will see it. The second step is to write code to direct the browser to send the data to the script and the information that the script will need to correctly process the submitted data.

Standard Elements and Attributes

As with every other XHTML functionality, creating forms requires knowing how to use a number of elements and attributes. In this section, we will begin to cover those items, as part of the discussion of how forms are built and how they should be properly deployed within your documents.

<form>

To be able to collect data from the user, all of your data collection boxes must be contained within the <form> element. If they are not, the data may not be passed on to the script, or, at worst, the input fields will not display.

The <form> element may contain any of the other elements itemized in this chapter; however, the <form> element may *not* contain another <form> element. Embedding forms within forms will cause the form to break. If you want more than one form on a page, you must end the first one before the second one begins.

The following code is the beginning of the customer service request form that we will be designing throughout this chapter:

```
<?xml version="1.0" encoding="UTF-8"?>
<!DOCTYPE html PUBLIC "-//W3C//DTD XHTML 1.0 Transitional//EN"
"http://www.w3.org/TR/xhtml11/DTD/xhtml1-transitional.dtd">
<html xmlns="http://www.w3.org/1999/xhtml" xml:lang="en" lang="en">
<head>
<title>Customer service request form</title>
</head>
<body>
<h1 align="center">Customer Service Request Form</h1>
<form>
...
</form>
</body>
</html>
```

The <form> element has three attributes: method, action, and enctype. The first two are required; they enable the form to send the collected data to the script. They are not, however, needed for displaying our form on the screen. (Because we are focusing initially on the design of our form, we will save the discussion of these attributes for later in the chapter.)

<input />

In most forms, the <input /> element will be the most commonly used input type. This element allows you to create text boxes (for items such as a user's name or address), checkboxes (from which users choose items on which they want information), radio buttons (from which users make exclusive choices, such as yes or no), password fields (to indicate information to be hidden from the screen), submit and reset buttons, and hidden fields (for passing information to the script that the user need not see).

The basic format for an input element is:

```
<input type="value" name="value" />
```

There are 10 available values for the type attribute: text, password, checkbox, radio, submit, reset, file, hidden, image, and button. Some of these values (text, password, checkbox, radio, and file) deal with the type of input we are asking for; therefore, they are considered design issues. The others (submit, reset, hidden, image, and button) deal with processing issues; they will be discussed later in the chapter.

type="text"

Of all the input types, text is the one you will probably use the most. It places a single-line box in the form that allows the user to type in the appropriate information.

Each text box placed in the form must have a unique fieldname attribute associated with it. There are several rules and guidelines for choosing effective fieldnames.

- Names cannot include spaces.

- Names are case-sensitive.

- Names should be descriptive of the field's content.

- Shorter is generally better than longer.

In addition to those four is a fifth rule: Almost every script will include certain reserved name values that the script is preprogrammed to process in a certain way. If you use that name in another situation, your data may not be properly processed. More on this later in the chapter, when we link our form to a script and process it.

The first thing we need to do in our example form is to ask for the user's first name, last name, and email address. To do this we will create text boxes that ask for that information. Here's the code for gathering that information, followed by its browser display in Figure 6.1:

```
<form>
<p>
First Name: <input type="text" name="firstname" />
Last name: <input type="text" name="lastname" /><br />
Email address: <input type="text" name="email" />
</p>
</form>
```

In addition to type="text", there are a few additional attributes that we can add to an <input /> element. These attributes are size, value, and maxlength, defined here:

size="n". Controls the width of the text box in the form in *n* number of characters. The default value for this box is 20. To make the box appear shorter or longer, we can add this attribute and resize the box. So, if we set size="30", the box will be 30 characters wide (in other words, will show no more than 30 characters at one time).

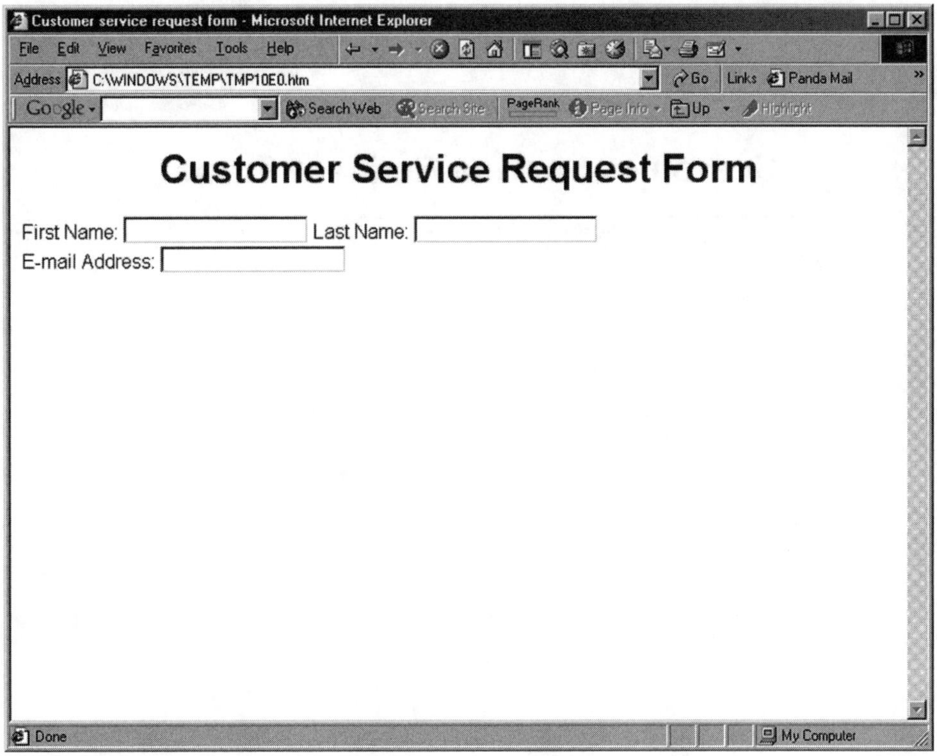

Figure 6.1 Beginning to gather customer information.

value="text". Enables us to place text in the box that will appear as soon as the form is loaded. This text is editable by the user.

maxlength="n". Allows us to limit the number of characters the box will accept. If we set this number to 10, the box will prevent an eleventh character being input.

Now, let's add another field to our form. We'll assume that all of our customers have been assigned a number that must be entered into the form before they can receive customer support. These customer numbers are limited to 8 digits in length, and are prefixed with the letter "C." Therefore, we want to limit the number of characters the box will accept to 8 and set the size of the box to match (because all the numbers begin with C, we put that into the box so the user doesn't have to). Here's the code for those additions, followed by the display in Figure 6.2:

```
</p>
<p>
Customer Number:
<input type="text" name="custnum" size="8" maxlength="8" value="C" />
</p>
</form>
```

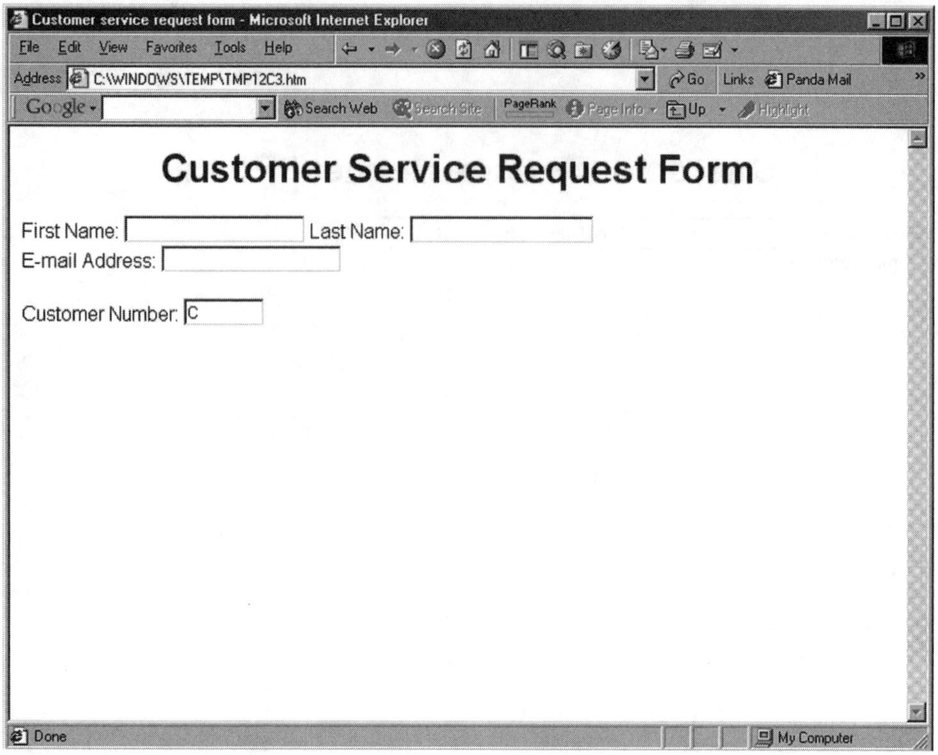

Figure 6.2   Adding the customer number field.

type="password"

The password type works the same as the text type, with one obvious difference. If you set type="password" then any characters entered into the box will be displayed on the screen as asterisks (*).

In this code, we'll add a new field to our form that asks users for the password issued to them when they registered at our site (see Figure 6.3 for the resulting browser display):

```
<p>
Customer Number:
<input type="text" name="custnum" size="8" maxlength="8" value="C" />
<br />
Password:
<Input type="password" name="password" size="10" maxlength="10">
</p>
</form>
```

There are three important pointers to keep in mind for implementing the password input type:

■ The information is not encrypted. From a security standpoint, encrypting would only prevent so-called shoulder surfing—someone looking over the

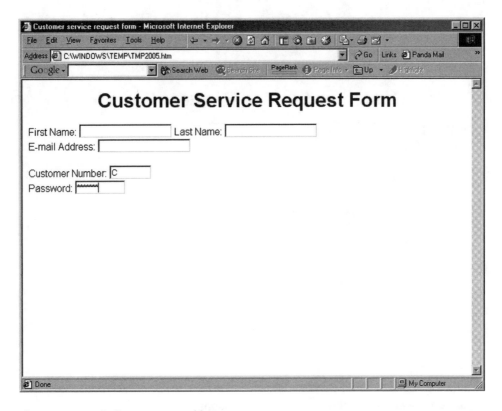

Figure 6.3 Including a password box.

user's shoulder to see what is on the screen—and since only asterisks appear in the box, this is not an issue.

■ The use of the value attribute is not recommended, as all text within the box will be unreadable by the user.

■ No validation is built into password boxes. Any validation must be taken care of by the script. (Note: The script we will be using does not do this for us.) We are only including this in our form to obscure this information from anyone that might be looking over our user's shoulder.

type="radio"

The radio button type is completely different from the text and password types. As described previously, it allows us to create a set of mutually exclusive choices. It is a toggle switch: if the user chooses one option, then changes his or her mind and chooses another, the first will be turned off and the new choice turned on.

In our example form, we'll assume we want to ask the user which of our products requires a customer support call. We'll also assume we have different customer support personnel for different products, so we need to design this aspect of the form so that the user can make a request for support on only one product at a time.

Here's the code, its browser display is shown in Figure 6.4. We'll explain the code after you've had a chance to examine it:

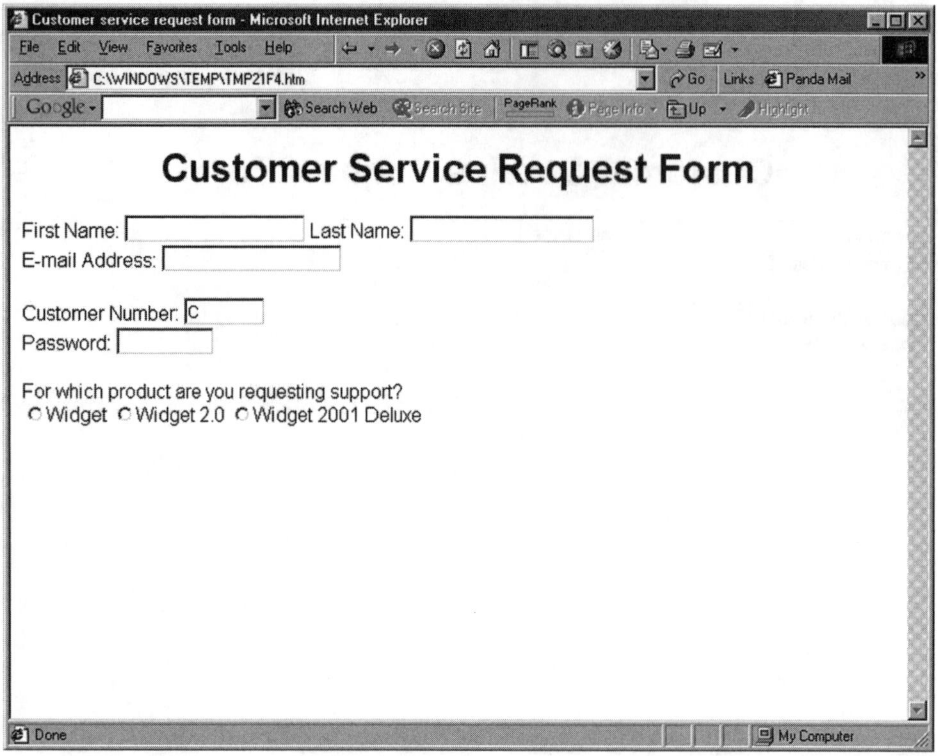

Figure 6.4 Setting up customer support radio buttons.

```
</p>
<p>
For which product are you requesting support?<br>
<Input type="radio" name="product" value="widget" />Widget
<Input type="radio" name="product" value="widget2" />Widget 2.0
<Input type="radio" name="product" value="widget2001deluxe" />Widget
2001 Deluxe
</p>
</form>
```

Unlike text boxes, each of which must have a unique name, radio buttons in a grouping must have the *same name but unique values*. If we give each of the radio buttons a different name, all three of them would be selectable, not what we want. (The rules for choosing values for radio buttons are the same as the first four for choosing field names.)

Once the data has been collected and submitted, each name in the data set can have only one value. In the case of a set of radio buttons, the name-value pair generated will come from the chosen radio button. In the set in our example, there are three possible results: product=widget, product=widget2, or product=widget2001deluxe.

This allows us to have another set of radio buttons later in our form. If we were to add another set, the buttons in the second set would share the same name, which is different from that of the first set.

type="checkbox"

The checkbox allows us to create a yes/no situation—with a small twist. First, let's update our form to present the user with the option of being on our mailing list (see Figure 6.5 for the resulting browser display):

```
</p>
<p>
<input type="checkbox" name="mailings" /> Yes, I would like to receive
mailings from Widgets, Inc.
</p>
</form>
```

Of course, we could have used radio buttons to handle this feature, but there are two benefits to using a checkbox in this situation. First, we use a lot less code to achieve our goal. This saves us typing time and the user loading time.

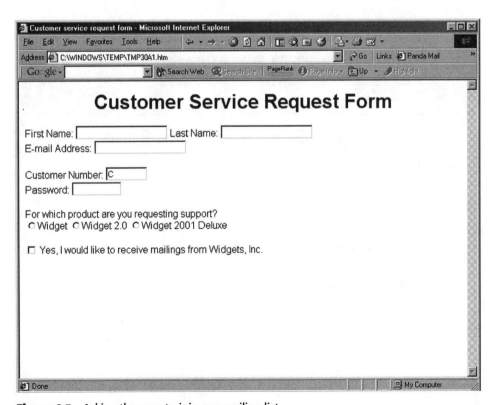

Figure 6.5   Asking the user to join our mailing list.

The second benefit is in how the results of this box are reported back to us after the script has processed the data. You may have noticed that we did not include a value attribute in this input element. And, unlike a text box, the value is not directly specified by the user since there is no way for the user to enter any actual text. Checkboxes, by default, have two binary-opposite values, on and off. If the checkbox is checked, the value for the box is "on"; if the box is unchecked, the value for the box is "off." The box will be reported only if the value is on. If the value is off, a name-value pair will not be sent to the script. In our example, if the user checks the box, indicating that he or she wishes to receive our mailings, then that information will be reported to us in the form of mailings=on. If the user does not check the box, then this fact will not be reported.

There are two additional ways that we can manipulate this box. The first is by changing the reported value. We can add a value attribute so that instead of the form reporting mailings=on, we can have it report mailings=yes, provided the user did check the box. For example:

```
<input type="checkbox" name="mailings" value="yes" />
```

The second way we can manipulate this checkbox is to have it checked by default. To do this, we need to add the checked attribute, as shown here (see Figure 6.6 for the resulting browser display):

```
<input type="checkbox" name="mailings" value="yes" checked="checked" />
```

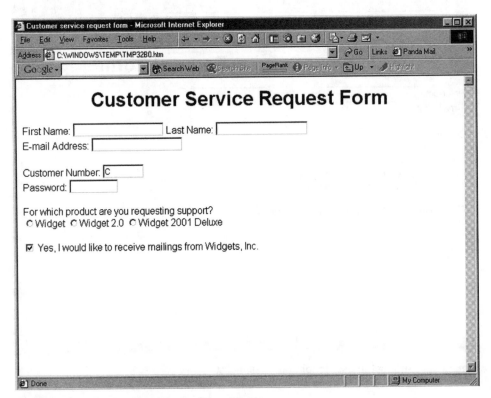

Figure 6.6   Changing the default of the checkbox.

A word of warning about this last action: By prechecking this box, the user *must* check the box if he or she does *not* want to receive our mailings. Many users resent this.

type="file"

The file input type gives users the ability to browse their computer for a file to attach to the rest of the submitted data. By using this type, a text box will appear in the form that is immediately followed by a Browse button, which, when clicked, will display an Open File dialog box, where the user can select the appropriate file. Once selected, the path to that file will display in the text box.

The following example shows our code updated to include this functionality (see Figure 6.7 for the resulting browser display):

```
</p>
<p>
Please send your Widget log file to us for analysis.<br>
<input type="file" name="logfile" />
</p>
<p>
<input type="checkbox" name="mailings" /> Yes, I would like to receive
```

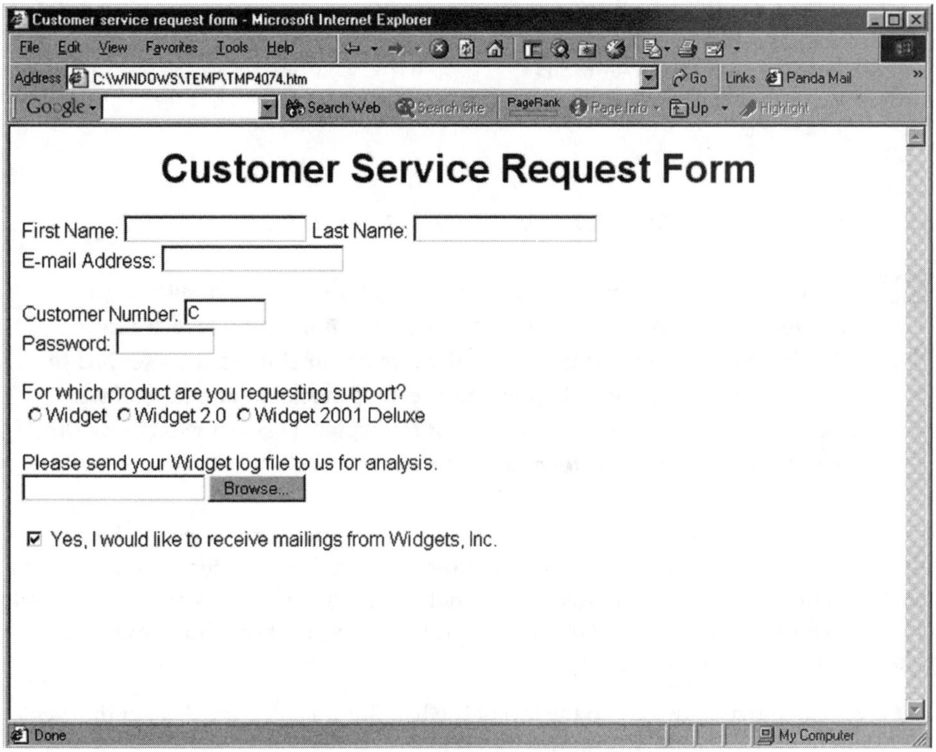

Figure 6.7   Adding an upload field to our form.

<select> and <option>

The <select> element allows us to create drop-down lists from which the user can choose one or more <option>s. By default, selections work like radio buttons, creating mutually exclusive lists of choices. However, selections can allow for multiple choices and can take up less space than radio buttons.

Single Options

In the next example, we'll add a field to our form asking the user for the day on which the problem with his or her widget occurred. Yes, we could offer them a text box to enter this information, but not everyone enters day names in the same format. By using <select>, we ensure that we get the day name in the format we want (in our case, non-abbreviated). Here's the code using <select> and <option> to ask for the day the problem occurred (see Figure 6.8 for the resulting browser display):

```
<input type="radio" name="product" value="widget2001deluxe" />Widget
2001 Deluxe
</p>
<p>Please tell us the day on which the problem with your Widget first
occurred.
<select name="day">
     <option>Monday</option>
     <option>Tuesday</option>
     <option>Wedneday</option>
     <option>Thursday</option>
     <option>Friday</option>
     <option>Saturday</option>
     <option>Sunday</option>
     </select>
</p>
<p>
Please send your Widget log file to us for analysis.<br>
```

NOTE As mentioned earlier, we could have used a set of radio buttons to achieve the same set of mutually exclusive choices. But in this case, a drop-down list is a much better choice due to the number of choices the user has to pick from. In the drop-down list, only one choice is available at a time. If we had used radio buttons, we would have had to display all seven choices on the screen and use up valuable screen real estate.

The name of the item is established by the name attribute on <select>. The value is established by whichever option is selected by the user. The first item in the list is the default choice, in this case, Monday. But, what if we want Thursday to be the default choice, because we have noticed that most widget errors occur on Thursdays? We have two options for making this change:

- We can move Thursday to the top of the list. But this puts the days of the week out of order, and might confuse the user.

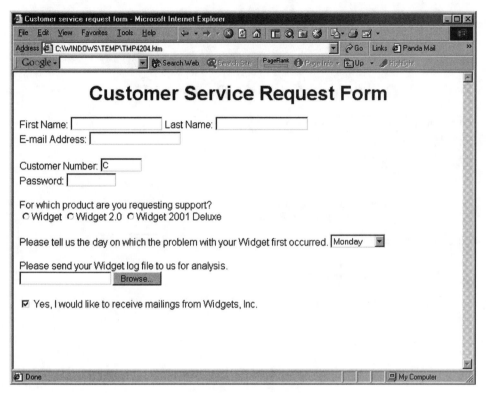

Figure 6.8 Updating our form to ask for the day the problem occurred.

■ The alternative, and better solution, is to add the <select> attribute to the option that we want to be the default choice.

The following code shows our code updated to display Thursday as the default option (see Figure 6.9 for the resulting browser display):

```
<select name="day">
    <option>Monday</option>
    <option>Tuesday</option>
    <option>Wedneday</option>
    <option selected="selected">Thursday</option>
    <option>Friday</option>
    <option>Saturday</option>
    <option>Sunday</option>
    </select>
```

Multiple Options

Let's now use <select> to give the user multiple <option>s. For this scenario, let's say we now want to know what other software users have installed on their computers; and we'll list software that is known to have problems with the widget. In this case, a user may have more than one of the software programs in our list, so we need to allow

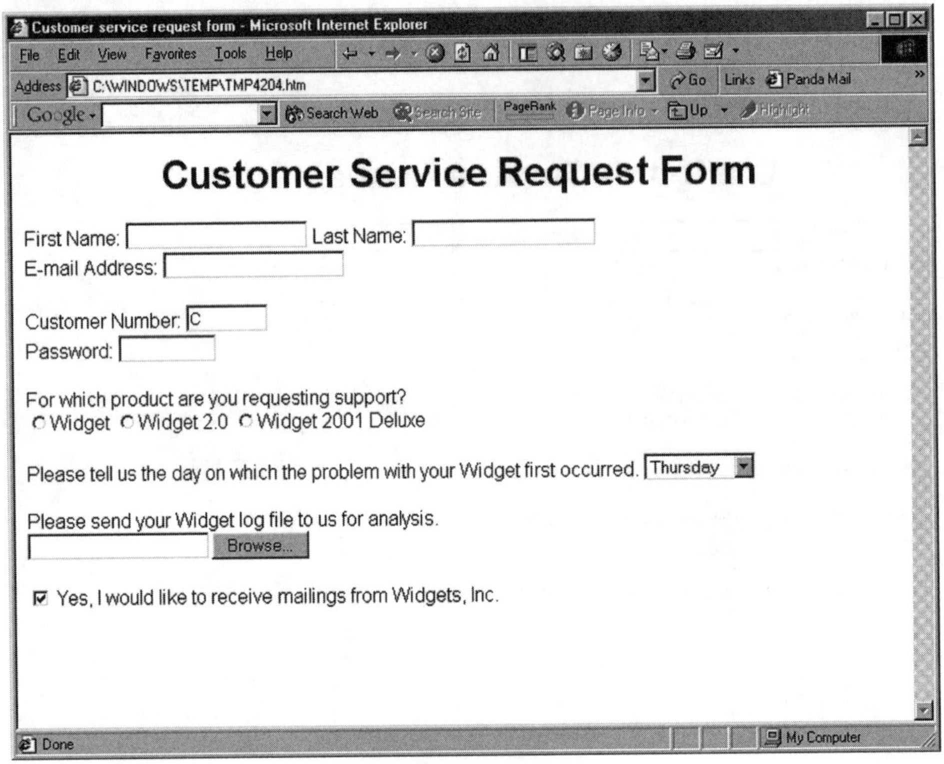

Figure 6.9 Making Thursday the new default option.

them to choose more than one option. We do this by adding the multiple attribute to the <select> element, as shown here:

```
        </select>
    </p>
    <p>
    Please let us know if you have any of the following programs installed
    on your computer.
        <select multiple="multiple" name="othersoftware">
        <option>Microsoft Word</option>
        <option>Microsoft Excel</option>
        <option>Microsoft FrontPage</option>
        <option>Microsoft Project</option>
        <option>Microsoft Outlook</option>
        <option>Corel WordPerfect </option>
        <option>Corel QuattroPro</option>
        <option>Adobe PageMill</option>
        <option>Adobe Acrobat</option>
        <option>Adobe Pagemaker</option>
        </select>
    </p>
    <p>
    Please send your Widget log file to us for analysis.<br>
```

Figure 6.10 shows how this code displays in Internet Explorer 5.x, and Figure 6.11 shows it in Netscape 4.x.

As you can see, Netscape 4.x automatically displays all of the available choices while Internet Explorer only displays *five* of the choices.

To solve this display inconsistency, we can add the size attribute to the <select> element, as shown here:

```
your computer.
    <select multiple="multiple" name="othersoftware" size="4">
    <option>Microsoft Word</option>
```

As you can see, we have three different vendors, Microsoft, Adobe, and Corel in our list. Later in the chapter we will discuss the use of <optgroup> to create groups within our option list.

<textarea>

One sign of a well-designed form is when it includes an area where users can input any additional information they feel is relevant. Previously, this could be accomplished elec-

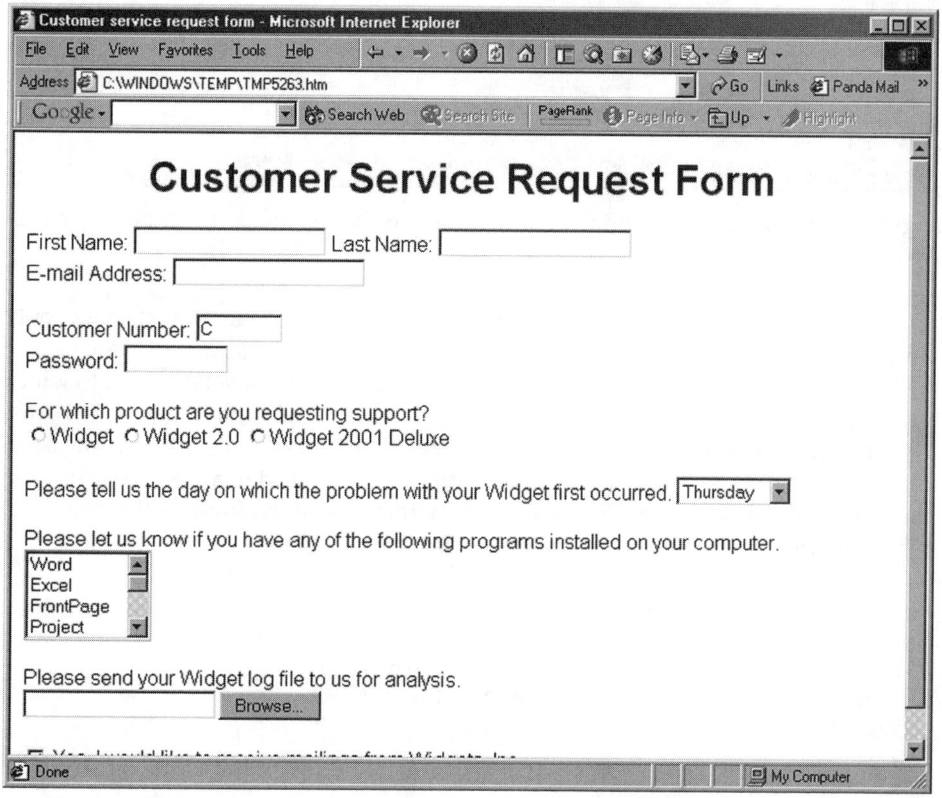

Figure 6.10   Internet Explorer 5.x display of the code with the multiple attribute <select> element.

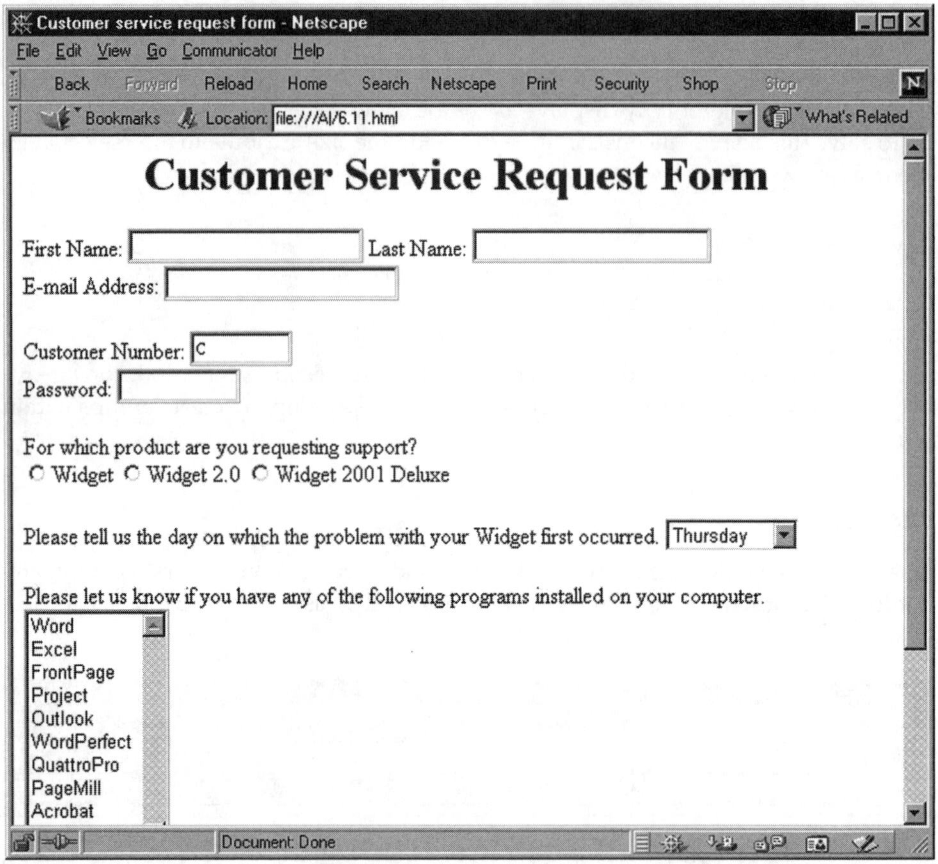

Figure 6.11 Netscape 4.x display of the code with the multiple attribute <select> element.

tronically only with text boxes. Unfortunately, as single-line elements, text boxes could not be made large enough to handle lengthier input. Enter the <textarea> element.

The <textarea> element gives us the ability to create a multiline text box into which users may enter as much material as they wish. Like the other input types we have discussed so far, textareas must be assigned unique names; this is done through the use of the name attribute. In addition, to establish the size of the textarea, you must also use the rows and cols attributes. You can see how this is handled in the following code, where we've added a comments box to the bottom of our form:

```
</p>
<p>
Please add any additional comments you may have.
<textarea name="comments" rows="3" cols="45"></textarea>
</p>
</form>
```

You can see how this looks in Figure 6.12.

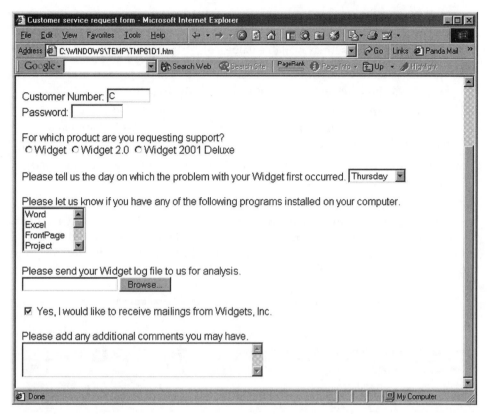

Figure 6.12   Adding a comments box to accommodate lengthier user input.

In looking at this code you may have noticed that <textarea> is not an empty element. This means that you can place content between <textarea> and </textarea>. When you do, this content will appear within the box displayed on the screen. That said, we do not recommend it, for two reasons. First, in most cases, the information you place in the textarea is not text you need reported to you, so why bother putting it where it will be? Second, any information placed within the box is editable by the user, which includes deleting it; so if you do need the information, this is not the place to put it.

It's also a good idea (providing you are not placing any content within the box) to always place the close element, </textarea>, on the same line as the open, <textarea>. If you put </textarea> on a different line, many browsers will assume there is content within the box and place several spaces within the box. This will cause the cursor to appear several spaces from the left edge of the box when the user moves into the box.

Wrapping in <textarea>

Another display issue we need to address with regard to the <textarea> element is text wrapping. As our sample code stands, when the user typing in the box reaches the right edge, the text will continue moving off, out of sight, unless the user presses the

Enter key. We can address this problem by adding the wrap attribute to the <textarea> element.

The wrap attribute has three available values: off, soft, and hard:

wrap="off". Means wrapping will not occur within the box. Users must press the Enter key to go to the next line. This is the default attribute.

wrap="soft". Creates what is known as "virtual" wrapping. Text will wrap when needed in the box on the screen, but hard returns will not be included in the data sent to the script unless the user presses the Enter key.

wrap="hard". Wraps the text in the box and adds hard returns to the submitted data wherever wrapping occurred.

Deciding whether to use the soft or hard value depends on how you want text sent to you. If you would like the text sent with the lines broken as the user typed, use hard. If you would prefer the text be sent as one long line, unless the user pressed Enter, use soft. We'll update our code to use soft wrapping (see Figure 6.13 for the resulting browser display):

```
<textarea name="comments" rows="3" cols="45" wrap="soft"></textarea>
```

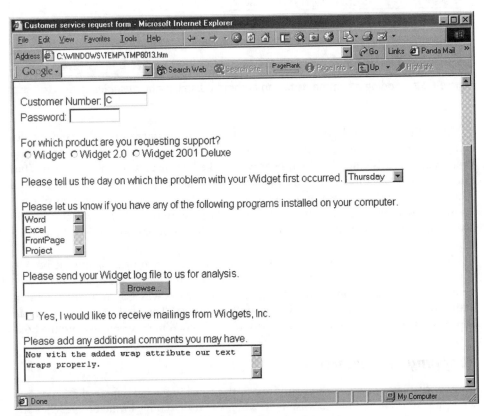

Figure 6.13 Using soft wrapping with the <textarea> element.

Implementing Recently Added Elements and Attributes

Though the elements described in this section are not new to XHTML—they were added to HTML 4.0—to date, they had been underused because of lack of browser support. With the advent of XHTML and increased browser implementation of the new standards, we really make appropriate use of these elements in our forms.

disabled="disabled"

You can add the disabled attribute to any form element so that it appears on the screen but renders the form element unusable. The field content will appear grayed-out, in the same way unavailable program menus are. Here's how a disabled field is set up in code; (Figure 6.14 shows the resulting browser display):

```
<input type="text" name="disabledtest" value="This field is disabled"
disabled="diabled">
```

readonly="readonly"

When readonly="readonly" is applied to a form element, the item will be displayed on the screen, and users can tab into it, but they may not edit the field in any way. The field

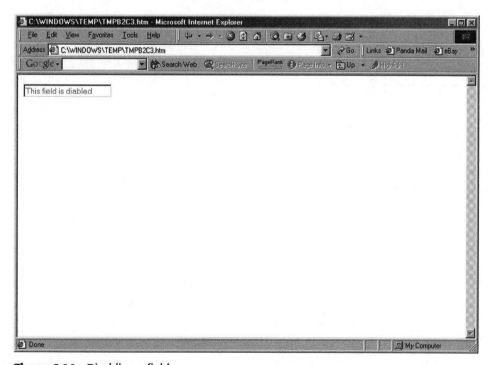

Figure 6.14   Disabling a field.

content will display as a normal field. The following is an example of a readonly field, first in code, then in the browser display shown in Figure 6.15:

```
<input type="text" name="readonlytest" value="This field is set to read-
only" readonly="readonly">
```

tabindex="n"

When used, the tabindex attribute is generally applied to all form elements. By default, when a user hits the Tab key to move through a form, the elements will be sequenced in the order in which they appear in the XHTML code. When the tabindex attribute is used, it assigns a number to each field, then orders them based upon those numbers, lowest to highest.

Thus, you might use tabindex when you have placed your form elements in a table and want the user to move, for example, down one column, and then the next. By setting the tabindex attribute, the user will move down columns instead of across rows, as shown in the following code:

```
<?xml version="1.0" encoding="UTF-8"?>
<!DOCTYPE html PUBLIC "-//W3C//DTD XHTML 1.0 Transitional//EN"
"http://www.w3.org/TR/xhtml11/DTD/xhtml1-transitional.dtd">
<html xmlns="http://www.w3.org/1999/xhtml" xml:lang="en" lang="en">
<head>
```

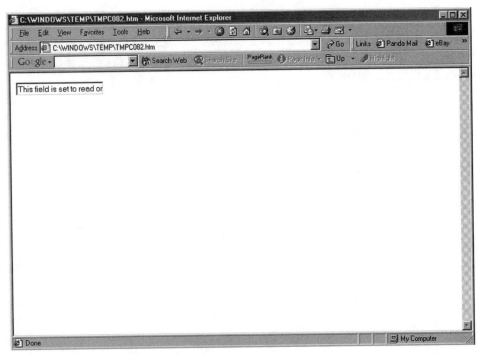

Figure 6.15 Browser display of the code for a readonly field.

```
<title>Using tabindex to move vertically through form elements</title>
<table border="1" width="75%" align="center">
<tr>
<td width="50%">First Name: <input tabindex="1" type="text" name="first-
name" /></td>
<td>Street: <input tabindex="4" type="text" name="street" /></td>
</tr>
<tr>
<td>Last name: <input tabindex="2" type="text" name="lastname" /></td>
<td>City, State: <input tabindex="5" type="text" name="citystate"
/></td>
</tr>
<tr>
<td>Email: <input tabindex="3" type="text" name="email" /></td>
<td>Zip code: <input tabindex="6" type="text" name="zip" /></td>
</tr>
</table>
</form>
</body>
</html>
```

<optgroup>

The <optgroup> element allows you to logically group a list of <option>s in a drop-down box. Recall our list with three logical company groupings, Microsoft, Corel and Adobe:

```
<select multiple="multiple" name="othersoftware">
<option>Microsoft Word</option>
<option>Microsoft Excel</option>
<option>Microsoft FrontPage</option>
<option>Microsoft Project</option>
<option>Microsoft Outlook</option>
<option>Corel WordPerfect </option>
<option>Corel QuattroPro</option>
<option>Adobe PageMill</option>
<option>Adobe Acrobat</option>
<option>Adobe Pagemaker</option>
</select>
```

Through the use of <optgroup> we can group those subsets as shown here:

```
<select multiple="multiple" name="othersoftware">
<optgroup label="Microsoft">
     <option>Word</option>
     <option>Excel</option>
     <option>FrontPage</option>
     <option>Project</option>
     <option>Outlook</option>
</optgroup>
```

```
<optgroup label="Corel">
    <option>WordPerfect </option>
    <option>QuattroPro</option>
</optgroup>
<optgroup label="Adobe">
    <option>PageMill</option>
    <option>Acrobat</option>
    <option>Pagemaker</option>
</optgroup>
</select>
```

With the addition of the label attribute, discussed next, we have now created our groups as displayed in Figure 6.16.

<label>, for="x" and id="x"

The label element allows you to give a title, or label, to a form element. So far in our form, a field element has been associated with a request for information by visual asso-

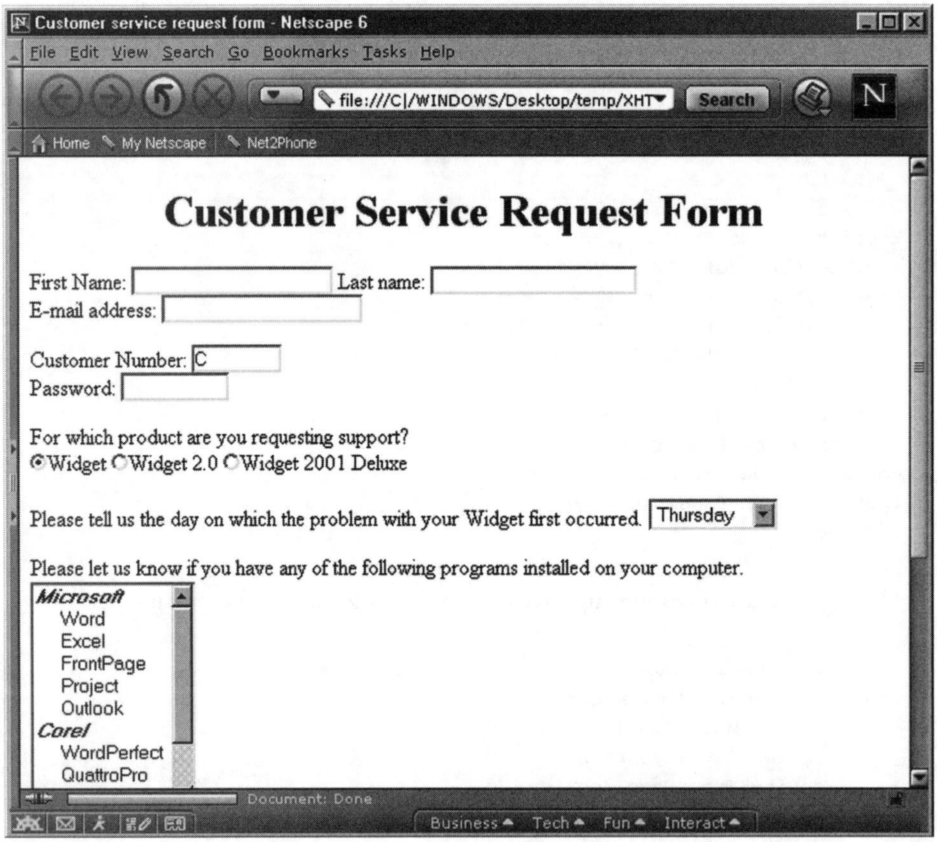

Figure 6.16 Creating option groups.

ciation only (the request, then the box). Through the use of <label> on the text, and id on the form element, the two can be associated at the code level. The following code shows our form updated with <label>s and ids:

```xml
<?xml version="1.0" encoding="UTF-8"?>
<!DOCTYPE html PUBLIC "-//W3C//DTD XHTML 1.0 Transitional//EN"
"http://www.w3.org/TR/xhtml11/DTD/xhtml1-transitional.dtd">
<html xmlns="http://www.w3.org/1999/xhtml" xml:lang="en" lang="en">
<head>
<title>Customer service request form</title>
</head>
<body>
<h1 align="center">Customer Service Request Form</h1>
<form>
<p>
<label for="fname">First Name:</label> <input id="fname" type="text"
name="firstname" />
<label for="lname">Last name:</label> <input id="lname" type="text"
name="lastname" /><br />
<label for="email">Email address:</label> <input id="email" type="text"
name="email" />
</p>
<p>
<label for="number">Customer Number:</label>
<input id="number" type="text" name="custnum" size="8" maxlength="8"
value="C" />
<br />
<label for="pass">Password:</label>
<input id="pass" type="password" name="password" size="10"
maxlength="10" />
</p>
<p>
<label for="product">For which product are you requesting
support?</label><br />
<input id="product" type="radio" name="product" value="widget" />Widget
<input id="product" type="radio" name="product" value="widget2" />Widget
2.0
<input id="product" type="radio" name="product" value="widget2001deluxe"
/>Widget 2001 Deluxe
</p>
<p><label for="day">Please tell us the day on which the problem with
your Widget first occurred.</label>
<select id="day" name="day">
     <option>Monday</option>
     <option>Tuesday</option>
     <option>Wedneday</option>
     <option selected="selected">Thursday</option>
     <option>Friday</option>
     <option>Saturday</option>
     <option>Sunday</option>
     </select>
```

```
</p>
<p><label for="software">Please let us know if you have any of the fol-
lowing programs installed on your computer.</label>
<select id="software" multiple="multiple" name="othersoftware">
<optgroup label="Microsoft">
      <option>Word</option>
      <option>Excel</option>
      <option>FrontPage</option>
      <option>Project</option>
      <option>Outlook</option>
</optgroup>
<optgroup label="Corel">
      <option>WordPerfect </option>
      <option>QuattroPro</option>
</optgroup>
      <optgroup label="Adobe">
<option>PageMill</option>
      <option>Acrobat</option>
      <option>Pagemaker</option>
</optgroup>
</select>
</p>
<p><label for="log">
Please send your Widget log file to us for analysis.</input><br />
<input id="log" type="file" name="logfile" />
</p>
<p>
<input id="mailings" type="checkbox" name="mailings" />
<label for="mailings">Yes, I would like to receive mailings from Wid-
gets, Inc.</label>
</p>
<p>
<label for="comments">Please add any additional comments you may
have.</label><br />
<textarea id="comments" name="comments" rows="3" cols="45"
wrap="soft"></textarea>
</p>
</form>
</body>
</html>
```

<button>

The <button> element allows you to create generic, nonsubmit or reset buttons in your form. (We will discuss the creation and functionality of the submit and reset buttons later in this chapter.)

For example, if you wanted to create a button that, when clicked, issues a print command to the browser, you could combine the <button> element with a JavaScript onclick command, as shown here:

```
<button onclick="javascript:window.print();">Print</button>
```

<fieldset> and <legend>

Through the use of the <fieldset> and <legend> elements, it is now possible to be more creative in laying out forms, without resorting to the use of tables, which makes code more complicated than it needs to be.

The <fieldset> element gives you the ability to group multiple field elements into logical groups surrounded by a common border. The <legend> element is then included within the <fieldset> to label that group.

The following code shows our updated form using the <fieldset> and <legend> elements to group our field elements into three logical groups: customer information, problem information, and additional information (see Figure 6.17 for the resulting browser display):

```
<?xml version="1.0" encoding="UTF-8"?>
<!DOCTYPE html PUBLIC "-//W3C//DTD XHTML 1.0 Transitional//EN"
"http://www.w3.org/TR/xhtml11/DTD/xhtml1-transitional.dtd">
<html xmlns="http://www.w3.org/1999/xhtml" xml:lang="en" lang="en">
<head>
<title>Customer service request form</title>
<style stype="text/css">
<!--
legend        {font-size: 120%}
-->
</style>
</head>
<body>
<h1 align="center">Customer Service Request Form</h1>
<form>
<fieldset>
<legend>Customer Information</legend>
<p>
<label for="fname">First Name:</label> <input id="fname" type="text"
name="firstname" />
<label for="lname">Last name:</label> <input id="lname" type="text"
name="lastname" /><br />
<label for="email">Email address:</label> <input id="email" type="text"
name="email" />
</p>
<p>
<label for="number">Customer Number:</label>
<input id="number" type="text" name="custnum" size="8" maxlength="8"
value="C" />
<br />
<label for="pass">Password:</label>
<input id="pass" type="password" name="password" size="10"
maxlength="10" />
</p>
</fieldset>
<fieldset>
<legend>Problem Information</legend>
<p>
```

```
<label for="product">For which product are you requesting
support?</label><br />
<input id="product" type="radio" name="product" value="widget" />Widget
<input id="product" type="radio" name="product" value="widget2" />Widget
2.0
<input id="product" type="radio" name="product" value="widget2001deluxe"
/>Widget 2001 Deluxe
</p>
<p><label for="day">Please tell us the day on which the problem with
your Widget
first occurred.</label>
<select id="day" name="day">
     <option>Monday</option>
     <option>Tuesday</option>
     <option>Wedneday</option>
     <option selected="selected">Thursday</option>
     <option>Friday</option>
     <option>Saturday</option>
     <option>Sunday</option>
     </select>
</p>
<p><label for="software">Please let us know if you have any of the fol-
lowing programs installed on your computer.</label>
<select id="software" multiple="multiple" name="othersoftware">
<optgroup label="Microsoft">
     <option>Word</option>
     <option>Excel</option>
     <option>FrontPage</option>
     <option>Project</option>
     <option>Outlook</option>
</optgroup>
<optgroup label="Corel">
     <option>WordPerfect </option>
     <option>QuattroPro</option>
</optgroup>
     <optgroup label="Adobe">
     <option>PageMill</option>
     <option>Acrobat</option>
     <option>Pagemaker</option>
</optgroup>
</select>
</p>
<p><label for="log">
Please send your Widget log file to us for analysis.</input><br />
<input id="log" type="file" name="logfile" />
</p>
</fieldset>
<fieldset>
<legend>Additional Information</legend>
<p>
<input id="mailings" type="checkbox" name="mailings" />
```

```
<label for="mailings">Yes, I would like to receive mailings from Wid-
gets, Inc.</input>
</p>
<p>
<labelnput for="comments">Please add any additional comments you may
have.</input><br />
<textarea id="comments" name="comments" rows="3" cols="45"
wrap="soft"></textarea>
</p>
</fieldset>
</form>
</body>
</html>
```

Finally, by adding a little CSS code to the head of our document, we can make the text contained in the <legend> elements somewhat larger than the regular form text. Cascading style sheets are covered in more detail in Chapter 8.

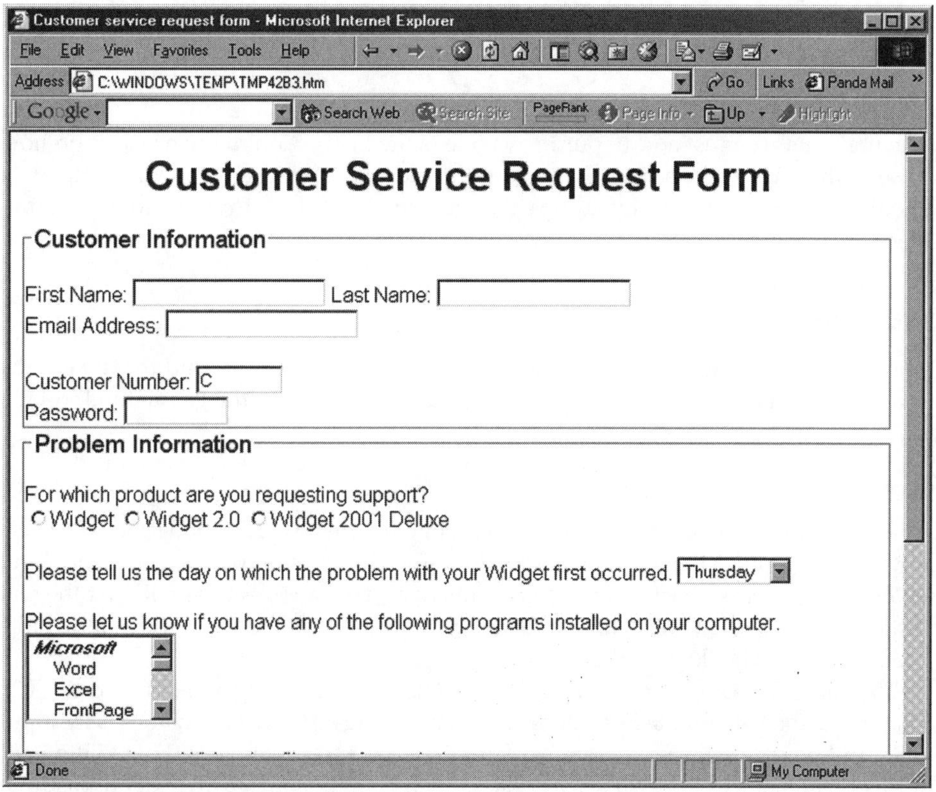

Figure 6.17 Updating the code to include fieldsets.

Processing Submissions

Once you have designed your form to accumulate all the information you need from your users, the next step is to code the form to send the collected name-value pairs off to a CGI script to be processed. As mentioned earlier, a CGI script can:

- Write the data to a file.
- Run the data against a database query.
- Email the data to someone.

For demonstration purposes here, we will choose to email the data to someone—in this case, ourselves. To do this we will be using the script FormMail, which is available for free download at www.worldwidemart.com/scripts/formmail.shtml.

NOTE To be able to do all of the exercises as written, you will need to install and configure FormMail on your server, following the directions provided at the previously listed URL. If, for any reason, you are unable or unwilling to install this script on your Web server, you can still benefit from the rest of this chapter, for all the concepts described herein are applicable to most others scripts.

Setting the Required Transmission Attributes

The first item we must add to our form code is the instruction to the browser on how to send the data to the script, along with the location of the script to which the data should be sent. We do this by adding the method and action attributes to the <form> element.

method

The method attribute tells the browser to use one of two ways to send the data to the script: to include the name-value pairs either as part of a URL (the get method) or as a separate file (the post method).

GET

The get method is used primarily on search-engine forms. This method sends the users data as part of a URL. For an example, go to the Google site (www.google.com) and enter a search term. Once you get the results page, take a look at the URL. At the end of the domain name you'll find a question mark (?), indicating that name-value pairs follow, and then q="keyword".

This method has two potential problems. The first is that URLs are limited to 1,024 characters: the total number of characters from the page's URL, field names, user input data, and field delimiters (=, ?, and +) cannot exceed 1,024 characters. Users filling out forms that enable extended user feedback, such as ours, may easily extend past that limit.

The second problem is one of security and/or privacy. URLs are commonly saved in log files, so if the form will gather data that you do not wish saved in log files, or you do not have control over those log files, then the get method is not the way to go.

POST

The post method creates a file from the user's data and sends that file to the script. This method has no limitations on length, and the file self-deletes after processing, thereby preventing the information from being stored in any server logs. If you are gathering extended user input and/or do not want to have the information stored in logs, post is the method for you.

Choosing a Method

To help you decide which method to choose, ask youself these three questions:

- *Will I be collecting a large amount of data?* If yes, post is the method of choice.
- *Do I want to prevent this information from being stored in server logs?* If no, go with post.
- *Does the script require one or the other method?* If your script requires a particular method, obviously that is the one you must use. If you do not like this restriction, you will need to find another script that lets you decide.

Because, as stated, our users' input might exceed the get method's character limit, we will use the post method, as shown in the following code:

```
<form method="post">
```

action

To that, we need to add the action attribute, to specify the path to, and the name of, the script to which the data needs to be sent. Typically, CGI scripts are stored in a server directory named cgi-bin. Therefore, a typical action attribute will look like this:

```
<form method="post" action="/cgi-bin/myscript.ext">
```

Next, we need to link our form to a CGI script, but before we do that, let's assume we do not have a script to work with, to learn the simplest action available: mailto:. The mailto: action does not involve any scripts. All it does is collect the data from the form in the specified method and email it to the user specified in the action. We can update our form to do this with the following code:

```
<form method="post" action="mailto:user@domain.com">
```

Unfortunately, this is not the most reliable way to deal with form data. For this to work, the user's browser must be configured to send email. If it is not (such as most workstations offering free public Internet access), the user will receive an error, not the data. Or the recipient will receive unformatted data, requiring extra steps to make the

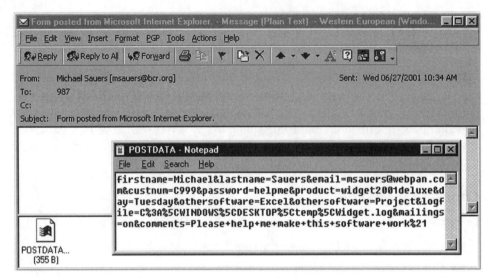

Figure 6.18   Email received from a form using a mailto: action.

data readable. Figure 6.18 shows an email received through the successful use of action= "mailto:".

> **NOTE**   You may be able to circumvent the formatting issue by using the enctype attribute, described in just a moment, but it will not solve any user configuration problems.

Obviously, using the mailto: action is highly unreliable, so we will use FormMail instead. By doing so, we will solve two problems: FormMail does not rely on the user's computer being configured to send outgoing mail; second, it will format the name-value pairs into something much more readable than mailto: did.

To use FormMail, we must change our action attribute as shown in this code sample. (Naturally, if you have installed FormMail into a directory other than cgi-bin, you will need to adjust this code accordingly.)

```
<form method="post" action="/cgi-bin/formmail.pl">
```

Optional Transmission Attributes

There are three additional attributes you can add to the <form> element, depending on your circumstances: enctype, accept, and accept-charset.

enctype

The enctype attribute specifies the file format in which the information should be submitted to the action. The default value for this attribute is application/x-www-form-urlencoded. (This is what causes the gibberish that is sent if you use the mailto: action.)

All of the name-value pairs will be encoded into one long string separated by ampersand (&) characters. As long as you are sending your data to a script, there is no need to include this attribute.

The other value for this attribute is multipart/form-data. You would want to set this value if you are using a mailto: action, as shown here:

```
<form method="post" action="mailto:user@domain.com"
enctype="multipart/form-data">
```

This will send each value from your form as a separate text file attached to the consequent email message. This, however, does not work with all browser/email client combinations. Thus, if it works at all, the results sent via a mailto: action will be much more readable, but it will not solve the user configuration issue associated with the mailto: action.

accept

The accept attribute specifies which file formats will be accepted when <input type="file" /> is used. Recall that we do use that input type in our form, so we need to include this information. By adding the code, as shown here, we can limit users to uploading text files only. This will prevent them from sending us large executable or other file types.

```
<form method="post" action="/cgi-bin/formmail.pl" accept="text/plain">
```

NOTE You will find a complete list of content types at ftp://ftp.isi.edu/in-notes/iana/assignments/media-types/.

accept-charset

The accept-charset attribute specifies which character sets the form will accept as input. You need to use this only when you are accepting input in non-Latin character sets.

NOTE A complete list of character sets can be found at ftp://ftp.isi.edu/in-notes/iana/assignments/character-sets.

The Other <input /> Types

Once we have instructed our form to send the name/value pairs in a certain format to a certain script, there are a few more items that we must include to make our form work. All of these items are based on the <input> element and the type attribute.

type="submit" and type="reset"

Both the submit and reset types are preprogrammed to create buttons that perform certain actions upon clicking by the user.

■ The submit button "activates" the form, causing it to gather the data and send it to the script through the methods established through the action attribute.

■ The reset button causes the form to revert to its original display state. All fields will be cleared and all selectable elements will revert to their default status.

Most browsers have default text that appears on each of the buttons. To change that text, you can add the value attribute to the <input> element.

The following is our updated code, with the two buttons added to the bottom of our form:

```
</fieldset>
<p>
<input type="submit" value="Submit Request" />
<input type="reset" value="Clear Form" />
</p>
</form>
```

Figure 6.19 shows how our form looks now, with the buttons added. Note we have edited our button text to read "Submit Request" and "Clear Form."

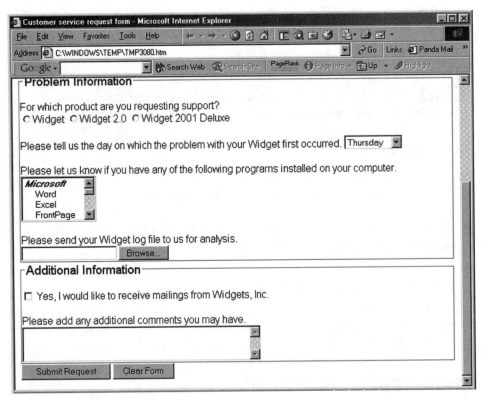

Figure 6.19 Our updated form with submit and reset buttons.

type="image"

If you would like to create a submit button that is more detailed than the one that comes with XHTML, you can use the type="image" attribute, as shown here:

```
<input type="image" src="filename.ext" border="0" />
```

type="button"

If you are designing for browsers that do not yet support the <button> element, you can use the older type="button" attribute on the <input /> element to create a generic button, as shown here:

```
<input type="button" name="print" onclick="javascript:window.print();"
/>
```

type="hidden"

Recall that we are planning to email the data collected by our form; therefore, we must provide a few pieces of information if that data is to reach its destination. The most obvious piece of information is the email address of the person to whom this data will be sent.

An aside is in order here, before moving on. The first reaction of many authors new to forms is to assume that this information should be included in the script that is processing the form's data. Although this is technically possible, it causes a couple of problems.

- If you are unaware of how to program in the language in which the script is written, adding this information may be difficult.

- You will lose the portability of the script. If you have multiple forms, each coded to send its data to different addresses, you will need to use multiple scripts, each with a different hard-coded address.

Fortunately, rather than include such information to the script itself, it is possible to include the information in the form. This allows you to use the same script for multiple forms, and does not force you to learn a new programming language.

Back to the subject at hand, supplying the information to get our data where it's going. This information must be sent to the script as name-value pairs, but it does not need to be displayed to the user. So the method we will use to include this information in the form, but hide it from the user, is to implement hidden fields. (Note: The user can still view this data by accessing the form's source code.) Hidden fields are traditionally placed immediately after the start of the form, and preceding any fields or other content that is displayed for the user.

Providing you are using a prewritten script (as we are with FormMail), the script's instructions should include all available hidden fields and what they do. This is where the fifth rule ("unless you are told otherwise"), discussed earlier, comes into play when naming fields. If a script specifies that a certain field name is reserved for a specific reason for the script, using it in another context may achieve an unintended result.

There are many hidden fields available in FormMail, but for the purposes of this chapter we will deal only with the five most commonly used ones. Once you understand how these five work, you will be able to apply that knowledge to the other fields and use them as you see fit.

name="email"

Early in the development of our form we took care of this field—although we did not treat it as a hidden field, but as one that asked the user to provide data. FormMail treats the value of email as the return address for the message sent by the script. In this case, we asked the user for the information that the script was looking for.

name="recipient"

The recipient field is where we generate a name-value pair that the script will use to address the resulting email message. In this case, the value of recipient needs to be the valid email address of the person receiving this message. (Note that you may include multiple addresses for this value by separating them with commas.) If an email address given in the value is not valid, the server will generate an error message and not send the message. The following code illustrates the format of the recipient hidden field:

```
<input type="hidden" name="recipient" value="address1,address2,etc" />
```

name="subject"

The subject field allows us to include a subject line in the email message being sent. The value of this field is the text you wish to appear in this line. The following code illustrates the format of the subject hidden field:

```
<input type="hidden" name="subject" value="text to appear in the email
message's subject line" />
```

name="required"

FormMail has a nice little feature that allows you to require that certain fields be filled in before the script will send the email message. The value for the aptly named "required" field is a comma-delimited list of the field names that you want to include. When the submit button is clicked, if any of the listed fields are not filled in, an error page will be generated, prompting the user to fill them in. The following code illustrates the format of the required hidden field:

```
<input type="hidden" name="required" value="fieldname,fieldname,etc" />
```

The required field comes with a few guidelines:

Use this feature sparingly. Use it only on fields that you absolutely must have. Requiring every field to be filled out will only annoy users.

Do not expect this feature to validate user information. As long as the user inputs any data to the field, the requirement will be regarded as having been met. To validate data (e.g., to make sure that a legitimate email address was entered in the email field), you will need to use JavaScript, which is covered fully in Chapter 9.

Always mark required fields. Typically, you can do this by adding a note to the top of the form and an asterisk by the name of the respective field. This prevents the user from having to guess which fields may or may not be required. (Note: Do not use color to indicate required fields ([e.g., "required fields are in red"]), because some browsers do not display colors, and some individuals are color-blind).

name="sort"

The sort field allows you to establish the order in which the fields are sent in the email message. There are two good reasons for using this field:

- It allows you to establish a data sequence that may be different from the order in which the fields are displayed on the screen. For example, maybe the first thing you want to see is the product name causing the problem, instead of the user's name.

- FormMail has a small quirk that returns the fields in a random order unless you have specifically established an order in the sort field.

The value for sort always starts with order: followed by a comma-delimited list of your field names in the order you want them to be sent. The following code illustrates the format of the sort hidden field:

```
<input type="hidden" name="sort" value="order:fieldname,fieldname,etc"
/>
```

name="title"

Once FormMail has successfully processed the submitted data and emailed it to the specified recipient(s) it will generate a screen for the user that echoes the data they submitted. Through the title-hidden field you can specify the text that the user will see at the top of that page. The value of the title field is the text that you wish to have appear. The following code illustrates the format of the title-hidden field:

```
<input type="hidden" name="title" value="text you want to appear at the
top of the results page" />
```

Putting Them All Together

The following is our updated code with hidden fields and marked required fields (note that you will need to type your own email address in the recipient field):

```
<p>Required fields are marked with an asterisk (*).</p>
<form>
<input type="hidden" name="recipient" value="user@domain.com" />
<input type="hidden" name="subject" value="Customer Service Request" />
<input type="hidden" name="required" value="firstname,lastname,email" />
```

```
<input type="hidden" name="sort"
value="order:firstname,lastname,email,custnum,password,product,day,soft-
ware,log,mailings,comments" />
<input type="hidden" name="title" value="Thank you for submitting your
request." />
<fieldset>
<legend>Customer Information</legend>
<p>
<label for="fname">*First Name:</label> <input id="fname" type="text"
name="firstname" />
<label for="lname">*Last name:</label> <input id="lname" type="text"
name="lastname" /><br />
<label for="email">*Email address:</label> <input id="email" type="text"
name="email" />
</p>
```

Testing Our Form

At this point, our form is complete and should be working. As with any document, especially interactive ones such as forms, it is always a good idea to test before releasing it for general use. Here are a few guidelines to keep in mind when testing forms.

- Make sure all field names in the hidden fields exactly match the actual field names, including character case. If they do not, the hidden field will not work appropriately.

- Make sure all recipient email addresses are valid. If not, the form will generate an error message the user will not understand.

- Make sure all required fields work as specified. To verify this, fill out the form leaving out one required field at a time. Also fill out the form leaving all required fields blank.

- Make sure your sort order works as you intended. Fill out all fields to confirm that the results will be sent in the intended order.

The Future of Forms

For all that we can do with forms today, they still have limited implementation. Though HTML 4.0 went a long way to make them more universally capable and flexible, as yet they cannot stand on their own. For instance, you must combine some type of client-side or server-side scripting to validate the data being entered by the user in a form—you don't want to be missing a digit in a phone number or street address. It is also impossible for a user to start the process of filling out a form, and then come back to finish a day later from another computer. And though there are some basic tags in HTML 4.0 that allow you to better develop forms for multiple devices, device-independence still does not exist in form implementation.

Because of these limitations, the W3C continues to work on improving forms, through the XForms Working Group, a successor to the HTML Working Group. Still in its infancy, a lot of progress has been made on the effort. A Requirements draft has been published, and work has begun on the next generation of forms. Unlike earlier HTML forms, XForms will enable not just the submission of XHTML documents, but other languages, as well, including XML, SMIL (Synchronized Multimedia Integration Language), and SVG (Scalable Vector Graphics). The basic idea is simple: separate purpose from presentation.

The XForms Working Group is concentrating on three distinct areas:

- User interface
- Data model
- Submit protocol

NOTE Still in a Working Draft state, a lot may change before XForms becomes a full W3C recommendation. For this reason, we will not discuss language semantics or syntax here. We will focus instead on the general breakdown of XForms, and introduce you to the concepts therein.

User Interface

The XForms user interface (UI) includes those aspects that define how the form will be presented to the user, in much the same way that CSS provides presentation information for XHTML documents. The XForms user interface, however, is different from CSS in that it includes extra levels of control that developers need, not only within Web browsers, but also within wireless devices or for print purposes.

The XForms UI currently comprises two parts. The first is the actual interface "widgets," the buttons, checkboxes, and text entry areas. These represent the elements that you will use to create the necessary look and feel to your forms. The second part is the foundation "binding" between those widget instances and the data model underneath. More on the model in the next subsection; here just be aware that it represents the method by which the widgets communicate to the form functionality. This is especially important as you begin to develop forms to be rendered across a variety of devices.

Model

The XForms model consists of the nonvisual aspect of forms. It was created to serve three purposes. First and foremost, of course, it defines the items in the model itself, as summarized in Figure 6.20, and describes the structure of all instances of XForms data. Second, it defines the reusable model elements, as well as any limits or restrictions on the items. Finally, as in all XML-based languages, it defines the relationships and any dependencies between items within the model.

You can clearly see the model's two main parts in the figure. The first part, Data Structures, is inherent to XML. XForms is based on the future XML schema standard, which is currently in a Candidate Recommendation state; therefore, it inherits all the benefits of defining languages in schema rather than DTDs. (Note: Schema is often considered somewhat more complex than the DTDs of today, so a comment is included

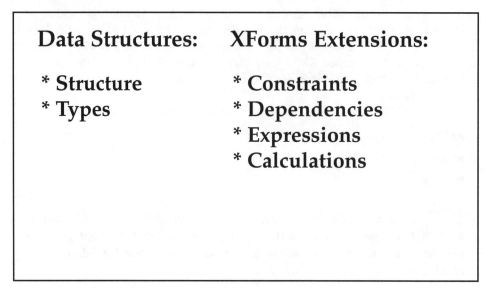

Figure 6.20   The XForms model.

in the current XForms Working Draft to the effect that the Working Group is looking into a simpler syntax.)

The second part of the model, XForms Extensions, involves constraints, dependencies, expressions, and calculations—aspects we were only able to accomplish through the use of a client-side scripting language like JavaScript before. This potentially adds the capability to apply a dependency or constraint on elements within forms. For example, if a form included a field for Company Name, it would be possible to require the user to fill out the Company's Address field. Moreover, simple calculations, such as decimal arithmetic, often used to calculate the costs of items in an online shopping cart, will become possible. These four types of functionality—constraints, dependencies, expressions, and calculations—are being referred to collectively as the Dynamic Constraints Language.

The model will also enable authors to include instance data. This means that you, as an author of an XForms instance, can submit data to the server as a complete XML document, and that you can prepopulate instances with data. It might even mean that your users will be able to save the state of their form to complete at a later time.

Submit Protocol

Currently, the XForms Working Group is soliciting requirements for a submission protocol. Historically, forms have had the capability to push user-entered data to the server in sets of name/value pairs, as well as to upload multipart MIME-encoded data. XForms, of course, will need to be able to support this type of functionality, but will most likely do so in a completely different manner.

As mentioned, the group is also working to support the capability to allow a user to stop entering information in a form when it becomes inconvenient to do so, and to resume it at a later time. Ideally, this would cross not only the time barrier, but also the user-agent barrier, meaning that a user might start filling out a form, say a credit card application, within his or browser at work, then resume it on his or her home computer or Web-enabled mobile phone later that evening.

Summary

Forms continue to be a very powerful mechanism by which Web authors can collect information from visitors to their Web sites. But for authors to make the most of them, forms must be designed carefully and implemented properly. In the future, we can look forward to greater possibilities, thanks to the effort being made by the W3C XForms Working Group.

Frames

Frames in HTML have a long and problematic history. When first implemented in HTML 2.0, many authors were quick to use this new design feature. Unfortunately, many of those authors lacked a thorough understanding of frames; this was exacerbated by poor support at the browser end, making for a poor user experience. Though much of the stigma attached to frames has dissipated over the last several years, some still do not like to use sites designed with frames.

The coding for frames has not changed in the upgrade from HTML to XHTML, so this chapter will serve primarily as a review. That said, note that the last section, *Avoiding Frame Problems*, is a must read, even for those experienced with frames, for it explains how to avoid common problems when implementing frames.

Implementing Frames in XHTML

As in HTML, frames have a singular purpose in XHTML: to give you, the author, the ability to present to the user multiple documents at the same time. This can be done through two methods: *fixed frames* and *floating frames*.

Fixed frames allow you to divide the screen into regions; subsequently, you indicate which document displays in each region. To do this, you must first create the individual document, then a frameset document that includes the code that details how to divide the window, and instructs the browser which document to display in which frame. Thus, you will be creating $n+1$ pages. n being the number of documents to be displayed; the plus-one document being the frameset document. So, to create a page that displays three documents, for example, you must create four documents, the three that will display, plus the frameset document.

The other method of displaying multiple documents to use a floating frame. In this case you create a document as usual, then create a floating frame, which is a space in the larger document that contains another document. Using this method, you create only the number of documents you wish to display. No frameset document is involved, as the floating frame is coded directly into the larger document.

Coding Fixed Frames

The only items that have changed in the coding of frames in XHTML are the larger issues, such as lowercase elements and quoted attribute values, the elements and attributes have not changed from HTML to XHTML.

NOTE For the examples used in this discussion, we assume that the documents being displayed within the frames have already been created. Thus, we focus only on the creation of the frameset document.

\<frameset\>

A frameset document tells the browser how to split up the window, and in which frame to display which document. Frameset documents start out as nonframe documents, do as shown here (be sure to change your !DOCTYPE statement to the one needed for a frameset document):

```
<?xml version="1.0" encoding="UTF-8"?>
<!DOCTYPE html PUBLIC "-//W3C//DTD XHTML 1.0 Frameset//EN"
"http://www.w3.org/TR/xhtml11/DTD/xhtml1- frameset.dtd">
<html xmlns="http://www.w3.org/1999/xhtml" xml:lang="en" lang="en">
<head>
<title>Simple html document to be converted to xhtml</title>
</head>
...
</html>
```

But note that, in a frameset document, there is no \<body\>. Instead, you must use the \<frameset\> element. In fact, in most instances, if you do include the \<body\> element after \</head\>, any frameset information will be ignored by the browser. Thus, you can regard the \<frameset\> element as a replacement for the body element.

Adding the \<frameset\> element, we end up with the following code:

```
<?xml version="1.0" encoding="UTF-8"?>
<!DOCTYPE html PUBLIC "-//W3C//DTD XHTML 1.0 Frameset//EN"
"http://www.w3.org/TR/xhtml11/DTD/xhtml1-frameset.dtd">
<html xmlns="http://www.w3.org/1999/xhtml" xml:lang="en" lang="en">
<head>
<title>Simple html document to be converted to xhtml</title>
</head>
```

```
<frameset>
...
</frameset>
</html>
```

Nested within <frameset>...</frameset>, only three other elements may appear:

<frame>. Used to establish the window areas.

<noframe>. Used to display alternate information for browsers that do not support frames.

<frameset>. Used for combining rows and columns.

We will deal with each of these elements in turn.

Just adding the <frameset> element does not tell the browser anything that it needs to know. It's similar to inserting an <img> element without specifying the src attribute. So, in this case, we also have an element that is required to actually accomplish anything.

The two attributes that you have to choose from to use with <frameset> are rows and cols. Which you use depends on the direction in which you would like to divide the browser window. To help you make this decision, it's a good idea to first take pencil and paper and sketch out what you want the browser window to look like. Doing so will make it much easier to code your frameset document and keep track of which frame is which.

To start, we'll work with rows. Let's say we want to create a window that displays two documents. The first document will display in the top 25 percent of the window, and the second will take up the bottom 75 percent of the window. Following is the code we'll use to divide our window into two portions:

```
<?xml version="1.0" encoding="UTF-8"?>
<!DOCTYPE html PUBLIC "-//W3C//DTD XHTML 1.0 Frameset//EN"
"http://www.w3.org/TR/xhtml11/DTD/xhtml1-frameset.dtd">
<html xmlns="http://www.w3.org/1999/xhtml" xml:lang="en" lang="en">
<head>
<title>Simple html document to be converted to xhtml</title>
</head>
<frameset rows="25%, 75%">
...
</frameset>
</html>
```

Because we have used the rows attribute, the browser will generate two frames, divided horizontally, based on the percentages we assigned. If we had used the cols attribute, the frames would have been established vertically.

Rows and Cols Value Types

Four methods are available to you for establishing the size of frames through the values set in the rows and cols attributes. These four methods can be used individually or in combination with each other:

Percentage (<frameset rows="25%, 75%">). Allows you to set a certain percentage of the available window aside for a frame, based upon the available window space. Note that problems may occur if you are designing on a high-resolution monitor and the user is viewing on a low-resolution monitor.

Integer (<frameset rows="100, 300">). Lets you tell the browser to establish the frames using an exact pixel size. In this example, we have established two rows: the top is 100 pixels in height, the bottom 300 pixels in height. The inherent problem with this method: the sum of the integers must be the same as the available number of pixels in the user's window. In this example, our total is 400 pixels. The chances of that matching the number of pixels available in any user's window are slim to none. However, don't rule out the use of integer values, as we can combine them with other types of values.

Asterisk (<frameset rows= "100, *">). As in DOS and Unix conventions, the asterisk is a wild card value. Asterisks are generally used in combination with percentage or integer values to indicate whatever is left. Here, we solved the problem caused in our integer example by changing the second value to an asterisk. We now have a top row of 100 pixels and a bottom row of whatever is left. In this way, our sum will total the amount of space in the user's browser, whatever that number might be. Asterisks can also be used in conjunction with percentage values. For example, we could rewrite our code to match.

Integer/Asterisk combination (<frameset cols="*, 4*">). Allows you to establish a relative value to your frame sizes. This is similar to the percentage value, but instead of the values being relative to the size of the browser window, the sizes will be relative to each other. Here we have created two column frames (left to right) in which the right frame will be four times as wide as the left frame. The left frame will take up one-fifth of the available space, and the right frame will take up four-fifths of the available space. (An asterisk by itself is the same as writing 1*.)

The following change to our code uses a combination of percentage and asterisk values:

```
<frameset rows="25%, *">
...
</frameset>
```

<frame />

Once we have established the layout of our frames in the <frameset> element, we must then indicate which documents are to be displayed within those frames. This we do through the <frame> element. Here are the rules to follow for using the <frame /> element.

- Because <frame /> is an empty element, you must close it, according to the new XHTML rules.

- The number of <frame /> elements you include in your document must equal the number of frames you have established in the <frameset> element. If you have established two frames in the <frameset> element, you must include two

<frame /> elements. Leaving out <frame /> elements or including too many <frame /> elements may prevent the document from displaying correctly.

Let's update our sample document to include <frame /> elements to tell the browser which files to display within those frames. Here's the code:

```
<?xml version="1.0" encoding="UTF-8"?>
<!DOCTYPE html PUBLIC "-//W3C//DTD XHTML 1.0 Frameset//EN"
"http://www.w3.org/TR/xhtml11/DTD/xhtml1-frameset.dtd">
<html xmlns="http://www.w3.org/1999/xhtml" xml:lang="en" lang="en">
<head>
<title>Simple html document to be converted to xhtml</title>
</head>
<frameset rows="25%, 75%">
     <frame />
     <frame />
</frameset>
</html>
```

Just as with the <img /> element, the <frame /> element requires the src attribute. This attribute instructs the browser which file to display in that location. Here is our code updated with the src attribute:

```
<?xml version="1.0" encoding="UTF-8"?>
<!DOCTYPE html PUBLIC "-//W3C//DTD XHTML 1.0 Frameset//EN"
"http://www.w3.org/TR/xhtml11/DTD/xhtml1-frameset.dtd">
<html xmlns="http://www.w3.org/1999/xhtml" xml:lang="en" lang="en">
<head>
<title>Simple html document to be converted to xhtml</title>
</head>
<frameset rows="25%, 75%">
     <frame src="toc.html" />
     <frame src="welcome.html" />
</frameset>
</html>
```

Figure 7.1 shows the resulting browser display.

Combining Rows and Cols

So far, in all of the examples, our window is split into just two rows (or if we want columns instead, we can just replace the rows attribute with cols). Now it's time to divide our document into rows *and* columns. This is where we will use multiple <frameset> elements.

Let's say we want to take the bottom frame of our document and split it in half vertically. This requires us to use a rows-based frameset and to split the lower frame using cols, as shown here:

```
<frameset rows="25%, 75%">
     <frame src="toc.html" />
```

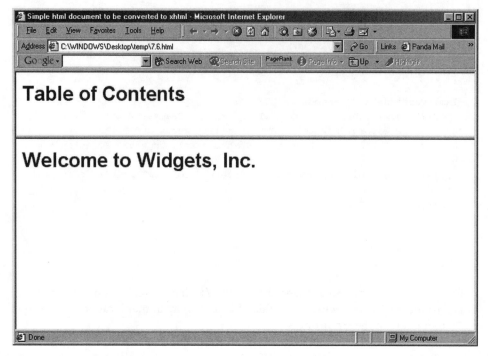

Figure 7.1   Including the src attribute.

```
<frameset cols="50%, 50%">
        <frame src="left.html" />
        <frame src="right.html" />
</frameset>
</frameset>
```

See Figure 7.2 for the resulting browser display.

In this example, the browser has split the window into two horizontal frames and placed the file toc.html into the top frame. To fill in the bottom frame, the <frameset> element instructs it to split that frame into two vertical frames, each taking up half of the available space, and to place the file left.html into the left frame and right.html into the right frame. (Probably now you can understand why sketching this out might help.)

Controlling Frame Display Options

XHTML offers several ways to control how your frames display to the user. You can modify frame borders, scrollbars, margins, and whether to allow the user to resize the frames.

Frame Borders

In some cases, you may find it more visually appealing to hide frame borders. To do this, you must add the frameborder attribute to the appropriate <frame /> elements and set its value to zero, as shown here (see Figure 7.3 for the resulting browser display):

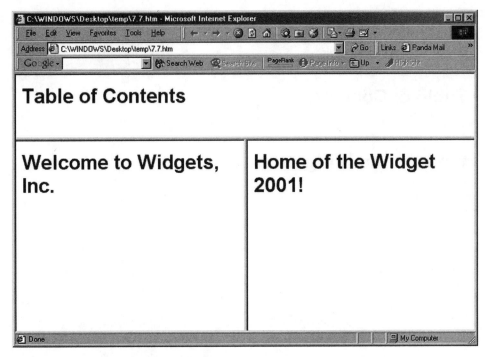

Figure 7.2 Splitting a screen vertically.

```
<frameset rows="25%, 75%">
    <frame src="toc.html" frameborder="0"/>
    <frame src="welcome.html" frameborder="0"/>
</frameset>
```

Frame Scrollbars

To control when and if a frame displays its scrollbar, you add the scrolling attribute, also on the <frame /> element. The scrolling attribute has three possible values:

scrolling="auto". The default value. The browser will display the frame's scrollbar if it is needed. This will happen when the content of the frame exceeds the available space.

scrolling="yes". The browser will display both the horizontal and vertical scrollbars in the frame whether they are needed or not.

scrolling="no". The browser will not display any scrollbars on the frame regardless of whether they are needed.

If you are thinking that scrolling="yes" is useless, we would have to agree with you. We are not aware of a single situation in which an author would want to turn on the scrollbars if they were not needed. This would take up valuable frame real estate and not look good.

The scrolling="no" value seems to have some potential, however, when used in combination with frameborder="0". This would allow you to smoothly integrate a

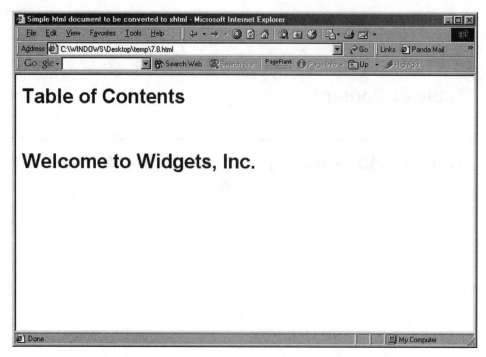

Figure 7.3 Using the frameborder attribute to hide the border.

frame into the rest of the document without any borders or scrollbars getting in the way. As it turns out, however, this is a dangerous assumption. Why? Because by doing so your users may be prevented from accessing some of your content. A real-life story will serve to demonstrate.

A small private Christian university library had a wonderfully designed site that used two frames, right and left. The left frame served as a table of contents to the library's resources, which appeared in the right frame. (We'll discuss linking frames shortly.) The document in the left frame had a background image, which, when there were no frame borders or scrollbars, smoothly integrated with the background image on the document in the right frame. If, however, a border or scrollbar appeared on the left frame, the look of the background image was destroyed. To fix this, the site set frameborder="0" and scrolling="no" on the left frame. But one problem remained.

The result was visually appealing and functional, as long as the user was viewing the site on a resolution of 800×600 or higher, where there was enough space on the screen to display the complete contents of the left frame. If, however, a user was viewing the site at a lower resolution, the bottom content of the left frame was cut off and inaccessible, as no scrollbars were available. Ironically, one of the links that disappeared was to the library's Bible resources.

The lesson is, unless you can guarantee that all of your users will be viewing your site at a resolution that renders all of your content accessible, don't use scrolling="no".

Locking Frames

Did you know that users can use their mouse to grab the borders between your frames and resize them by dragging the border? Although this does make the page much more flexible for the user, it tends to defeat the purpose of designing your frameset and setting the frame sizes to meet your specific needs, especially if you use integer values.

Fortunately, it is possible to turn off the ability for the user to do this by adding the noresize attribute to any and all <frame /> elements. Take a look at the following code, then try to resize the frames in your browser:

```
<frameset rows="25%, 75%">
    <frame src="toc.html" noresize="noresize"/>
    <frame src="welcome.html" noresize="noresize"/>
</frameset>
```

Setting Frame Margins

We think it odd that the folks who wrote the HTML specification enabled us to set the margins on frames. This has been carried over to XHTML. Why odd? Because in HTML and XHTML, we cannot set the margins on nonframe documents without using additional code, such as CSS.

Nevertheless, to the <frame /> element we can add the marginheight and margin-width attributes:

marginheight="n". Sets the size of the top and bottom margins of the frame in *n* pixels.

marginwidth="n". Sets the size of the left and right margins of the frame in *n* pixels.

Note that to set the margins on frames in nonpairs, you will need to use the CSS methods available to you on the actual XHTML document appearing within the frame. CSS is discussed in the next chapter.

Linking Frames Using the Target Attribute

Once we have our window split into the frames we want, and have the frames looking the way we want, with the correct documents displaying within those frames, the next step is to make the frames interact with each other.

In this section we'll create a frames-based newsletter site. Here, we would like to give the user the ability to click on an issue date in the left frame and have that issue appear in the right frame. As our site exists now, this is not possible. To set it up so that our frames interact in this way, we must follow a two-step process: name the frames and set our link targets.

Naming the Frames

The first step is to give each of our frames a name. We do this by adding the name attribute to the <frame /> element in our frameset document.

There are three guidelines to follow for choosing good frame names. Keep in mind that:

■ Names are case-sensitive. They can be in any case combination that you wish, but your use of case must be consistent between the naming of a frame and any other reference to that frame name in your code. For example, if you name a frame "Home", you must the link to the frame "Home". If you link to "home", a match will not be made and your link will not work.

■ Names should be descriptive.

■ Names may not contain spaces.

In our code, as you can see, the names appear in all lowercase, contain no spaces, and are descriptive of their content:

```
<frameset cols="25%, 75%">
    <frame src="toc.html" name="toc" />
    <frame src="welcome.html" name="display" />
</frameset>
```

Setting Targets

The next step in this process is to set targets on our hyperlinks. We do this in the documents that are being displayed in the frames, not in the frameset document. In fact, it's impossible to do in our frameset document because it does not contain any hyperlinks.

The following code shows the updated hyperlinks in the toc.html file to include the target attribute:

```
<p><a href="nov00.html" target="display">November 2000</p>
<p><a href="dec00.html" target="display">December 2000</p>
<p><a href="jan01.html" target="display">January 2001</p>
<p><a href="feb01.html" target="display">February 2001</p>
<p><a href="mar01.html" target="display">March 2001</p>
<p><a href="apr01.html" target="display">April 2001</p>
<p><a href="may01.html" target="display">May 2001</p>
```

However, there is a much more efficient way of doing the same thing. If a majority of our hyperlinks are going to the same target, we can set a default target on the whole document by adding some code, as in the following, within the head of our document:

```
<?xml version="1.0" encoding="UTF-8"?>
<!DOCTYPE html PUBLIC "-//W3C//DTD XHTML 1.0 Transitional//EN"
"http://www.w3.org/TR/xhtml11/DTD/xhtml1-transitional.dtd">
<html xmlns="http://www.w3.org/1999/xhtml" xml:lang="en" lang="en">
<head>
<title>Acme, Inc. Newsletter Archive Table of Contents</title>
<base target="display">
</head>
<body>
<div align="center">
<p>Acme, Inc. Newsletter Archive</p>
```

```
<p>Please select the issue you wish to view.</p>
<hr width="50%" />
<p><a href="nov00.html">November 2000</p>
<p><a href="dec00.html">December 2000</p>
<p><a href="jan01.html">January 2001</p>
<p><a href="feb01.html">February 2001</p>
<p><a href="mar01.html">March 2001</p>
<p><a href="apr01.html">April 2001</p>
<p><a href="may01.html">May 2001</p>
</div>
</body>
</html>
```

By adding a base target, all links within the document will go to that target—unless there is a target specified on a particular link. If a particular link has its own target attribute, that target will be given precedence over the document's base target.

Reserved Targets

XHTML has four built-in targets specifically designated to do certain things. They are: _self, _top, _blank, and _parent (note these reserved targets are all prefixed with an underscore):

target="_self". Instructs the browser to load the next document into the same frame as the document that contained the link. This is the default target, providing no other target has been specified either on the link or in the document head.

target="_top". Instructs the browser to load the next document into the full window, not within a frame. This is best used when linking to a document from another site. (We'll deal with this issue in more detail later in the chapter.)

target="_blank". Instructs the browser to load the next document into a new browser window. A word of caution: Don't overuse this target, or you risk annoying users.

target="_parent". Instructs the browser to load the next document into the parent frameset of the current document. If no parent is available, it will be treated as target="_self".

<noframes>

The <noframes> element allows you to specify alternate content to be displayed when the browser in use does not support frames. This element is placed between the </frameset> and </html> elements, as demonstrated in the following code:

```
</frameset>
<noframes>
<p>This content will be displayed in browsers that do not support
frames.</p>
</noframes>
</html>
```

Further details on the proper, and improper, use of <noframes> are discussed in the last section of this chapter.

Coding Inline Frames

Floating, or inline, frames allow you to create a master document and to display secondary documents within an area of that document. These frames are so named because the browser window is not split up and these areas can be placed at the discretion of the author.

<iframe>

Coding an inline frame is similar to coding an image; the only difference is that you use </iframe> to properly close the element. As with an image, the first step is to determine where within the document you would like the area to appear and what you want to appear within that area.

There are five elements that you can use to create your inline frame. The first three are required; the last two are optional:

src="filename.ext". The source file to be displayed within the inline frame.

height="n". Specifies the height of the inline frame in pixels.

width="n". Specifies the width of the inline frame in pixels.

frameborder="n". Specifies the thickness of the border around the frame. The larger the number, the thicker the border. Set the value to 0 if you don't want a border.

align="left | right | center". Specifies the alignment of the frame on the line. This alignment works the same as the alignment on an <img /> element. Left is the default value.

You will notice in the following code that establishing inline frames is similar to setting up images. Here, you can see the XHTML code you would use to insert an inline frame to the right of the paragraph, starting with "another paragraph" (see Figure 7.4 for the resulting browser display):

```
<p> This is a paragraph. This is a paragraph. This is a paragraph. This
is a paragraph. This is a paragraph. This is a paragraph. This is a
paragraph. This is a paragraph.</p>
<iframe src="otherfile.html" height="180" width="150" align="right">
</iframe>
<p> Another paragraph. Another paragraph. Another paragraph. Another
paragraph. Another paragraph. Another paragraph. Another paragraph.
Another paragraph. Another paragraph. Another paragraph.</p>
```

You will notice that <iframe> is not an empty element. This is because you can place content within the inline frame, similar to placing content within a <textarea> in a form. The significant difference is that the content will appear only if the user's browser does not support inline frames (see Figure 7.5). The following code illustrates how to add alternative inline frame content.

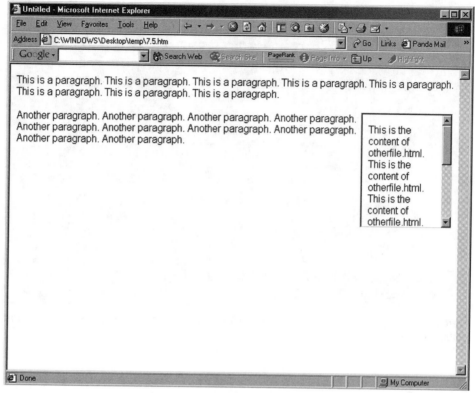

Figure 7.4 Setting the code to insert an inline frame.

```
<p> This is a paragraph. This is a paragraph. This is a paragraph. This
isa paragraph. This is a paragraph. This is a paragraph. This is a para-
graph. This is a paragraph.</p>
<iframe src="otherfile.html" height="180" width="150" align="right">
<a href="otherfile.html">Fetch the missing content.</a>
</iframe>
<p> Another paragraph. Another paragraph. Another paragraph. Another
paragraph. Another paragraph. Another paragraph. Another paragraph.
Another paragraph. Another paragraph. Another paragraph.</p>
```

Such content is best used as a link to the file in the src attribute. This gives the user the ability to access the content without your having to duplicate it.

Avoiding Frame Problems

We began this chapter by commenting on the problematic history of frames. Still, today, many new users are not aware of what a frames-based site is until examples are shown to them. A primary problem was that early browsers (Netscape 2.x for one) would treat all browsing within a frames-based site as one click. This meant that the

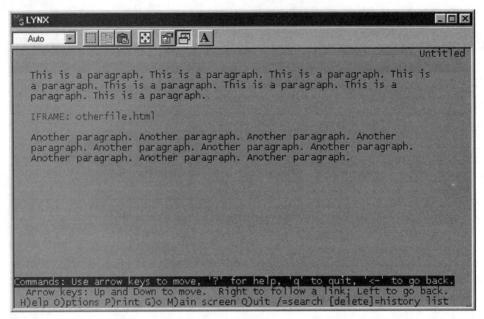

Figure 7.5 Displaying alternate content in DOSLynx, a browser that does not support inline frames.

moment a user clicked the Back button he or she was sent not back one page, but back to the site he or she was at before entering the frames-based site.

Many such problems have long been solved. However, you still need to be aware of problems you may unintentionally cause your users when coding frames. This section is intended to help you avoid those problems, by establishing some guidelines to follow.

Use Descriptive Frame Names

Current text-only browsers can handle frames-based pages only in a limited way. As shown in Figure 7.6, DOSLynx (a text-only browser that does not display frames, but links to individual documents) provides the user with a list of frames that he or she can choose to view. In this case, the Ask Jeeves site has properly descriptive frame names, AdBannerFrame, LinksFrame, and AnswerFrame.

Here, the user is looking for the answer to a question, so he or she should be able to determine which frame contains the information he or she is looking for: the Answer-Frame.

If a site contains names such as Frame1, Frame2, and Frame3, obviously the user will be unable to choose the correct frame; they will be forced to guess—and will be unlikely to return to your site in the future.

Take Advantage of <noframes>

As mentioned earlier, the <noframes>...</noframes> area of a frameset document allows you to place text in the document that can be seen by users whose browsers cannot display frames. Here is a little more detail on why you should do this.

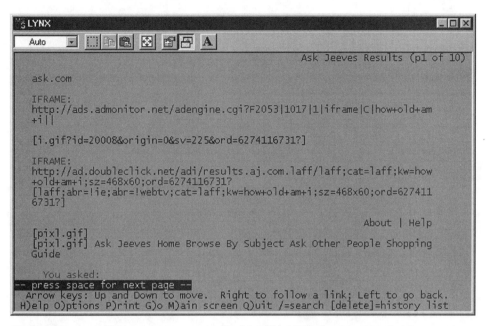

Figure 7.6   An Ask Jeeves answer page displayed in DOSLynx.

Today's text-only browsers offer better access to frame content through links, as discussed previously. However, older text-only browsers do not provide those links. They can display only the content of the <noframes> area. So, by including this type of content, you take into consideration users with older hardware and software.

That said, you should consider carefully what you include in that <noframes> area. As shown in Figure 7.6, the Ask Jeeves site encourages users to upgrade their software. As polite as this message is, it does not take into account that some people may not be able to upgrade their software for one reason or another. A better idea is to present as much information as possible in the <noframes> area. At a minimum, present a link to the information the user is looking for. (Ask Jeeves has done this.)

Another good reason to use the <noframes> element has to do with search engines. Most major search engines, upon encountering a frameset document, will not continue to index the documents listed in the frame elements. These search engines will, however, index text contained within the <noframes> area. (Metadata—that is, data about data—will also be indexed as usual.) By including not just a link, but actual content within the <noframes> area, your document will be better indexed and thus easier to find by users.

The following code shows good use of the <noframes> area. Not only is descriptive information included for indexing purposes, but it also reproduces the content of the left-hand "TOC" frame, giving users direct access to the material if they are using a text-only browser:

```
The frameset document
<?xml version="1.0" encoding="UTF-8"?>
<!DOCTYPE html PUBLIC "-//W3C//DTD XHTML 1.0 Transitional//EN"
```

```
"http://www.w3.org/TR/xhtml11/DTD/xhtml1-transitional.dtd">
<html xmlns="http://www.w3.org/1999/xhtml" xml:lang="en" lang="en">
<head>
<title>Acme, Inc. Newsletter Archive</title>
</head>
<frameset cols="25%,75%">
    <frame src="TOC.html" name="TOC" />
    <frame src="welcome.html" name="Documents" />
</frameset>
<noframes>
<body>
<div align="center">
<p>Acme, Inc. Newsletter Archive</p>
<p>Please select the issue you wish to view.</p>
<hr width="50%" />
<p><a href="nov00.html">November 2000</p>
<p><a href="dec00.html">December 2000</p>
<p><a href="jan01.html">January 2001</p>
<p><a href="feb01.html">February 2001</p>
<p><a href="mar01.html">March 2001</p>
<p><a href="apr01.html">April 2001</p>
<p><a href="may01.html">May 2001</p>
</div>
</body>
</noframes>
</html>


toc.html
<?xml version="1.0" encoding="UTF-8"?>
<!DOCTYPE html PUBLIC "-//W3C//DTD XHTML 1.0 Transitional//EN"
"http://www.w3.org/TR/xhtml11/DTD/xhtml1-transitional.dtd">
<html xmlns="http://www.w3.org/1999/xhtml" xml:lang="en" lang="en">
<head>
<title>Acme, Inc. Newsletter Archive Table of Contents</title>
<base target="display">
</head>
<body>
<div align="center">
<p>Acme, Inc. Newsletter Archive</p>
<p>Please select the issue you wish to view.</p>
<hr width="50%" />
<p><a href="nov00.html">November 2000</p>
<p><a href="dec00.html">December 2000</p>
<p><a href="jan01.html">January 2001</p>
<p><a href="feb01.html">February 2001</p>
<p><a href="mar01.html">March 2001</p>
<p><a href="apr01.html">April 2001</p>
<p><a href="may01.html">May 2001</p>
</div>
</body>
</html>
```

```
welcome.html
<?xml version="1.0" encoding="UTF-8"?>
<!DOCTYPE html PUBLIC "-//W3C//DTD XHTML 1.0 Transitional//EN"
"http://www.w3.org/TR/xhtml11/DTD/xhtml1-transitional.dtd">
<html xmlns="http://www.w3.org/1999/xhtml" xml:lang="en" lang="en">
<head>
<title>Acme, Inc. Newsletter Archive Welcome Screen</title>
</head>
<body>
<h1 align="center">Welcome to the Acme, Inc. newsletter archive</h1>
<p align="center">Please select the issue you wish to view from the menu
on the left.</p>
</body>
</html>
```

Figure 7.7 has the resulting Internet Explorer browser display, and Figure 7.8 has the display in DOSLynx.

Of course, because the example has the identical content of the toc.html file reproduced in the frameset document, we now have two copies of the same material to keep up to date. When the June 2001 issue of the newsletter becomes available, we will need

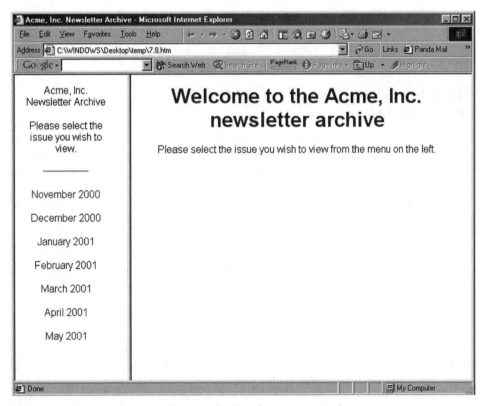

Figure 7.7 The <noframes> element displayed in Internet Explorer.

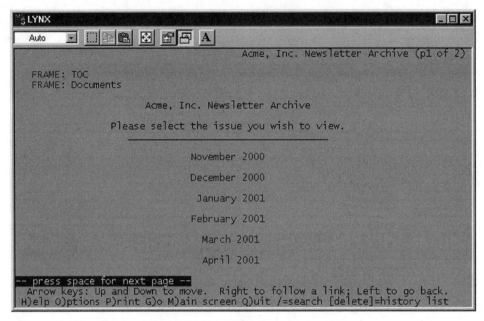

Figure 7.8 The same code displayed in DOSLynx.

to update not only the toc.html file but also the noframes area of the frameset document. This is double the work, but worth it to increase the accessibility of your information.

Use a Small Number of Reasonably Sized Frames

You may have noticed that all of the examples for frames-based documents in this chapter have used only two or three frames, sufficiently sized to present the information they contained. We raise this issue because one of the major complaints users have regarding frames is that often they are too small for the content they contain. One frames-based site for a former U.S. Senator had no fewer than nine frames. When displayed on a low-resolution monitor, many of the frames were too small to be useful. When printed out, one frame contained a four-page document. On the screen at a 640×480 resolution, that frame displayed about 10 words at a time. The chances that any visitor to that site actually read that document were quite small. The point is, if you design your site at a high resolution, be sure it also works at lower resolutions.

Don't Use Frames in Frames

As mentioned earlier, it is possible to put a frameset document in a frame, to include multiple frames within a single frame. But doing so can be problematic to code.

The moment you place frames within frames, you compound code complexity. Just keeping track of all the documents involved and the names of all the individual frames is difficult. The more complex your code, the greater the chances of causing the other problems discussed in this section, most of which end up affecting the user's experience in a negative way.

Don't Enable Access to Other Sites within Frames

There are two major reasons you should not enable users to open someone else's documents within your frames: user confusion and potential legal issues.

To illustrate the user confusion issue, consider this real-life online database product designed for libraries. This database allowed users to search for full-text resources and texts on authors from around the world. The system linked users not only to content provided by the database vendor, but also to the rest of the Web. For example, a search on Mark Twain would present the user with links to material offered by the company running the database, as well as links to universities that had their own material on Mark Twain available online.

The problem was that the database site used frames; at the top in the left-hand frame was the company logo; in the right-hand frame the results were displayed. When a user clicked on a link in the left frame, the result was shown in the right frame, regardless of who owned that content. Clearly, users would think they were still accessing vendor data, even if they had gone to a university site, since the vendor's logo was always in the left frame. This kind of "mistaken identity" obviously can lead to legal as well as ethical dilemmas. (In lawsuits resulting from cases such as this, the "framed" party usually wins.)

To avoid such situations, use target="_top" whenever you are linking to content that is not yours. This will cause the content to appear in the full window and display the correct URL.

NOTE You may hear or read the suggestion to open new content in a new window. We recommend against this, as whenever you open new windows, you increase the chances of user confusion, which is exactly what you should be working to avoid.

Summary

There are not many differences between the coding of frames in HTML and XHTML. Therefore, in this chapter, we focused on the pitfalls to avoid when designing frames. When designing with frames, your goal should always be to give the user a rewarding browsing experience.

Formatting with Style Sheets

HTML was created as a markup language to specify document structure, that is, to define where items in a document start and end. This is most evident in such elements as <html>, <head>, <body>, <hx>, and <p>. However, with the advent of graphical browsers, Web designers quickly became frustrated by the lack of layout and style control in the early versions of HTML. Quickly, style elements such as <b>, <i>, and <u> were added. Later, layout controls such as tables (though unintentionally) and alignments were added. Still, HTML is, at its core, designed to establish document structure. Even with such tricks as no-border tables, blank GIFs, and proprietary solutions, designers do not have the control they want over the layout of their documents.

With the release of XHTML, most of the stylistic elements have disappeared, elements such as <b>, <i>, and <u> have been officially removed from the specification. Attributes such as align are now discouraged from being used. So how can you, an author, implement style on your Web documents? The answer is cascading style sheets (CSS).

Cascading Style Sheets

The cascading style sheet specification was developed by the W3C in response to designer demands. CSS gives you complete control over the look and layout of a document, down to pixel-level positioning.

The most significant drawback to CSS today is the lack of support in older browsers. Even with proper implementation of CSS, many users may not see the document as you intended. Therefore, the key to successful use of CSS today is to make sure that your document is presentable and usable in older browsers. Even if your documents don't look exactly as you intended in these older browsers, as long as users can find the information they need, the problem should be regarded as a minor one.

> **NOTE** Keep in mind that the topic of this book is XHTML. We cover CSS here because it is the preferred method for formatting XHTML documents. That said, this chapter should not be regarded as comprehensive coverage of CSS. For more on CSS and its available options, we recommend *XHTML 1.0 Language and Design Sourcebook* and *XHTML 1.0 Web Development Sourcebook* by Ian Graham (John Wiley & Sons, Inc., 2000).

Understanding CSS Code Format

CSS codes have two parts: the *selector* and the *declaration;* the declaration has two sections: the *property* and the *value*. The following illustrates the CSS code format:

```
selector {property: value}
```

The selector must come first and be followed by at least one space. The declaration is enclosed in curly brackets ({ }). Within the brackets, the property must come first, followed by a colon and at least one space, then the value. The following is a simple example of CSS:

```
body {color: black}
```

In this example, body is the selector (what we are controlling) and the part starting with the open curly bracket, ({), and ending with the close curly bracket, (}), is the declaration (what we are doing to the selector.)

Within the declaration, color is the property (the particular part of the selector we are controlling) and black is the value (what we would like the property to be).

In many cases, your selector will be an XHTML element. (You also can make up your own, and we will get to that later.) The property is usually the same or an equivalent of an HTML attribute.

CSS declarations can also be stacked onto one selector. If we want the background white, the text color black, and the font a 12-point sans-serif face, we can make multiple declarations, separating them by semicolons. This eliminates the need to repeat the selector multiple times for multiple formatting changes. The following code shows a stacking of CSS declarations:

```
body {background: white;
      color: black;
      font-size: 12pt;
      font-family: sans-serif}
```

Notice in this example that the code is not tightly formatted. But as long as the information is in the proper order and the required single spaces appear, your code will be interpreted properly. You could just as easily write your CSS as in the next example, but you will quickly notice that it is not as easy to read for later human editing:

```
body {background: white; color: black; font-size: 12pt; font-family:
sans-serif}
```

Including CSS in Your Document

There are three ways to include CSS information in a document: in the document head, in a separate file, and inline with XHTML.

In the Document Head

If the style information applies only to one document, you would include it within the document head, enclosing it in <style> and </style>. You should also "comment out" the style code so as to avoid problems with browsers that do not support CSS.

To specify the background color of the document as white, we would write:

```
<head>
<style type="text/css">
<!--
body                   {background: white;
                        color: black;
                        font-size: 12pt;
                        font-family: sans-serif}
h1                     {color: red}
p                      {text-align: justify}
blockquote             {font-size: 14pt;
                        font-style: italic;
                        border: groove}

-->
</style>
</head>
```

In a Separate File

If you have style sheet information that you would like to apply to more than one document, it would be a waste of time to type (or even copy and paste) the style information into each document. Even if you did, making changes to all documents would present an ongoing tedious process.

With CSS, it is possible to put all of your style information into a separate text file and then point to it in the document's code. For example, let's create the following with the filename masterstyle.css:

```
body                   {background: white;
                        color: black;
                        font-size: 12pt;
                        font-family: sans-serif}
```

```
h1, h2, h3          {color: red}
p                   {align: justify}
blockquote          {font-size: 14pt;
                     font-style: italic;
                     border: groove}
```

In the head of this document, we would just need to add one line of HTML code to implement this style sheet:

```
<head>
<link rel="stylesheet" type="text/css" href="masterstyle.css" />
</head>
```

Inline with XHTML

Finally, if you want to implement a style on a particular instance of an element, you can add the style attribute to the element, as shown here:

```
<h1 style="color: purple">This is a purple header</h1>
```

However, this defeats the purpose of CSS, which is to separate the style from the XHTML. Although this is valid XHTML, we recommend that designers avoid this method and use classes and IDs instead to apply styles to certain instances of an XHTML element (discussed later in this chapter).

Selector Methods

There are seven different methods for using selectors: *type, descendant, adjacent sibling, attribute, pseudo, class,* and *ID.* Class and ID selectors are significantly different from the first five, so we will address them in a separate section.

Type

Type selectors are the most common selectors, and so far we have been using them. Any single element listed as a selector is a type selector, such as the following:

```
h1 {color: yellow}
```

Type selectors can also be stacked if you separate them by commas. This allows you to set the same declaration to multiple selectors, as shown here:

```
h2, h3, h4 {color: green}
```

Descendant

The descendant selector allows for style selection based on the context of the element. For example, when you use a foreign language word in traditional publishing, you italicize it. When you are quoting a whole paragraph in Italian, you italicize it. If that paragraph includes a word in English, you cannot double-italicize it, so you need to, in

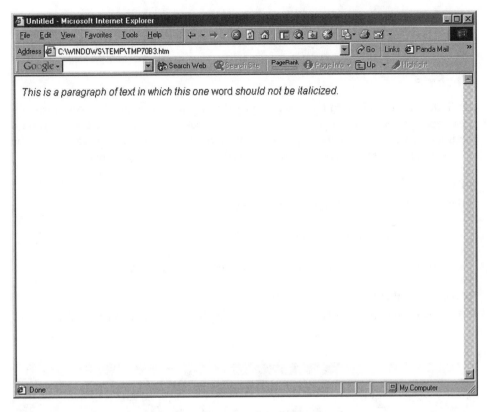

Figure 8.1 Using the descendant selector to deitalicize a word.

essence, "deitalicize" that word. You can use the following CSS to accomplish this (see Figure 8.1 for the resulting browser display):

```
p.foreign    {font-style: italic}
p.foreign i  {font-style: none}
<p class="foreign">This is a paragraph of text in which this one
<i>word</i> should not be italicized.</p>
```

NOTE Descendant selectors do not use commas, as type selectors can.

Adjacent Sibling Selectors

Adjacent sibling selectors are similar to descendant selectors, but specify that the second element must immediately follow the first:

```
blockquote {text-indent: 5cm}
p + blockquote {text-indent: 0}
```

In this example, blockquotes should be indented 5 centimeters, except those that immediately follow a start paragraph. So if we combine that with the following HTML code, we would end up with the following (see Figure 8.2 for the resulting browser display):

```
<p>This is a paragraph with a blockquote immediately following it.</p>
<blockquote>This is the blockquote that immediately follows the para-
graph.</blockquote>
```

Attribute

Attribute selectors allow you to specify styles that are applied only when certain attributes appear on a particular element. Attribute selectors are specified by enclosing a modifier in square brackets ([ ]) immediately after the selector. Attributes can be matched in any of four ways, as described in the following subsections.

[attribute]

If the attribute appears, then apply the style.

```
q[cite] {background: yellow}
```

In this example, quotes that have a citation will be given a yellow background.

[attribute=value]

If the attribute appears, and equals a particular value, the style will be applied.

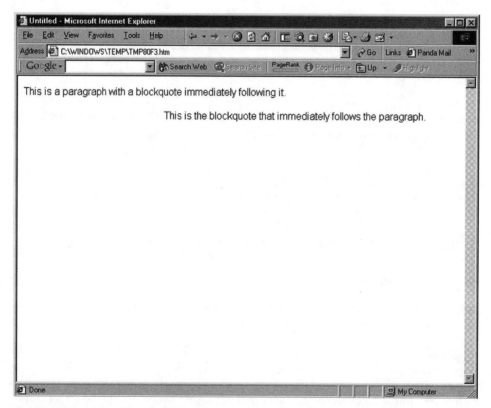

Figure 8.2   Using adjacent sibling selectors to specify order.

```
table[width="50%"] {color: red}
```

In this example, tables that have a width of exactly 50 percent of the browser window will have red text.

[attribute~=value]

Allows you to specify a style to be applied when a particular word appears within a descriptive attribute on a particular element.

```
table[summary~="library"] {font-family: fantasy}
```

In this example, tables that have a summary attribute in which the word "library" occurs will use a fantasy font.

[attribute|=value]

The | = (pipe equals) specifies a value list separated by hyphens. This is mainly used in language attributes, as that is the one place where the hyphen is required as part of the value (e.g., "en-US").

```
*[lang|=fr] {font-style: oblique}
```

In this example, any element that is in French will be printed oblique. Note also that an asterisk can be used in place of an element to specify any element.

Pseudo Selectors

Pseudo selectors receive influence from factors outside of the XHTML code. In some cases, they are based on a certain portion of a complete element; in others, they are based upon user actions. Currently, there are not many examples of pseudo selectors, so we'll take the time to go over all of them.

Anchors

Since the anchor element is one of the most common elements that authors use in their documents, you will find immediate benefit in the use of pseudo selectors.

All Web users quickly realize that anchors have two different states: not clicked and previously clicked. This is noticeable because, traditionally, nonclicked links display blue and clicked links display purple. There are, however, four states to links: *normal*, *selected*, *visited*, and *hover*. The following outlines the differences between these states:

Normal. A link that has not been clicked on. This is the default state, so there is no identifier for it. The default color for this state in most browsers is blue.

Selected. The state links are in while they are being clicked on—that is, while the mouse button is depressed but has not yet been released. In most cases, this state is not visible to users since a mouse-click is done quickly.

Visited. A link that has been clicked on recently. The default color for links in this state is purple.

Hover. The state a link is in while the mouse cursor is over the link, regardless whether the mouse button has been clicked or the link has been previously visited.

Many Web designers recommend against changing the colors of links since users are familiar with the standard blue and purple color scheme. Though not in complete agreement with this opinion, we do recommend that you consider your users (novice or experienced) before making such significant changes to your site's interface. Besides, there are other things you can do to anchors using pseudo selectors, which we will discuss later in this chapter.

To change the colors of your links, you can do the following:

```
a              {color: green}
a:selected     {color: yellow}
a:visited      {color: red}
a:hover        {color: blue}
```

In these examples, the links are now green by default (the normal state); links that are being clicked on are yellow; visited links are red. While the mouse pointer is over the link, the link is blue. (Instead of the normal blue, blue, purple, blue scheme.)

Block-Level Elements

The two other pseudo selectors are applied to block-level elements such as paragraphs, blockquotes, and headers. In these examples, we will stick to paragraphs as they are the most commonly used block-level elements.

The first of the block-level pseudo selectors is *first-line*. This allows us to apply a style to the first line of its associated XHTML element. For example, if we wanted to present all of the characters in the first line of paragraphs in small-caps, we could use:

```
p:first-line {text-transform: small-caps}
```

A browser that correctly handles this pseudo selector would automatically adjust the font of the first line of the paragraph accordingly. The flexibility of the pseudo selector is demonstrated by the fact that the first line of a paragraph may contain a larger or smaller number of words based upon the screen resolution of the user's browser. The browser should look for this and adjust accordingly.

The other block-level pseudo selector is *first-letter*. This allows us to apply a style to the first character in a particular block-level element. For example, the following illustrates the code needed to change the font of the first letter in paragraphs:

```
P:first-letter {font-family: elephant}
```

Unfortunately, this pseudo selector is not widely supported by browsers. An alternative method is shown here (unfortunately, this is not as elegant, but it does work):

```
CSS
.firstletter {font-family: elephant}

XHTML
<p><span class="firstletter">T</span>he first letter in this paragraph
is in the elephant font.</p>
```

Playing Cool Tricks with Pseudo-Selectors

More and more sites these days are changing the way their hyperlinks interact with the user's mouse. Here are some of the thing you can do to your hyperlinks with just a line or two of code:

- If you would prefer that your hyperlinks do not have underlines, regardless of what the user has their browser set for, you can change the text-decoration property:

  ```
  a {text-decoration: none}
  ```

- If your page is a sea of hyperlinks, you may want to make it clear to your users which link they will select if they click their mouse button. To add a highlight, change the background property for hovered links:

  ```
  a:hover {background: yellow}
  ```

- Another way to alert your user to which hyperlink they are selecting is to change the link's size, by modifying the font-size property:

  ```
  a:hover {font-size: 115%}
  ```

- If you are taking advantage of the accesskey attribute in XHTML to make your pages more accessible to users with disabilities by adding a keyboard shortcut to your links, you can make your links look like Windows-based program menus by underlining just the letter associated with the keyboard shortcut. To do this, you must turn off link underlining, and create an underlined class to be applied to just the particular letter, as shown here:

  ```
  CSS
  a               {text-decoration: none}
  .linkletter     {text-decoration: underline}

  XHTML
  <a href="http://www.yahoo.com" accesskey="Y">
  <span class="linkletter">Y</span>ahoo</a>
  ```

NOTE A much more complex example of this can be found at www.bcr.org/~msauers/css/accesskey.html.

And, for a more stylistic look, you can create drop caps, letters at the beginning of a paragraph that are significantly larger than the rest of the paragraph's characters and around which the others wrap. You can also change the font to one more ornamental to add additional style to your document, as shown here:

```
CSS
p:first-letter.start{font-size: 400%;
 float: left}
```

```
XHTML
<p class="start">The first letter of this paragraph will be a drop
cap.</p>
```

NOTE If you do not classify the paragraph with the drop cap, all paragraphs will have drop caps.

Although the previous example is the most efficient method of creating a drop cap, most browsers do not yet support the first-letter pseudo class. However, here is an alternative method for creating a drop cap that will work today:

```
CSS
.dropcap      {font-size: 400%;
  float: left}
```

```
XHTML
<p><span class="dropcap">T</span>he first letter of this paragraph will
be a drop cap.</p>
```

Using Classes and IDs

The idea behind classes and IDs is to give you the ability to create styles that can be applied to any element on a case-by-case basis. Initially, classes and IDs may seem very similar, but there are significant differences that you need to realize.

Implementing IDs

Let's say that you have a document in which there are two paragraphs. You would like the first paragraph to be printed in 24-point type and the second in 6-point type. In this instance, you have the same selector, p, but two different styles that you would like applied to that selector. One method for solving this problem is to identify those two different paragraphs in a method so as to associate them with particular styles.

To use the ID selector, create the name for the ID. This can be almost anything you wish as long as you adhere to these simple rules:

- IDs are case-sensitive. As long as you are consistent, you will have no problems. This is the same as when you name a frame. You may use any case combination you wish, but always remember that the id in the CSS and the id in the XHTML must match case in order to work. Spaces are not allowed.

- Name should be descriptive of the style being applied or the type of element being modified.

- In the CSS code, IDs must be preceded by a pound symbol (#).

In this example, we have decided to have two paragraphs print in two different point sizes, one large and one small. So we have created two IDs, #large and #small. For each, we have then followed with the appropriate declaration:

```
#large {font-size: 24pt}
#small {font-size: 6pt}
```

Once we have created the IDs, we can then apply them to elements as needed in the XHTML code. To do this, we add the id attribute to an element; its value will be the name of the ID to be used, sans the pound sign (#), as shown here (see Figure 8.3 for the resulting browser display):

```
<p id="large">This is 24pt text</p>
<p id="small">This is 6pt text</p>
```

Because they are intended to be applied to only their first instance of use in the XHTML code, IDs are limited in scope. If we were to reuse our ID, as in the next example, the style should be applied only to the first use of the ID large:

```
<p id="large">This is 24pt text</p>
<p id="small">This is 6pt text</p>
<p id="large">This is not 24pt text</p>
```

Although this is an invalid use of ID, most current browsers will allow this and apply the style anyway.

IDs can also be set up to apply to only certain XHTML elements. In the previous example, we could have used the IDs on any element we wanted, not just paragraphs.

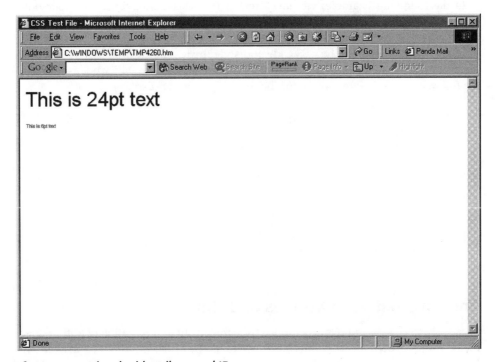

Figure 8.3 Using the id attribute and ID name.

If we wanted to be sure that the IDs could only be used on paragraphs, we could modify our CSS code to read:

```
p#large {font-size: 24pt}
p#small {font-size: 6pt}
```

By specifying an element at the beginning of the selector, we have forced the large and small styles to be applied only when identifying paragraphs. This would allow us to create multiple instances of #large, letting the style change depending on the element it is tied to, as shown here:

```
p#large              {font-size: 24pt}
blockquote#large     {font-size: 20pt}
```

Implementing Classes

You now know that IDs are designed to work only on one instance of an element. But what if you need to create a style that you want to use over and over again? This is where the more flexible class—for classification—comes in. Classes give you the ability to create multiple types of styles for the same element.

Classes are created in the same way, following the same rules and guidelines, as IDs, with the minor difference that they are preceded by a period (.) instead of a pound sign (#).

In the following example, we have created two classes: .business and .personal. Then, in our XHTML code we have specified which items in an unordered list are to be classified as business and which are to be classified as personal. When classified, the browser will refer back to the CSS code and style the text appropriately. In this example, businesspeople will be in bold and personal friends will be italicized, as shown in the following code (see Figure 8.4 for the resulting browser display):

```
CSS
.business {font-weight: bold}
.personal {font-style: italic }

XHTML
<ul>
<li class="business">Jim Hensinger</li>
<li class="personal">Denice Adkins</li>
<li class="business">Ellen Fox</li>
<li class="personal">Bob Dylan</li>
</ul>
```

Choosing between Classes and IDs

Because both classes and IDs accomplish the same result—the creation of author-specified designs—you may be wondering which to use in which situation. To answer that, let's take a moment to differentiate the two:

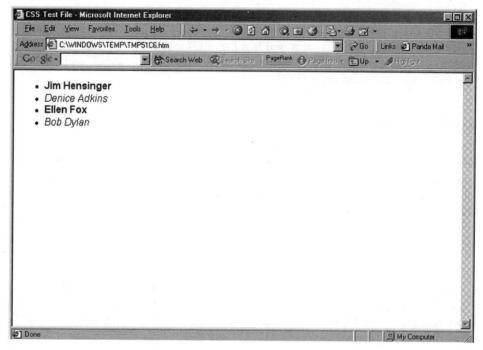

Figure 8.4   Using class to classify content.

■ IDs are designed for use in single instances.

■ Classes are designed to be reusable.

Once you understand these two points, and can remember which goes with which, the solution to the dilemma seems clear. If you will only be using the style once, use an ID; if you will be using the style more than once, use a class.

However, it may not be that simple. What if you create a style using ID, intending to use it but once, and later discover that you want to use it again? Sticking to the rules, you cannot, since IDs are single use. Under this circumstance, the decision between ID and class is not clear. Therefore, we recommend that whenever you come to the question of whether to create an ID or a class, create a class. Classes are much more flexible and can be used once or multiple times. If you create a class, you have the ability to reuse it. If you create an ID, you've locked yourself in.

Changing Font Properties

The method for changing a font in HTML was to use the font element along with its many attributes, including face, color, and size. For example, if you wanted to increase the size of the font in a particular paragraph you would have done the following:

```
<p><font size="+1">This is a paragraph</font></p>
```

Although this did achieve the result desired, it was neither exact (just what size is +1 anyway?) nor efficient. In order to apply this to text in a table in older versions of Netscape Navigator you were required to repeat the font element in every cell.

With the advent of XHTML, the font element has been discarded, and has been replaced with font formatting via CSS.

Font Families

CSS replaced the <font face="fontname"> HTML code with the font-family property. In its simplest form, this property works just as HTML's face attribute did. For example, you can specify a particular font or a list of particular fonts, as shown here (note that the first font will be tried first; if it does not exist on the user's computer, the next font will be tried, and so on):

```
body {font-family: arial}
body {font-family: arial, helvetica}
```

This property not only allows you to specify a particular font or set of fonts, but also a category or family of fonts. There are five available font families: Serif, Sans Serif, Cursive, Fantasy and Monospace. As you can see in Table 8.1, the default fonts used in these families vary from browser to browser and OS to OS.

Best-Choice Fonts

Because of this variation in appearance, many designers avoid these families, instead choosing to specify specific fonts. This decision has its own set of problems since you cannot be sure which fonts are installed on user machines. For example, if you specify that the Arial font should be used, this will work on Windows-based computers; but

Table 8.1   Default Font Families by Browser Version and OS

FONT FAMILY	NS 4.X WIN	NS 4.X MAC	NS 6.X WIN	IE 4.X WIN	IE 5.X WIN	IE 4.X MAC
Serif	Times New Roman	Times	Times New Roman	Times New Roman	Times New Roman	Times
Sans serif	Arial	Times	Arial	Arial	Arial	Times
Cursive	Arial	Times	Comic Sans MS (bold)	Comic Sans MS	Comic Sans MS	Times
Fantasy	Arial	Times	Arial (bold)	Ransom	Brush Script MS	Times
Monospace	Courier	Times New	Courier New	Courier New	Courier New	Monaco

Table 8.2 Best-Choice Fonts for MS Windows and MacOS

WINDOWS	CROSS-PLATFORM	MACOS
Arial	Arial/Helvetica	Chicago
Comic Sans	Times New Roman/Times	Courier
Courier New	Courier New/Courier	Geneva
Modern		Helvetica
MS Sans Serif		Monaco
Symbol		New York
Times New Roman	Palatino	
Wingdings	Symbol Times Zapf Dingbats	

the MacOS does not include a font named Arial—it has a similar font named Helvetica. Therein lies the problem.

Table 8.2 shows the fonts that come with a plain, clean installation on both the Windows and Mac operating systems. These are the only fonts you can reliably assume are on a user's computer. The middle column shows the matches across platforms, Windows on the left, MacOS on the right.

In short, to solve all of these issues, the best suggestion is to do something like the following:

```
body {font-family: arial, helvetica, sans-serif}
```

This code takes into consideration Windows, using the Arial font, MacOS, using the Helvetica font, and other OSes that may not have either, a final default to a sans serif font.

Font Appearance

Beyond specifying the actual font used, CSS allows you to modify the font in many ways, including its size, style, and weight. Table 8.3 shows the six available font properties and each of their available values.

Several of these have equivalents in HTML, but there are newer options that authors have been wanting for years. Here are some examples of those newer options.

Previously in HTML, authors were limited to a positive or negative size value, relative to the size of the current text. With CSS, not only can you set the size of text based on relative values (percentage, smaller, larger, etc.), but you can now set the exact size you wish to use in points, ems, inches, and centimeters. The following is an example of setting the body's text to 12 points:

```
body {font-size: 12pt}
```

Table 8.3   Font Appearance Properties and Available Values

font-size	(pt, em, cm)| n% | xx-small | x-small | small | medium | large | x-large | xx-large | smaller | larger
font-style	normal | italic | oblique
font-weight	bold | extra-bold | bolder | lighter | n (100-900)
font-variant	small-caps
text-transform	capitalize | uppercase | lowercase | none
text-decoration	underline | overline | line-through | blink | none

Next is an example of the font-variant property. This is an interesting property, not only for what it accomplishes, but also because there is only one valid value for this property, small-caps. Here's some example code:

```
p.caps {font-variant: small-caps}
```

Box and Text Properties

HTML authors have also dreamed of being able to control the white space in a document (the area not containing text or images, though not always literally the color white) without having to rely on tricks such as "blank" GIFs and creative use of borderless tables. With the box and text properties in CSS, you are given the power over that white space via margins, borders, indents, and alignment.

Margins

Most HTML authors quickly learned to use tables when they figured out that doing so was the only reliable way to make their pages appear as if they had margins. This workaround was, however, a misuse—though an acceptable one—of tables, which was easier for some than others. It also, in many cases, added much code to the document and therefore slowed down load time. It also significantly slowed down display time since the browser had to read the contents of the whole table before it could display any of the information in that table. This is why many pages load the beginning of their text (not in a table) quickly, then stall before displaying the rest of the document (within a table).

With margin control in CSS, you finally have true control over the margins; it's no longer necessary to use tables to simulate margins. Table 8.4 shows the available margin properties and their value formats.

The available margin properties in CSS are somewhat different from other types of properties, in that you can use any combination of the first four properties or the fifth one. For example, in the following example, we set the margins of our document to 1 inch on the top and bottom and 1.5 inches on the left and right, one side at a time:

Table 8.4 Margin Properties and Their Values

Margin-top	n(in, cm, px, pt)
Margin-right	n(in, cm, px, pt)
Margin-bottom	n(in, cm, px, pt)
Margin-left	n(in, cm, px, pt)
Margin	n(in, cm, px, pt) n(in, cm, px, pt) n(in, cm, px, pt) n(in, cm, px, pt)

```
body {margin-top: 1in;
      margin-left: 1.5in;
      margin-right: 1in;
      margin-bottom: 1.5in}
```

However, using the margin property shown here, we can create more efficient code:

```
body {margin: 1in 1.5in 1in 1.5in}
```

Both examples achieve the same result. The only difference is that the second example is more efficient. So why, if the second example is the better way, can we do it the first way? The answer to that question lies in the fact that you do not have to set all four sides, which is the only way you can set margins by using the margin property.

For example, if you only wanted to set a margin on the left side of the screen, the margin property would not work, because that only allows you to set all four sides. The following is an example of how to set a single margin:

```
body {margin-left: .5cm}
```

The next example sets two margins:

```
body {margin-left: .5cm;
      margin-top: .25cm;}
```

Alignment

In terms of alignment, CSS maintains HTML's capability to horizontally align text, but extends the capability to align text and images by adding the float property. Table 8.5 lists the alignment properties along with their values.

HTML's align attribute was generally confusing to many authors, because when used on text, it had one result: it shifted the content of the whole element in the desired

Table 8.5 Alignment Properties and Their Values

text-align	Left | right | center | justify
float	Left | right

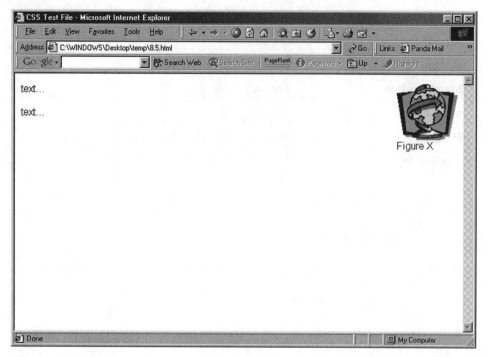

Figure 8.5 Using the float property to keep a caption with its corresponding image.

direction. But it had another result when used on images: it moved the image to the left or right and allowed adjacent elements to wrap around the image.

The float property is similar to the align attribute as applied to images, allowing other elements to wrap around the image, but it was renamed to clear the confusion, then extended to include any block-level elements, including text.

For example, if you had an image that you wanted to align to the right margin, with the adjacent text wrapped around it, you would have used the following code in HTML:

```
<img src="filename.gif" align="right">
<p>text...</p>
<p>more text...</p>
```

But what if you wanted that image to have a caption that stayed with the image? In HTML, that is impossible. This is the type of situation the float property was made for. The following example shows the code necessary to accomplish this task (see Figure 8.5 for the resulting browser display):

```
CSS
.figure     {float: right}

XHTML
<div class="figure">
```

```
<img src="filename.gif"><br>
Figure X
</div>
<p>text...</p>
<p>text...</p>
```

By creating a class that floats to the right and then applying it to a div (div was discussed in Chapter 2, "Getting Started with XHTML"), we have created an independent area in which anything in that area is aligned to the right margin around which the other elements will wrap. This allows us to place multiple images, or even blocks of text, within that area. By adding a border to that class (which we explain how to do later in this chapter), you can create a sidebar that stands out from the rest of your text.

Indentation

The indent property indents the first line of the element a positive (as in a paragraph in a novel) or negative amount (called a "hanging margin"). Table 8.6 contains this property's values.

NOTE Do not confuse this property with the first-line pseudo selector. The pseudo selector is used when you want to modify the first line of an element in any way *other* than indenting it.

Many new designers use the word indenting in a more generic way, meaning to shift all the text away from the left margin. To do so, they use the text-indent property. With this in mind, take a look at the following code:

```
p.example {text-indent: 1in}
```

Now compare it to:

```
p.example {margin-left: 1in}
```

The difference between these two examples is the amount of the paragraph that is indented. The results of these two code samples, as displayed in a browser, are shown in Figures 8.6 and 8.7, respectively.

The code shown in Figure 8.7 will create the desired effect *as long as the paragraph is less than one line long* and therefore does not work in our example since we have a multiline paragraph. However, if our paragraph was less than a line long, this would only be an illusion, just as using tables to create margins is. If the screen is resized so as to cause the single-line paragraph to wrap, the illusion will be broken.

Table 8.6 Indentation Property and Its Values

text-indent	n(in, cm, px, pt) | -n(in, cm, px, pt)

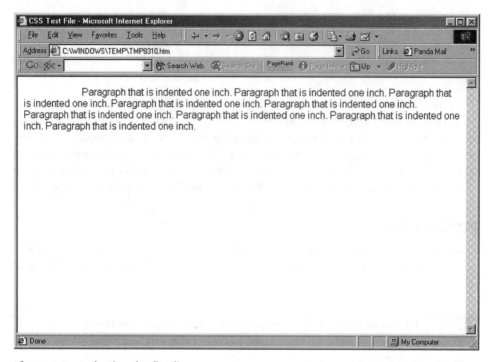

Figure 8.6 Indenting the first line.

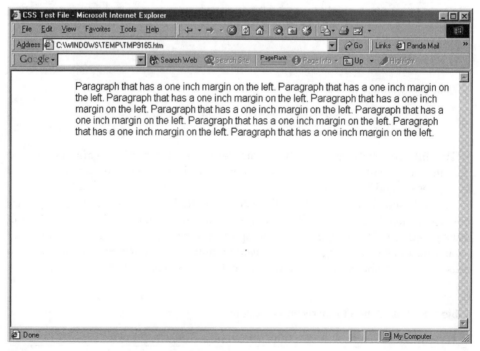

Figure 8.7 Indenting the entire paragraph.

Borders

The border properties available in CSS greatly improve the ability to put a border around an element or group of elements beyond what HTML offered (which was to create a single-row, single-cell table and place the content inside).

You may now assign a border around a section of a document and modify that border's color, style, and width. Table 8.7 describes the three border properties and their values.

Just as the margin property can be subdivided, all three border properties may also be subdivided, into top, right, bottom, and left subproperties. Therefore beyond the three properties shown in Table 8.7, you actually have the following properties also available: border-top-color, border-left-color, border-bottom-color, border-right-color, border-top-style, border-left-style, border-bottom-style, border-right-style, border-top-width, border-left-width, border-bottom-width, and border-right-width.

Earlier, we mentioned that you could use the float property in combination with the border property to create a sidebar. This is possible with the following code (see Figure 8.8 for the resulting browser display):

```
CSS
.figure        {float: right;
                border-style: solid;
                border-width: medium}


XHTML
<div class="figure" width="150">
<p>Text of your sidebar...</p>
</div>
<p>text...</p>
<p>text...</p>
```

Previously, we established the width of the float area based on the width of the image within. But because we did not use an image in this example, we had to establish the width of the sidebar using the width attribute on div.

Indicating Color in CSS

There are five ways to represent colors in CSS:

Table 8.7 Border Properties and Their Values

border-color	See the next section Indicating Color in CSS
border-style	Dotted | dashed | solid | double | groove | ridge | inset | outset
border-width	Thick | medium | thin

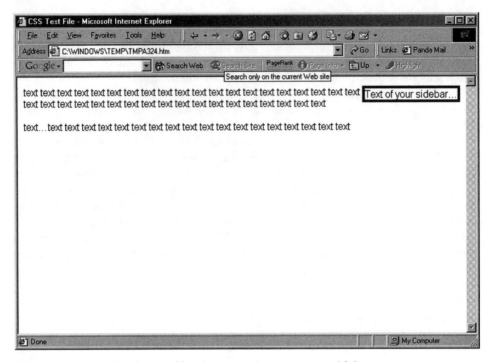

Figure 8.8 Using the float and border properties to create a sidebar.

NOTE All of these examples will produce the same result: set the text color to red.

Body {color: red}. Specifies one of the 16 basic colors. This is one of the two methods remaining from HTML.

body {color: #ff0000}. Uses the standard hexadecimal (hex, base 16) notation. A two-character representation each for the values of red (R), green (G), and blue (B). This is the other method left over from HTML.

body {color: #f00}. New in CSS; enables a three-character hex representation. Each of the three characters will expand by doubling to form a standard six-character hex value. This example will give the same result as the previous one.

body {color: rgb(255,0,0)}. Also new in CSS. Each value for R, G, and B can be represented by a whole number decimal value ranging from 0 to 255. This method removes the need for the author to convert the values to hexadecimal notation.

body {color: rgb(100%,0%,0%)}. The last new method in CSS. Known as an RBG float range. This method allows you to specify a percentage of the potential values for R, G, and B. Since possible RGB values range from 0 to 255, 0%=0, 50%=127.5, and 100%=255. Technically allows for more than the 16 million-plus possible colors.

Using URLs in CSS

In CSS, you can use a URL to point to a remote source for a particular declaration. The pointer to the remote source is used as the value. The format for this value is url("url"):

```
body {background: url("http://www.bcr.org/image.gif")}
```

In this example, the file image.gif will be used for the background of the document. A relative URL can also be used:

```
body {background: url("image.gif")}
```

In this instance, image.gif will be looked for in a location relative to the style sheet specified in the link statement, not the location of the XHTML file. So, if you write your document as:

```
CSS File
body {background: url("image.gif")}

XHTML File
<link rel="stylesheet" href="http://www.site.org/junk/masterstyle.css">
```

the location of the background image will be read as if it were written as:

```
body {background: url("http://www.site.org/junk/bcrback.gif")}
```

Visual Formatting Properties

With the creation of CSS level 2 (CSS2), the final shot was fired in the war against using tables for layout. The "bullet" is the ability to position elements in your document, whether at a specific location or relative to another element.

NOTE Unfortunately, the bullet has yet to reach its target, and will not do so until full implementation of CSS has been achieved by browsers.

Positioning

Every HTML author, at one point in his or her Web page design lifetime, has wished for the ability to exactly position an element, usually an image, on a page. Many varied methods have been attempted over the years to simulate this, including creating transparent images to generate artificial white space around an image, as well as elaborate table layouts, usually involving embedding tables within tables, a coding nightmare.

With the development of CSS2, some of the first properties suggested were the positioning properties. Now, with position, top, left, right and bottom, you can position elements on a document exactly where you want them.

When using positioning properties, you treat all elements as boxes. The boxes are then positioned as requested.

Positioning Properties and Their Values

Table 8.8 gives an overview of the five positioning properties and their available values. We will then discuss them each in detail.

position

The position property sets the type of positioning for the element. Following are its values:

Static. The box positioning is laid out as part of the normal flow of the document.

Relative. The box positioning is laid out as part of the normal flow, then is offset relative to its normal position.

Absolute. The box positioning is set by the left, right, top, and/or bottom properties and is not part of the normal document flow.

Fixed. The box positioning is figured in the same method as absolute but with regard to another element.

Inherit. The box positioning will be the same as the parent element.

top

The top property is used in conjunction with the absolute value of position, and places the box based upon the top of the document. Following are the top values:

n. Sets a length value in pixels.

n%. Sets a length in a percentage of the available space.

Auto. The default value for the box as established by the box content.

Inherit. Takes on the same property as the parent element.

bottom

The bottom property is used in conjunction with the absolute value of position, and places the box based upon the bottom of the document. Following are the bottom values:

Table 8.8   Positioning Properties and Their Values

Position	static, relative, absolute, fixed, inherit
top	n, n%, auto, inherit
right	n, n%, auto, inherit
bottom	n, n%, auto, inherit
top	n, n%, auto, inherit

n. Sets a length value in pixels.

n%. Sets a length in a percentage of the available space.

Auto. The default value for the box as established by the box content.

Inherit. Takes on the same property as the parent element.

right

The right property is used in conjunction with the absolute value of position, and places the box based upon the right side of the document. Following are the right values:

n. Sets a length value in pixels.

n%. Sets a length in a percentage of the available space.

Auto. The default value for the box as established by the box content.

Inherit. Takes on the same property as the parent element.

left

The left property is used in conjunction with the absolute value of position, and places the box based upon the top of the document. Following are the left values:

n. Sets a length value in pixels.

n%. Sets a length in a percentage of the available space.

Auto. The default value for the box as established by the box content.

Inherit. Takes on the same property as the parent element.

Examples

As just described, the position property has five possible values. The absolute value is the easiest to understand, the most used, and the most supported so we will focus our examples on absolute positioning.

The following is our first example of positioning:

```
<p style="position: absoulte; left: 40">This paragraph will be posi-
tioned 40 pixels from the left edge of the document.</p>
```

Here we have specified that the box, in this case a paragraph, be placed 40 pixels off the left edge. Since we have not specified a top value, the box will be placed vertically wherever it lands in the normal layout of the document.

The best way to visualize absolute positioning is to view the document with x,y coordinates, with the upper left corner of the document being x=0 and y=0 or 0,0. The more you move down, the larger x becomes. The more you move right the larger y becomes.

If we next decide to specify that the upper left corner of an image will appear at 60 pixels down from the top edge of the document and 40 pixels from the left edge of the document, coordinate 40,60, we would use the following code:

```
<img class="test" src="logo.gif" style=" position: absoulte; left: 40;
top: 60" />
```

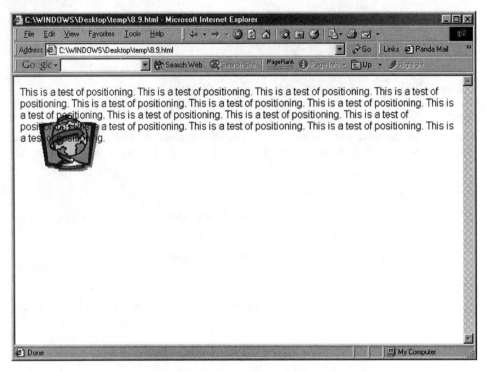

Figure 8.9   Positioning text to appear on top of an image.

As you can see, when we set the position style to absolute, the normal flow of elements in the document does not apply; any text in the document will continue to flow without regard to the image.

Layering

In addition to the control of the two dimensions that CSS2 offers us, we are also given control over the third dimension: depth. We can now determine how elements appear in front of or behind other elements. This is known as the z-index property. (This means we can plot a point on all three plains, x, y, and z.)

The z-index property is always used in conjunction with the position property, and has three available values: n (a positive or negative number), auto (default), and inherit (has the same value as its parent element).

In dealing with the numeric values, the lower the number, the more to the back the item will appear; the higher the number, the more to the front the item will appear.

Positioning Text on Top of an Image

In the next example, we have adjusted our code to force the text to appear on top of (more to the front than) the image (see Figure 8.9 for the resulting browser display):

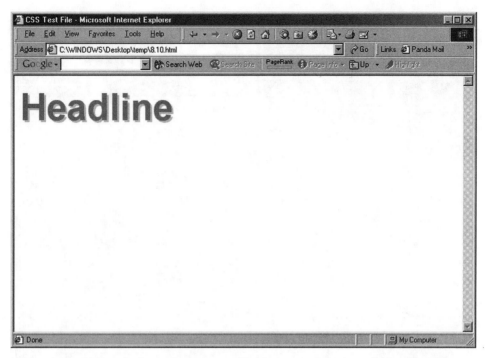

Figure 8.10 Using z-index and relative positioning to create a drop shadow text effect.

```
<p style="position: absoulte; z-Index: 2">This is a test of positioning.
This is a test of positioning. This is a test of positioning. This is a
test of positioning. This is a test of positioning. This is a test of
positioning. This is a test of positioning. This is a test of position-
ing. This is a test of positioning. This is a test of positioning. This
is a test of positioning. This is a test of positioning. This is a test
of positioning. This is a test of positioning. This is a test of posi-
tioning.</p>
<img class="test" src="logo.gif" style="position: absoulte; left: 40;
top: 60; z-index: 1" />
```

Creating a Drop Shadow Effect

By using a combination of z-index and relative positioning, you can create some interesting text effects without having to resort to graphics. Take a look at the following example. This code creates a level-one header with a drop shadow. The second header is placed 3 pixels to the left, 3 pixels down, and behind the first one (see Figure 8.10 for the resulting browser display):

```
<h1 style="position: absolute; color:red; font-size: 45pt; z-index:
2">Headline</h1>
<h1 style="position: relative; top: 3px; left: 3px; color:cccccc; font-
size: 45pt; z-index: 1">Headline</h1>
```

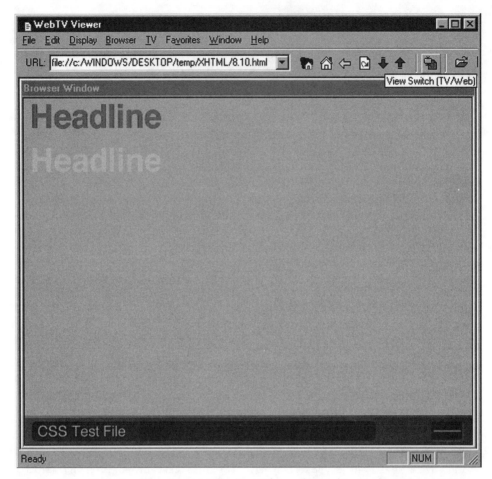

Figure 8.11   Nonsupporting browser display of the code used to produce Figure 8.10.

A word of caution is in order for using such an effect: You are putting two copies of the same text on the screen. In a browser that supports CSS2 positioning, one will be mostly hidden under the other. Unfortunately, in a browser that does not support CSS2 positioning, you will get what is shown in Figure 8.11. Therefore, only use this effect if you are sure that visitors are using browsers that support this code.

Media Types

Another CSS2 development is media types. Media types allow you to specify different style sheets based upon the medium on which the document is being displayed.

For example, you may create a style sheet for your document that is colorful when displayed on a user's monitor, but realize that it prints only in black and white. In another situation, you may be using a rather large font size in your document, which is fine for a full-size computer monitor, but it displays only one line at a time on a hand-held computer.

The use of CSS media types solves the problems inherent in such situations. CSS includes eight media types: Aural, Braille, Emboss, Handheld, Print, Projection, Screen, TTY, and TV. For the purposes of this discussion, we will focus our examples on the Print and Screen media types.

Media types are specified by an "at rule," which specifies that you are defining a set of commands that will be applied when called for. In the case of media types, the "at rule" is as shown here:

```
@MEDIA MEDIATYPE {selector {declaration}}
```

The browser will automatically call the MEDIATYPE specified when it loads the document.

In the following code, when the document is displayed on a screen, the user will be presented with white text on a black background. But that color arrangement does not always print well, so we can specify that the document have black text on a white background when it is printed, by using the following code:

```
@MEDIA SCREEN       {body   {color: white;
  background: black}}
@MEDIA PRINT {body   {color: black;
  background: white}}
```

You can equate an "at rule" to an if-then statement in programming. In the previous example, "if the media type is screen, then follow the white on black style"; "if the media type is print, then follow the black on white style."

NOTE Unfortunately, at this time, the major browsers do not support media types.

CSS Validation

Unlike XHTML code, which depends on validation to create well-formed code, CSS is a little more flexible. As with HTML, if the browser doesn't understand what it's being told, it will just ignore that code.

That said, be aware that the more complex your CSS files become, the more difficult they will be to troubleshoot. To assist in that troubleshooting effort, there are CSS validators available online. The main one, supplied by the W3C, is located at http://jigsaw.w3.org/css-validator/.

The validator is available for use through four methods:

Download the validator. You can download an executable version of the CSS validator for offline use. This version will run faster than the online methods.

Enter a URI (URL). If you have created a CSS file, and have already published it to a Web server, this version will allow you to enter the URL of the file to be tested.

Enter code in a text area. This method will present you with a box in which you can enter, through typing or copy-paste, your CSS code. This works well for short, nonpublished CSS code.

Upload your file. Allows you to upload your CSS file to the server for validating. This works better than entering code in a text area for longer, nonpublished CSS files.

The Future of CSS

At the time of the writing of this book (early 2001) the key focus for the future of CSS is modularization. According to the W3C:

As the popularity of CSS grows, so does interest in making additions to the specification. Rather than attempting to shove dozens of updates into a single monolithic specification, it will be much easier and more efficient to be able to update individual pieces of the specification. Modules will enable CSS to be updated in a more timely and precise fashion, thus allowing for a more flexible and timely evolution of the specification as a whole.

For resource constrained devices, it may be impractical to support all of CSS. For example, an aural browser may be concerned only with aural styles, whereas a visual browser may care nothing for aural styles. In such cases, a user agent may implement a subset of CSS. Subsets of CSS are limited to combining selected CSS modules, and once a module has been chosen, all of its features must be supported.

You can keep up with the development of CSS3 through the W3C Web site at www.w3.org/Style/CSS/current-work.

Summary

This chapter served as an overview of cascading style sheets (CSS) as they apply to formatting XHTML documents. As you have seen, most of the formatting-related elements have been removed from the XHTML specification. With those elements gone, you need to learn CSS to format your documents. This chapter has given you the information required to get started. Once you have the basics of CSS down, we recommend that you purchase a CSS reference book to learn more.

JavaScript

JavaScript, like cascading style sheets, is external to XHTML itself. And just as important as the applicability of CSS within the XHTML world is the inclusion of a scripting language within your documents—specifically, JavaScript can often be used for form data validation and to add interactivity. Therefore, the purpose of this chapter is to introduce you to the preferred scripting language for XHTML documents.

We will cover the basic syntax, semantics, and the common objects of JavaScript, which you will need to know for scripting your documents. We will focus on the language itself in this chapter, not how it applies to XHTML, for that is the topic of Chapter 10.

NOTE Comprehensive coverage of the JavaScript programming language is beyond the scope of this book. The objective in this chapter is to introduce you to the basics of this language, to serve as the foundation for the next chapter, where we will use some of what we learn here.

Learning the Fundamentals

JavaScript is an object-based language designed to allow developers and programmers to easily create interactive documents. It offers basic characteristics of an object-oriented language, like Java and C++, without many of the complicated features.

JavaScript also has a relatively small vocabulary that is easy to understand, but does not limit what can be accomplished with a browser.

When first released by Netscape in its Navigator 2 browser suite, JavaScript was a Netscape-only technology, but Microsoft soon followed with an implementation called JScript. Since that time, the language has been submitted to the ECMA (European Computer Manufacturers Association), a standardization body, which standardized the language based primarily on implementations from Netscape and Microsoft. Dubbed the ECMA-262 standard, in practice it is referred to as ECMAScript.

NOTE Want more information on ECMAScript? Check out the ECMA Web site at www.ecma.ch.

Understanding How It Works

Each time a document is requested and loaded by a user agent that supports JavaScript, the code is interpreted and executed within the application. Depending on the actions of the user and other events that can occur within the document, portions of the embedded script or scripts are executed. Suppose, for instance, you created a document to collect contact information from users visiting your site. This could be accomplished with a form that included name, address, and telephone number fields.

Traditionally, once users filled out the form and pressed the Submit button, the form passed to a program on the server for processing. If a user left out required information, the program would respond with a new document asking for the missing data. Again the user had to submit the form, whereby the server program again had to validate it. In this model is a lot of room for error—and wasted time going back and forth to the server. Here is where JavaScript can be handy.

Using JavaScript, you can validate the data on the client-side before the user submits it. You can check to make sure all fields have information entered into them, look for unsupported characters, or confirm that the phone number is in the proper format. And you can perform all of this, along with alerting the user to his or her mistakes, before the form is submitted. This saves both time and server processing power, which benefits you and the user.

NOTE This chapter focuses on how you can use JavaScript to perform tasks after an event has been invoked. Events themselves are covered in more detail in Chapter 12.

Embedding Scripts

This section introduces you to the syntax of the language and explains how scripts can be embedded into your XHTML documents. There are two ways to include JavaScript within your XHTML documents: embed them in the document within an instance of the <script> element, or include them as the value of an *intrinsic event* attribute and sometimes as the value of the href attribute of a support element. (Don't worry about the meaning of *intrinsic event* at this time—we will discuss it later.) Additionally, scripts can be stored in an external file and included into the current document through the use of the src attribute of the <script> element.

To give you an idea of these three types of methods of embedding scripts work, take a look at this simple example (Figure 9.1 shows how this will look after you click the <a> link):

```
<!DOCTYPE html PUBLIC "-//W3C//DTD XHTML 1.0 Transitional//EN"
    "http://www.w3.org/TR/xhtml1/DTD/xhtml1-transitional.dtd">
<html xmlns="http://www.w3.org/1999/xhtml" lang="en" xml:lang="en">
<head>
 <title>XHTML Essentials</title>
 <script type="text/javascript" src="/scripts/mycode.js"></script>
</head>
<body>
<p>
 <script type="text/javascript">
  document.write("Hello World!");
 </script>
 <a href="javascript:alert('You clicked!')">Embedded in href</a>
</p>
<form action="null">
 <input type="button" value="Click Me"
     onclick="alert('You pressed the button!')" />
</form>
</body>
</html>
```

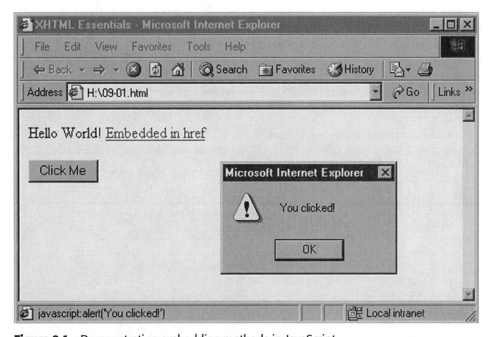

Figure 9.1 Demonstrating embedding methods in JavaScript.

Table 9.1 Attributes of the <script> Element

ATTRIBUTE	DESCRIPTION
defer	A Boolean attribute that provides a hint to the user agent regarding whether the code in the element is used to modify any of the page content.
language	A deprecated attribute, in favor of type, that was originally used to specify the language used in the element.
src	Specifies the URI of an external script library.
type	Specifies the content-type, and therefore language of the element's content. This should be set to "text/javascript" for the JavaScript language.

First in this example, we have included an instance of the <script> element in the <head> portion of the document. Here we have specified an external-source JavaScript library to be loaded for the document. This library can contain variables, functions, or other valid JavaScript code as if it were actually included in the document.

In the <body> of the document, we have included another instance of the <script> element. This time we have included our code, to write out "Hello World!" inline. Following this instance, we have a form with a single button, which includes the onclick event handler that will execute the JavaScript alert( ) method when clicked. Table 9.1 defines the attributes of this element.

Another element is worth mentioning here: <noscript>. This element should be used to specify text to be rendered by nonsupporting user agents. To our previous example we can add <noscript> entries like the following:

```
<!DOCTYPE html PUBLIC "-//W3C//DTD XHTML 1.0 Transitional//EN"
    "http://www.w3.org/TR/xhtml1/DTD/xhtml1-transitional.dtd">
<html xmlns="http://www.w3.org/1999/xhtml" lang="en" xml:lang="en">
<head>
 <title>XHTML Essentials</title>
 <script type="text/javascript" src="/scripts/mycode.js"></script>
</head>
<body>
<p>
 <script type="text/javascript">
  document.write("Hello World!");
 </script>
 <noscript>
  Your browser does not support JavaScript, so no text will be written.
 </noscript>
 <a href="javascript:alert('You clicked!')">Embedded in href</a>
</p>
<form action="null">
 <input type="button" value="Click Me"
     onclick="alert('You pressed the button!')" />
```

```
<noscript>
  Your browser does not support JavaScript, so this button
  will not work.
</noscript>
</form>

</body>
</html>
```

Implementing Syntax

Like any programming language, JavaScript has a certain way of handling different items and elements. There are also specific keywords and reserved words to avoid. JavaScript, as we mentioned earlier, is an object-based language, and like Java any sub-objects, properties, methods, or constants of the parent objects are accessed through a "dot" notation. This can take on the form of any of the following:

```
parentobject.childobject.property
parentobject.childobject.method
parentobject.childobject.constant
parentobject.property
parentobject.method
parentobject.constant
```

Remember that in the first example we called the write( ) method of the document object to write some text to the page; this was accomplished using the document.write( ) syntax. There are some methods, such as alert( ), which is a method of the window object, that do not need the reference to the parent object—it is implied. So a shorthand way of writing window.alert( ) is to just use alert( ).

As for the reserved words, you'll find a current listing in Table 9.2. As you define variables, which we will cover later, you will need to avoid naming any of them after these.

In addition to these reserved words, there are a few rules to follow when defining your own names (variables, functions, methods, properties, etc.). They are:

Table 9.2   JavaScript Reserved Words

abstract	final	public
boolean	finally	return
break	float	short
byte	for	static
case	function	super
catch	goto	switch
char	if	synchronized
class	implements	this

continues

(Continued)

const	import	throw
continue	instanceof	throws
debugger	in	transient
default	int	true
delete	interface	try
do	long	typeof
double	native	var
else	new	void
enum	null	volatile
export	private	while
extends	package	with
false	protected	

- Begin all names with either a letter or an underscore (_).
- Use letters, digits, or underscores for all subsequent characters.
- Letters include all uppercase and all lowercase characters.
- The sequence of characters should not include any spaces.
- Digits include the characters 0 through 9.

Versions

As Netscape, Microsoft, and other leading companies have been improving the core ECMAScript standard and their individual implementations, JavaScript has seen many new versions of the language, which often coincide with new versions of their browsers. Table 9.3 provides a list JavaScript, JScript, and ECMAScript versions, along with the browser support. There may be some slight discrepancies, but these are the baseline associations.

Special Characters

Like any language, JavaScript has the capability to represent special characters, such as newlines or tabs. Table 9.4 contains a list of these special characters and what they represent.

Let's look at an example to better understand how this works. If you want to emulate a newline character with the text of an alert box, you would use the \n representation. This is helpful if the amount of text you need to include in the alert box is too long, or if you simply need parts of the text to appear on a different line, which is how we use \n in the following example (see Figure 9.2 shows how this looks when clicked):

Table 9.3 JavaScript's Relationship to JScript

JAVA SCRIPT	JSCRIPT	ECMA SCRIPT	SUPPORTING NETSCAPE BROWSER	SUPPORTING MICROSOFT BROWSER
1.0	n/a	n/a	Navigator 2	n/a
1.1	1.0 - 2.0	n/a	Navigator 3	Internet Explorer 3.0
1.2	3.0 - 4.0	1st Edition	Netscape Communicator 4 - 4.05	Internet Explorer 4.0
1.3	5.0 - 5.1	2nd Edition	Netscape Communicator 4.06 - 4.7	Internet Explorer 5.0
1.5	5.5	3rd Edition	Netscape 6	Internet Explorer 5.5
n/a	5.6	3rd Edition	n/a	Internet Explorer 6

```
<!DOCTYPE html PUBLIC "-//W3C//DTD XHTML 1.0 Transitional//EN"
    "http://www.w3.org/TR/xhtml1/DTD/xhtml1-transitional.dtd">
<html xmlns="http://www.w3.org/1999/xhtml" lang="en" xml:lang="en">
<head>
 <title>XHTML Essentials</title>
 <script type="text/javascript">
  function myAlert(){
   alert("Your data is invalid. Please check the following\n" +
      " * Name\n * Address \n * Phone Number");
  }
 </script>
</head>
<body>
<form action="null">
 <input type="button" value="Click Me"
     onclick="myAlert()" />
</form>
</body>
</html>
```

Figure 9.2 Using the \n special character.

Table 9.4   JavaScript Representations of Special Characters

REPRESENTATION	DESCRIPTION
\b	Backspace
\f	Form feed
\n	Newline
\r	Carriage return
\t	Tab
\\	Backslash
\'	Single quote
\"	Double quote

NOTE If we had enclosed the text in our alert( ) method with single quotes ('), rather than double quotes ("), the \n representation would have been interpreted literally, rather than as a special character. Try both and you will see what we mean.

Variables

Variables, which are similar to properties, are used to store values in your code. Let's say, for instance, that you needed to store a name or maybe a dollar amount in your script. To do this, you would declare a variable and assign that variable a value. This would look like:

```
var myString = "Allen Wyke"
var myDollar = 5.00
```

The var keyword declares the variables myString and myDollar in our samples, while the = sign assigns the values to these variables. Note that you do not have to assign a value to a variable when it is declared. When taking this approach, you can even declare more than one variable on the same line of code; doing so will save time and space. For instance, variables a, b, and c are all declared in the following sample:

```
var a, b, c
```

There are several points about variables that we need to discuss, so let's get to it.

Naming

A variable name is made up of one or more letters, digits, or underscores. As we mentioned before, the name cannot begin with a digit, but it can include all uppercase and lowercase characters. Although the length of a variable is limited only by a device's memory, you should keep lengths to a practical size. And keep in mind that JavaScript is case-sensitive and therefore considers the following two as different:

```
var myVar
var MyVar
```

NOTE It is common practice to use all lowercase letters when naming single-word variables in JavaScript, while using two or more words often results in the first word being all lowercase and capitalization of the first letter of all words thereafter.

Types

When storing a value in our variables, JavaScript automatically categorizes it as one of the core data types. Table 9.5 contains a list of the primary types and a description of each.

Typically, programming languages require that you define the type of data when the variable is declared. Although it is not required within JavaScript because it is a loosely typed language, it is good programming practice and is encouraged. Here are some samples of how this might be done:

```
var myString = new String();
myString = "Hello World";
var myBool = new Boolean();
myBool = false;
var myNum = new Number();
myNum = 8.968;
```

The type of data you have is important, which is why we recommend that you declare it. Let's say, for instance, you have the following line of code. Does it mean to add the two numbers together, to concatenate them? Basically, is the + symbol acting as the addition (mathematical) operator or the concatenation (string) operator? And here is a more interesting question: What happens if you enclose the value within double quotes or declare one as a string?

```
var first = 5;
var second = 5;
var results = first + second;
```

Table 9.5   JavaScript Data Types

TYPE	DESCRIPTION
Number	Holds either an integer or a real number.
Boolean	Holds either true or false.
String	Holds any string literal that is assigned to it, including an empty string.

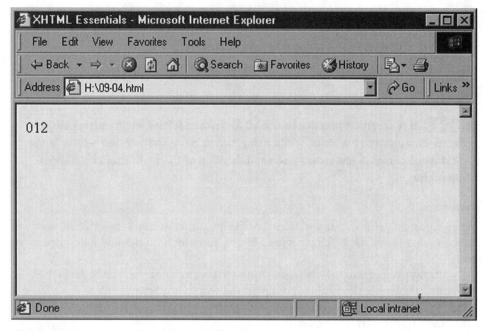

Figure 9.3 Demonstrating global variables.

> **NOTE** Want to know more about data types and type conversion? Check out http://developer.netscape.com and http://msdn.microsoft.com/scripting.

Scope

The scope of a variable is another important area to understand. It defines the boundaries in which a variable can be accessed. This becomes an obvious issue if you have two variables of the same name, which can often occur if you are using variables to hold the current count of an item.

In JavaScript, if you declare two variables within the same <script> element, and they are *not* part of any function or looping statement, these variables are considered to be global, which means any script in the current document can access them. But, if the variables are declared within functions or looping statement, they are considered local and are not always accessible by every script.

Here is an example to help explain this characteristic. In this example we declare a global variable called counter, in the <head> of the document. We then define a function that defines another counter and returns its value. In the <body> of the document we write out the value of the counter, which will be our first instance, and then we declare another counter. Since this counter and our original counter are within the same scope, it overwrites the first one with a new value. After writing out counter again, 1 this time, we call our function and write out its results, which will be 2, as shown in the following code example (see Figure 9.3 for the resulting browser display):

```
<!DOCTYPE html PUBLIC "-//W3C//DTD XHTML 1.0 Transitional//EN"
    "http://www.w3.org/TR/xhtml1/DTD/xhtml1-transitional.dtd">
```

```
<html xmlns="http://www.w3.org/1999/xhtml" lang="en" xml:lang="en">
<head>
 <title>XHTML Essentials</title>
 <script type="text/javascript">

  // declare a global counter
  var counter = 0

  // create a function that declares counter, and return its value
  function myCount(){
   var counter = 2;
   return counter;
  }
 </script>
</head>
<body>
<script type="text/javascript">

 // writes out our 0 counter
 document.write(counter);

 // declare another counter, which actually re-declares our
 // original one. Then write out its value
 var counter = 1;
 document.write(counter);

 // call out function and write out its value
 var result = myCount();
 document.write(result);

</script>
</body>
</html>
```

Comments

Another important aspect to know and understand within JavaScript, and any programming language for that matter, is comments. So far we have used XHTML comments in our documents, but we have not explained comments with scripts.

There are two ways to specify comments with JavaScript. The first is a single-line comment, which precedes your text with the // characters, as shown here:

```
// Here is a single-line comment
```

The second method is a multiline comment. This is accomplished in much the same fashion as XHTML comments, through the user of a beginning /* set and a concluding */ set. When this method is used, all text and whitespace in between these are ignored by the language. Here's the code:

```
/* Use this method to include
multiple lines of comments */
```

Functions

In a couple of our examples we have defined functions. Until now, we have not really talked about functions, nor have we talked about how they operate. In its simplest form, a function is nothing more than a block of code you can call by name at any time. This allows for easy code reuse, as well as the ability to control when a block of code is executed. Let's say, for instance, that you did not want to perform a task until the user clicked a form button. You would define all relevant code within a function and then invoke it when the user clicked.

Functions are declared using the *function* keyword, and are often located either in the <head> of your document or in external source libraries (loaded through the src attribute of the <script> element). This allows them to be preloaded and ready to be executed as your <body> scripts begin processing. The syntax for functions is:

```
function functionName(param1, param2, ..., paramN){
  code;
}
```

The name you wish to give your function is located at *functionName*. If you want to pass the function parameters, although not required, they are passed as *param1*, *param2*, and so on. Once called, the function will process any *code* within its beginning and ending curly brackets ({})

Let's say, for instance, you wanted to create a function that would add two values. This could be done with the following:

```
<!DOCTYPE html PUBLIC "-//W3C//DTD XHTML 1.0 Transitional//EN"
    "http://www.w3.org/TR/xhtml1/DTD/xhtml1-transitional.dtd">
<html xmlns="http://www.w3.org/1999/xhtml" lang="en" xml:lang="en">
<head>
 <title>XHTML Essentials</title>
 <script type="text/javascript">

  function myAdd(first, second){
   return first + second;
  }
 </script>
</head>
<body>
<script type="text/javascript">

 var num1 = new Number();
 num1 = 5;

 var num2 = new Number();
 num2 = 7;

 document.write(myAdd(num1, num2));

</script>
</body>
</html>
```

NOTE Want to try something fun? Define the variables as String types rather than Number, and enclose the 5 and 7 in quotes and see what happens.

Invoking Operators

At this point we have given you the basics on the JavaScript language. But we have not given you any information that allows you to really use the language and perform operations. This is where operators come into play. Operators are the symbols and identifiers that represent the way data is changed or the way a combination of expressions is evaluated. The JavaScript language supports several types of operators, including binary, unary, and arithmetic; we will narrow our focus in this chapter to cover:

- Arithmetic
- Assignment
- Comparison
- Boolean

Doing Arithmetic

The first type of operator we are going to look at is the arithmetic set of operators. These you should be intimately familiar with from grade school.

The most basic operator of the group is the plus sign (+), which is used to add two values. Of course there is the minus sign (-), which subtracts one value from another, and the asterisk (*), which multiplies two values. Finally, there is the forward slash (/), which is used to divide one value by another, and the percent sign (%), which refers to the modulus operation of returning the remainder between two values.

Like other computer languages, when JavaScript encounters one of these operators, it reads them right to left. For example, the following will store the value of 56 in the variable a:

```
var a = 52 + 4
```

Once the value is stored in a variable, we can use it as part of the mathmatical operations that could further change its value. Let's say, for instance, we wanted to add 5 more to our variable a. We could accomplish this with:

```
a = a + 5
```

This approach works not only for addition, but subtraction, multiplication, division, and modulus as well. There are also some incremental and decremental operations you have at your side. These you invoke by placing a double minus sign (--) or a double plus sign (++) before or after a value or variable. If placed before, the value will be incremented or decremented before the variable or value is read. If placed after, the value will change after the value is read. Here is an example to help you understand how this works.

```
<!DOCTYPE html PUBLIC "-//W3C//DTD XHTML 1.0 Transitional//EN"
      "http://www.w3.org/TR/xhtml1/DTD/xhtml1-transitional.dtd">
<html xmlns="http://www.w3.org/1999/xhtml" lang="en" xml:lang="en">
<head>
 <title>XHTML Essentials</title>
</head>
<body>
<script type="text/javascript">

var num = new Number();
num = 5;

// writes 5, changes value to 4
document.write(num--);

// changes value to 3, and writes it
document.write(--num);

// writes three again, changes to 4 after
document.write(num++);

// changes value to 5 and writes it
document.write(++num);

// writes final value, which is 5
document.write(num);

// final text written is: 53355

</script>
</body>
</html>
```

In this example, we performed a postdecrement of our variable (initialized to 5), then a predecrement, writing the value of both to the page. Next, we performed a postincrement followed by a preincrement, again writing both to the page. Finally, we wrote out the final value of our variable. When executed in a browser, as shown in Figure 9.4, the result is 53355. This process is commonly used for counters that must enumerate up or down on each iteration, so keep that in mind when we talk about control structures later in the chapter.

The modulus operator will find the modulus, or remainder, of two values after dividing the first by the second. Let's look at an example where we write out the remainder of dividing 13 by 5, which is 3.

```
<!DOCTYPE html PUBLIC "-//W3C//DTD XHTML 1.0 Transitional//EN"
      "http://www.w3.org/TR/xhtml1/DTD/xhtml1-transitional.dtd">
<html xmlns="http://www.w3.org/1999/xhtml" lang="en" xml:lang="en">
<head>
 <title>XHTML Essentials</title>
</head>
<body>
```

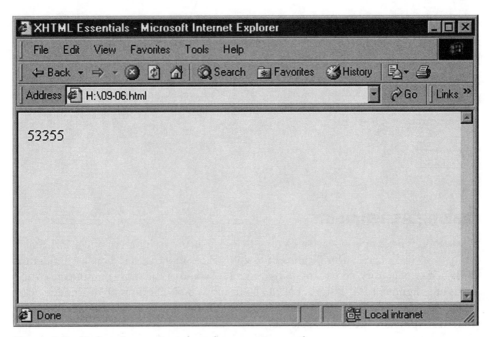

Figure 9.4 Performing post- and predecrement operations.

```
<script type="text/javascript">

var num1 = new Number();
num1 = 5;

var num2 = new Number();
num2 = 13;

// writes 3 (remainder of dividing 13 by 5)
document.write(num2 % num1);

</script>
</body>
</html>
```

The final type of arithmetic operator we want to mention here is the unary negation operator (-) It is used to change a numerical value from positive to negative, or vice versa. For example, if you have a positive 5 value, you can place the unary negation operator in front of it and turn it into –5. Here is a quick example that does just that:

```
<!DOCTYPE html PUBLIC "-//W3C//DTD XHTML 1.0 Transitional//EN"
     "http://www.w3.org/TR/xhtml1/DTD/xhtml1-transitional.dtd">
<html xmlns="http://www.w3.org/1999/xhtml" lang="en" xml:lang="en">
<head>
 <title>XHTML Essentials</title>
</head>
```

```
<body>
<script type="text/javascript">

 var num = new Number();
 num = 5;

 // writes -5
 document.write(-num);

</script>
</body>
</html>
```

Making Assignments

The second type of operator we are going to look at is the assignment operation, which we have already used several times to assign values to variables. This assignment is fairly self-explanatory, so we are going to look at some of the more complex uses and types of assignment. An assignment can be used in combination with arithmetic operators to create arithmetic assignment instances. A list of these combinations, along with their descriptions, is given in Table 9.6.

Here is an example that uses one of these combination operators. Here we apply the += operator to a variable that has a value of 5, adding 6 to it. When the result is written to the page, the value is 11, as shown in Figure 9.5:

```
<!DOCTYPE html PUBLIC "-//W3C//DTD XHTML 1.0 Transitional//EN"
      "http://www.w3.org/TR/xhtml1/DTD/xhtml1-transitional.dtd">
<html xmlns="http://www.w3.org/1999/xhtml" lang="en" xml:lang="en">
<head>
 <title>XHTML Essentials</title>
</head>
<body>
<script type="text/javascript">

 var num = new Number();
```

Table 9.6 Combination of Assignment and Arithmetic Operators

OPERATOR	EXAMPLE	MEANING
+=	x += y	x = x + y
-=	x -= y	x = x - y
*=	x *= y	x = x * y
/=	x /= y	x = x / y
%=	x %= y	x = x % y

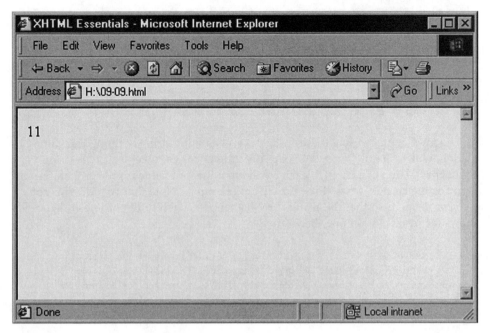

Figure 9.5 Using the += combination operator.

```
num = 5;

num += 6;

// writes 11 (5 + 6)
document.write(num);

</script>
</body>
</html>
```

NOTE This method also uses *bitwise* operators, which we do not cover here. For more information, go to http://developer.netscape.com/docs/ manuals/js/core/jsguide15/expr.html#1008505.

Making Comparisons

Comparisons are something we are exposed to everyday, so this concept should be familiar to you. Simply, comparison operators are used for comparing expressions. The result is either a Boolean true or false. Entering in a password, for instance, invokes this process whereby an application will compare what you entered with its stored password. If the comparison evaluates to true, as in a match, you are allowed to log in. If they do not match, a false is returned, and at that time the application can decide how to handle the incident.

You have several comparison operators at your disposal within the JavaScript language, all of which are covered in Table 9.7. The basic syntax is, where [comparison operator] is replaced with one of the valid operators listed in the table, as shown here:

```
expression1 [comparison operator] expression2
```

A good example of using these operators is evaluating string or numerical values. In the following example, we will create two numerical variables and two string variables. For the numerical variables, we will see if the first value is greater than the second. For the strings, we will see if they are the same. (Note that we added a <br /> element instance so that the results are displayed on two different lines.) Figure 9.6 shows the results of running this example:

```
<!DOCTYPE html PUBLIC "-//W3C//DTD XHTML 1.0 Transitional//EN"
     "http://www.w3.org/TR/xhtml1/DTD/xhtml1-transitional.dtd">
<html xmlns="http://www.w3.org/1999/xhtml" lang="en" xml:lang="en">
<head>
 <title>XHTML Essentials</title>
</head>
<body>
<script type="text/javascript">

 var num1 = new Number();
 num = 5;
```

Table 9.7 Comparison Operators

OPERATOR	DESCRIPTION
==	The equal operator. Returns true if both of its expressions are equal.
!=	The not-equal operator. Returns true if its expressions are not equal.
>	The greater-than operator. Returns true if its left expression is greater in value than its right expression.
>=	The greater-than-or-equal-to operator. Returns true if its left expression is greater than or equal to its right expression.
<	The less-than operator. Returns true if its left expression is less than the value of its right expression.
<=	The less-than-or-equal-to operator. Returns true if its left expression is less than or equal to its right expression.

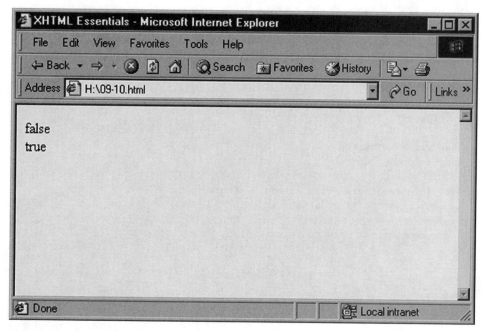

Figure 9.6   Comparing two expressions.

```
var num2 = new Number();
num2 = 7;

document.write((num1 > num2) + '<br />');

var str1 = new String();
str1 = "Hello";

var str2 = new String();
str2 = "Hello";

document.write(str1 == str2);

</script>
</body>
</html>
```

Using Boolean Operators

Boolean operators, which can also be referred to as logical operators, are used in conjunction with expressions to return logical values. The best way to understand this concept is to see these used with comparison operators. For instance, if you wanted to make sure that two variables had two specific values before performing a block of code, you could use the following:

```
<!DOCTYPE html PUBLIC "-//W3C//DTD XHTML 1.0 Transitional//EN"
    "http://www.w3.org/TR/xhtml1/DTD/xhtml1-transitional.dtd">
<html xmlns="http://www.w3.org/1999/xhtml" lang="en" xml:lang="en">
<head>
 <title>XHTML Essentials</title>
</head>
<body>
<script type="text/javascript">

 var first = "here";
 var second = "there";

 if((first == "here") && (second == "there")){
  document.write("They match");
 }else{
  document.write("They don't match");
 }

</script>
</body>
</html>
```

Figure 9.7 shows the results of running this example.

In this example, we assigned a value to two different variables; then within the condition of an if statement (which we will cover later), we check to see if both (an AND

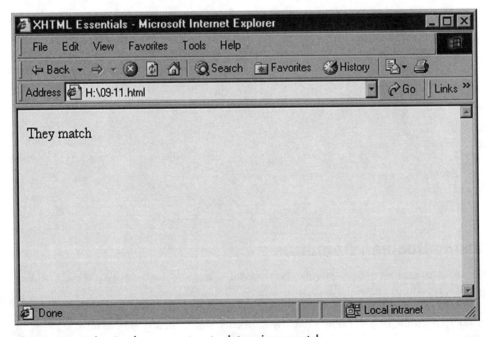

Figure 9.7 Using Boolean operators to determine a match.

Table 9.8 Boolean Operators

OPERATOR	SYNTAX	DESCRIPTION
&&	*exp1* && *exp2*	Logical AND operator. Returns true if both *exp1* and *exp2* are true. Otherwise, it returns false.
||	*exp1* || *exp2*	Logical OR operator. Returns true if either *exp1* or *exp2* is true. If neither is true, it returns false.
!	!*exp*	Logical NOT unary operator. Returns the opposite value of a Boolean *exp*. If *exp* is true, it returns false; if *exp* is false, it returns true.

operation with &&) evaluate to true. This could be used, for instance, to make sure a user entered the correct password. Table 9.8 lists the three Boolean operators that are available within JavaScript.

Determining Precedence

When creating expressions that use more than one operator, you must be aware of operator precedence. This is most likely a concept you learned in school, whereby one operator gets priority over another when an expression is evaluated. For instance, division and multiplication occurs before subtraction and addition. Here is an example:

```
var result = 3 + 4 * 5
```

Read this from left to write, you would think 3 and 4 would be added before the multiplication of 5. However, since multiplication has precedence over addition, 4 and 5 are multiplied, giving you 20, before 3 is added. The result variable ends up with the value of 23.

If it were necessary to add 3 and 4 together before the multiplication occurred, then you could do this without having to reorganize the expression. To do this, you use parentheses, ( ), which have a higher precedence than multiplication. If we add these to the same sample, as follows, we get 3 added to 4, giving us 7, and then multiplied by 5, yeilding 35 as the result.

```
var result = (3 + 4) * 5
```

For your reference, Table 9.9 shows operator precedence, from lowest to highest.

Table 9.9 Operator Precedence

OPERATOR NAME	OPERATOR
Comma	,
Assignment	= += – = *= /= %= <<= >>= >>>= &= ^= |=
Conditional	?:
Logical OR	||
Logical AND	&&
Bitwise OR	|
Bitwise XOR	^
Bitwise AND	&
Equality	== !=
Comparison	< <= > >=
Bitwise shift	<< >> >>>
Addition/subtraction	+ –
Multiplication/division	* / %
Negation/increment	! ~ – ++ – –
Call, data structure	( ) [ ] .

NOTE When expressions have operators of the same precedence, JavaScript evaluates from left to right. For example, the addition operator has the same precedence as the concatenate operator; therefore, JavaScript will evaluate all additions and concatenations from left to right throughout the statement.

Controlling Structures

So far we have discussed data types, how to assign values to variables, and operators, but we really have not discussed how they are put to use. We have hinted toward some control structure statements, such as if...else, but we really have not explained them in any detail. In this section, we are going to look at a few of these control structures, which really complete our coverage of the language semantics. Subsequently, we will look at some of the specific objects, methods, and properties that you can use within your scripts.

Making Statements

The main statement that you will use in your script is the if...else conditional statement, which will be the focus of this section. The syntax of this statement is very simple. You specify a *condition* that must evaluate to true for *code1* to execute. If the *condition* is false, AND there is an else statement present, its contents will be executed (*code2)* as shown here:

```
if(condition){
 code1
}else{
 code2
}
```

This is not the only way if...else statements can occur. It is also possible to include a condition for the else portion. This looks like:

```
if(condition){
 code1
}else if (condition){
 code2
}else{
 code3
}
```

Now that you understand how this works, look back at the last example in the Boolean operator section to see if you understand it better. A list of the other types of statements, brief descriptions, is given in Table 9.10.

NOTE For more information on these statements, check out the ECMA-262 standard at www.ecma.ch.

Looping

Loops are another important aspect of programming. Often, you may want to perform a set number of tasks over and over again until a certain number has been reached.

Table 9.10 JavaScript Statements

STATEMENT	DESCRIPTION
switch	Used to evaluate a single expression for multiple possibilities.
for..in	Iterates a specified variable over all properties of an object.
with	Specifies a default object for a set of statements.
throw	Throws an exception.
try...catch	Marks a block of statement to try, and specifies one or more responses should an exception be thrown.

Table 9.11   JavaScript Loops

STATEMENT	DESCRIPTION
for	Type of loop that will execute according to the condition and limits set.
do...while	Type of loop that will execute according to the condition and limits set.
while	Type of loop that will continue to execute until the condition is no longer true.

Table 9.11 contains a list of the loops available in the JavaScript language; and as you can see, this can be accomplished in a variety of ways.

To get your feet wet, we are going to show you a simple example of a for loop. In this loop we are going to initialize a counter to 0, loop through the code until the counter reaches 10, and increment it on each pass. The resulting page will have the numbers 0 to 9 printed, each on its own line. Figure 9.8 shows the results of running this example.

```
<!DOCTYPE html PUBLIC "-//W3C//DTD XHTML 1.0 Transitional//EN"
        "http://www.w3.org/TR/xhtml1/DTD/xhtml1-transitional.dtd">
```

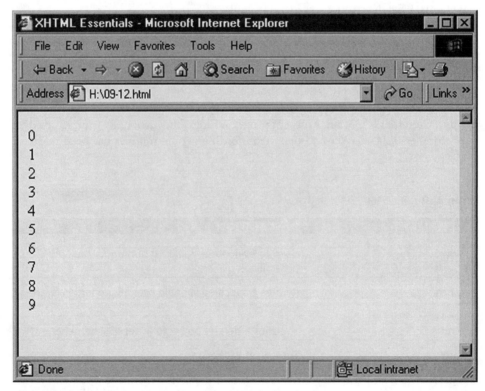

Figure 9.8   Learning to loop.

```
<html xmlns="http://www.w3.org/1999/xhtml" lang="en" xml:lang="en">
<head>
 <title>XHTML Essentials</title>
</head>
<body>
<script type="text/javascript">
 for(var i = 0; i < 10; i++){
  document.write(i + '<br />');
 }
</script>
</body>
</html>
```

Implementing JavaScript Objects

As we mentioned at the first of the chapter, the JavaScript language is now based on (and originally the foundation for) the ECMAScript language. The ECMAScript language contains the core language objects, such as Array, Math, and RegExp, used in the JavaScript and JScript implementations. JavaScript and JScript however, have additional host language objects that can be used. In this section we discuss both of these, and provide some insight on how they might be used.

Defining Core Objects

The core JavaScript language objects, which are defined by ECMAScript, lay the foundation for the language. At a minimum, these are the objects that you should be aware of and understand. They are "user-agent agnostic," meaning they should be present in all ECMAScript implementations—not just in browsers.

We will cover a sample of these objects to familiarize you with them as well as help you understand how they work. For your benefit, we have included a complete list of objects covered in ECMAScript, along with a brief description, in Table 9.12.

Table 9.12 Core JavaScript Objects

OBJECT	DESCRIPTION
String	Container for string-related methods and properties.
RegExp	Container for regular expression-related methods and properties.
Array	Container for array-related methods and properties.
Date	Container for date-related methods and properties.
Math	Container for mathematical-related methods and properties.
Boolean	Container for Boolean-related methods and properties.

continues

(Continued)

OBJECT	DESCRIPTION
Number	Container for numerical-related methods and properties.
Function	Container for a string of JavaScript code to be compiled as a function.
Global	Container for all top-level functions and properties that are not part of any object.

Array

The array is a common programming resource used in most all scripts. JavaScript is no exception in that it provides an array object for you to use. If, say, you wanted to create a "family" variable and store the names of all of your family members in it, rather than have a variable for each person, you would use an array to store this information.

The Array object has several methods and properties, which we have included in Table 9.13. The one you will probably use the most is the length property; it holds the total number of items in the array. For instance, if we had four people in our family array, it would contain the number 4.

Here's a quick example to help you understand how arrays work. In this example, we create an array that contains three words. We then use a for loop, which we mentioned earlier in the chapter, to write each of the values out to the page. Notice how we use the length property to act as a bound for the for loop:

```
<!DOCTYPE html PUBLIC "-//W3C//DTD XHTML 1.0 Transitional//EN"
      "http://www.w3.org/TR/xhtml1/DTD/xhtml1-transitional.dtd">
<html xmlns="http://www.w3.org/1999/xhtml" lang="en" xml:lang="en">
<head>
 <title>XHTML Essentials</title>
</head>
<body>
<script language="JavaScript"type="text/javascript">

//Create a new array that contains 3 words.
var myArray = new Array("you", "me", "them");

// using a for loop, write out each of the values.

for(var i = 0; i < myArray.length; i++){
 document.write(myArray[i] + '<br />');
}

</script>
</body>
</html>
```

Figure 9.9 shows what this looks like when displayed in a browser.

Table 9.13 Array Object Methods and Properties

TYPE	ITEM	DESCRIPTION
Property	constructor	Specifies the function that creates the Array object's prototype.
	index	Contains the original string against which a regular expression was matched (read-only).
	input	Contains the position of a regular expression match in a string (read-only).
	lastIndex	Contains the position after the last regular expression match in a string (read-only).
	length	Contains the number of elements in the array.
Method	concat()	Concatenates an array onto the end of an array.
	join()	Concatenates all elements of an array into one string.
	pop()	Deletes the last element from an array.
	push()	Adds elements to the end of an array.
	reverse()	Reverses the order of the elements in the array.
	shift()	Deletes elements from the front of an array.
	slice()	Returns a subsection of the array.
	sort()	Sorts elements in array.
	splice()	Inserts and removes elements from an array.
	toSource()	Converts elements to a string with square brackets.
	toString()	Converts elements to a string.
	unshift()	Adds elements to the front of an array.
	unwatch()	Removes a watchpoint.
	watch()	Sets a watchpoint.

String

The String object has one of the most extensive lists of methods and properties, mostly because of the formatting that can be applied to a string. When variables are assigned a value within quotes, such as "5", the values are stored, by default, as strings. Additionally, you can use the following method to explicitly create a variable of type string.

```
var myString = new String()
```

A popular use of the String object is for looking for the occurrence of specific characters. Although the RegExp (Regular Expression) object provides more flexibility, using the methods of the String object is a quick and easy way to accomplish the same

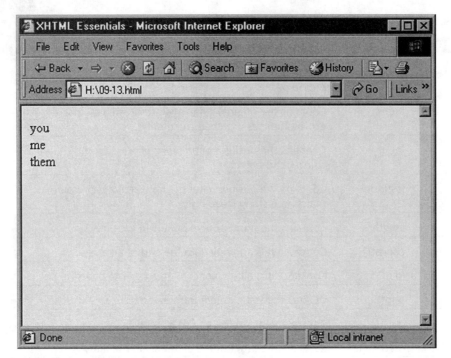

Figure 9.9 Using an array and a for loop.

thing. Let's say, for instance, you want to see if the letter "a" occurred in a string. The following code would accomplish this:

```
<!DOCTYPE html PUBLIC "-//W3C//DTD XHTML 1.0 Transitional//EN"
     "http://www.w3.org/TR/xhtml1/DTD/xhtml1-transitional.dtd">
<html xmlns="http://www.w3.org/1999/xhtml" lang="en" xml:lang="en">
<head>
 <title>XHTML Essentials</title>
</head>
<body>
<script type="text/javascript">

 var myStr = new String();
 myStr = "Hello there my friend";

 if(myStr.indexOf("a") == -1){
  document.write("The letter a was not found");
 }else{
  document.write("The letter a was found!");
 }

</script>
</body>
</html>
```

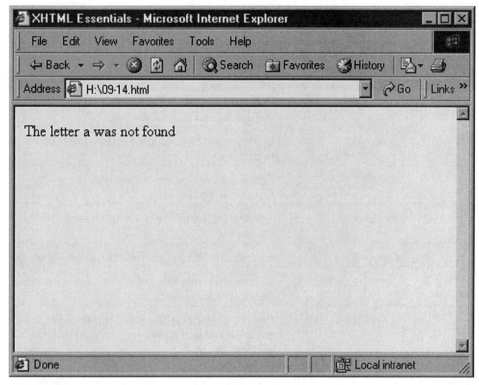

Figure 9.10 Using a String object to search for something.

Figure 9.10 shows the results.

As mentioned, String has many other properties and methods. Table 9.14 contains a complete list of these.

Table 9.14 String Object Properties and Methods

TYPE	ITEM	DESCRIPTION
Method	anchor( )	Creates an instance of the <a> tag with the name attribute set to the string passed to the method.
	big( )	Converts the string into an instance of the <big> tag.
	blink( )	Converts the string into an instance of the <blink> tag.
	bold( )	Converts the string into an instance of the <b> tag.

continues

(Continued)

TYPE	ITEM	DESCRIPTION
	charAt( )	Returns the character at the index passed to the method.
	charCodeAt( )	Returns the ISO-Latin-1 number of the character at the index passed to the method.
	concat( )	Concatenates the two strings passed to return a new string.
	fixed( )	Converts the string into an instance of the <tt>, fixed pitch font tag.
	fontcolor( )	Sets the color attribute of an instance of the <font> tag.
	fontsize( )	Sets the size attribute of an instance of the <font> tag.
	fromCharCode( )	Returns the string value of the ISO-Latin-1 number passed to the method.
	indexOf( )	Returns the index of the first occurrence of the string passed to the method within an instance of a String object.
	italics( )	Converts the string into an instance of the <i> tag.
	lastIndexOf( )	Returns the index of the last occurrence of the string passed to the method within an instance of a String object.
	link( )	Converts the string into an instance of the <a> tag and sets the href attribute with the URL that is passed to the method.
	match( )	Returns an array containing the matches found based on the regular expression passed to the method.
	replace( )	Performs a search and replace, using the regular expression and replace string passed to the method, on the instance of a String object that calls it.
	search( )	Returns the index location of the match found in the string passed to the method. An [ms]1 is returned if the string is not found.
	slice( )	Returns the string between the beginning and ending index passed to the method. If a negative number is passed, the index is referenced from the end of the string passed.
	small( )	Converts the string into an instance of the <small> tag.

(Continued)

TYPE	ITEM	DESCRIPTION
	split( )	Returns the string split into segments defined by the string and instance limit passed to the method.
	strike( )	Converts the string into an instance of the <strike> tag.
	sub( )	Converts the string into an instance of the <sub> tag.
	substr( )	Returns the string beginning with the indexed location and number of characters to return. If a negative number is passed, the index is referenced from the end of the string passed.
	substring( )	Returns the string between the beginning and ending index passed to the method.
	sup( )	Converts the string into an instance of the <sup> tag.
	toLocaleLowerCase()	Converts all the characters in the string to lowercase according to the host machine's current locale.
	toLocaleUpperCase()	Converts all the characters in the string to uppercase according to the host machine's current locale.
	toLowerCase( )	Converts all the characters in the string to lowercase.
	toSource( )	Returns the string representation of the String passed.
	toString()	Returns the characters passed as type string.
	toUpperCase( )	Converts all the characters in the string to uppercase.
	watch( )	Used to turn on the watch on a particular property.
	unwatch( )	Used to turn off the watch on a particular property.
Property	length	Returns the length of the string.
	prototype	Provides the ability for a programmer to add properties to instances of the String object.

Date

The Date object allows you to work with date and time values in JavaScript. Creating an instance of the Date object is similar to creating a String or Array instance. It is accomplished by using the new operator. Once the object is created, you can use one of several methods to either get or set date values. For example, to return the date of the current month, you would use the following code:

```
var myDate = new Date();
date = myDate.getDate();
```

To change the month defined for an instance of the Date object, you can use the following. You can then use the getMonth( ) method to check your change.

```
var myDate = new Date(2002, 01, 01);
myDate.setMonth(7);
alert(myDate.getMonth())
```

One of the most common uses of the Date object is to generate a random number, which will be our next example. To do this, we will use the getTime( ) method that returns the number of seconds since January 1, 1970. This guarantees our number to be unique when compared to other random numbers generated at other times. Notice the little trick we use to create the new Date instance *and* call the getTime( ) function at the same time. This saves us a line of code. Be sure to reload your browser several times to see the value change. Figure 9.11 shows the results of this example.

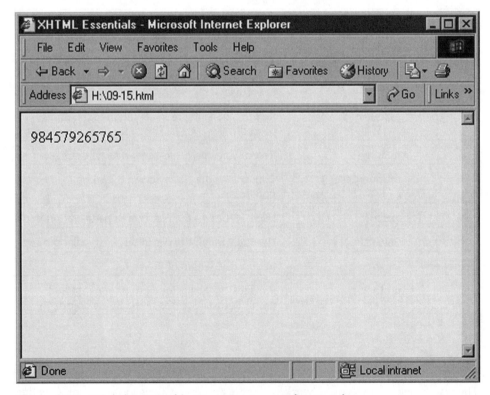

Figure 9.11   Using the Date object to generate a random number.

```
<!DOCTYPE html PUBLIC "-//W3C//DTD XHTML 1.0 Transitional//EN"
    "http://www.w3.org/TR/xhtml1/DTD/xhtml1-transitional.dtd">
<html xmlns="http://www.w3.org/1999/xhtml" lang="en" xml:lang="en">
<head>
 <title>XHTML Essentials</title>
</head>
<body>
<script type="text/javascript">

 var random = (new Date()).getTime();

 document.write(random);

</script>
</body>
</html>
```

In Table 9.15, we have included a list of the methods and properties of the Date object.

Table 9.15 Date Object Methods and Properties

TYPE	ITEM	DESCRIPTION
Property	constructor	Specifies the function that creates the Boolean object's prototype.
	prototype	Allows you to add new methods or properties to the Date object.
Method	getDate( )	Returns the day of the month.
	getDay( )	Returns the day of the week.
	getFullYear( )	Returns the year in local time in four digits.
	getHours( )	Returns the hour.
	getMilliseconds( )	Returns the milliseconds.
	getMinutes( )	Returns the minutes.
	getMonth( )	Returns the month.
	getSeconds( )	Returns the seconds.
	getTime( )	Returns the date and time in milliseconds.
	getTimezoneOffset( )	Returns the time zone offset from GMT in minutes.
	getUTCDate( )	Returns the day of the month converted to universal time.

continues

(Continued)

TYPE	ITEM	DESCRIPTION
	getUTCDay( )	Returns the day of the week converted to universal time.
	getUTCFullYear( )	Returns a four-digit representation of the year converted to universal time.
	getUTCHours( )	Returns the hour converted to universal time.
	getUTCMilliseconds( )	Returns the milliseconds converted to universal time.
	getUTCMinutes( )	Returns the minutes converted to universal time.
	getUTCMonth( )	Returns the month converted to universal time.
	getUTCSeconds( )	Returns the seconds converted to universal time.
	getVarDate( )	Returns the date in VT_DATE format.
	getYear( )	Returns the year as either four digits or two digits.
	parse( )	Converts a string, representing a date and time, into milliseconds.
	setDate( )	Sets the day of the month.
	setFullYear( )	Sets the year as a four-digit number.
	setHours( )	Sets the hour.
	setMilliseconds( )	Sets the milliseconds.
	setMinutes( )	Sets the minutes.
	setMonth( )	Sets the month.
	setSeconds( )	Sets the seconds.
	setTime( )	Sets the date and time from a millisecond representation of a date and time.
	setUTCdate( )	Sets the day of the month in universal time.
	setUTCFullYear( )	Sets the year as a four-digit number in universal time.
	setUTCHours( )	Sets the hour in universal time.
	setUTCMilliseconds( )	Sets the milliseconds in universal time.
	setUTCMinutes( )	Sets the minutes in universal time.
	setUTCMonth( )	Sets the month in universal time.
	setUTCSeconds( )	Sets the seconds in universal time.

(Continued)

TYPE	ITEM	DESCRIPTION
	setYear( )	Sets the year as either a four-digit or a two-digit number.
	toGMTString( )	Returns the data and time as a string in universal time (GMT).
	toLocalString( )	Returns the date and time as a string in local time format.
	toSource( )	Returns the source of the Date object.
	toString( )	Returns the date and time as a string in local time.
	toUTCString( )	Returns the data and time as a string in universal time (GMT).
	unwatch( )	Removes a watchpoint.
	UTC( )	Converts a universal date and time (GMT) to milliseconds.
	watch( )	Sets a watchpoint.

Math

For mathematical calculations, the JavaScript includes a host of mathematical constants and procedures in the Math object. This object is quite different from the other core objects, because you can already perform basic arithmetic calculations—including addition, subtraction, multiplication, and division—outside a Math object. The primary purpose of this object is to hold constants and provide methods for advanced mathematical calculations, such as taking the sine or tangent of a value.

Let's say, for instance, that you wanted to take the square root of PI (3.14...). You could do this with the following bit of code:

```
<!DOCTYPE html PUBLIC "-//W3C//DTD XHTML 1.0 Transitional//EN"
    "http://www.w3.org/TR/xhtml1/DTD/xhtml1-transitional.dtd">
<html xmlns="http://www.w3.org/1999/xhtml" lang="en" xml:lang="en">
<head>
 <title>XHTML Essentials</title>
</head>
<body>
<script type="text/javascript">

 document.write(Math.sqrt(Math.PI));

</script>
</body>
</html>
```

These are not the only methods and constants the Math object provides. Table 9.16 contains a list of remaining items.

Table 9.16 Math Object Methods and Constants

TYPE	ITEM	DESCRIPTION
Method	abs( )	Returns absolute value of a number.
	acos( )	Returns the arccosine of a number.
	asin( )	Returns the arcsine of a number.
	atan( )	Returns the arctangent of a number.
	atan2( )	Returns the arctangent of the quotient of its parameters.
	cos( )	Returns the cosine of a number.
	exp( )	Returns Ex, where x is a number.
	floor( )	Returns the largest integer less than or equal to a number.
	log( )	Returns the natural logarithm (base E) of a number.
	max( )	Returns the larger of two arguments.
	min( )	Returns the smaller of two arguments.
	pow( )	Returns base to the exponent power, baseexp.
	random( )	Returns a random number between 0 and 1.
	round( )	Rounds a number to its nearest integer.
	sin( )	Returns the sine of a number.
	sqrt( )	Returns the square root of a number.
	tan( )	Returns the tangent of a number.
	toSource( )	Creates a copy of an object.
	toString( )	Returns a string representation of an object.
	unwatch( )	Removes a watchpoint.
	watch( )	Sets a watchpoint.
Property	ceil	Returns the smallest integer greater than or equal to a number.
	E	Returns the value for Euler's constant.
	LN10	Returns the natural logarithm of 10

(Continued)

TYPE	ITEM	DESCRIPTION
	LN2	Returns the natural logarithm of 2.
	LOG10E	Returns the base 10 logarithm of E.
	LOG2E	Returns the base 2 logarithm of E.
	PI	Returns the value of PI.
	SQRT1_2	Returns the square root of _.
	SQRT2	Returns the square root of 2.

Adding Objects to Popular Browsers

When the ECMAScript language is implemented, it is done so within a host environment. Because many of these host environments have the need for additional objects, methods, properties, and constants, new items are added to the language specific to that host. Running JavaScript within a browser is no exception. It adds objects such as navigator, window, Frame, Form, and Link to the language. Table 9.17 contains a list of currently supported objects and their primary function.

Table 9.17   Current Browser Environment Objects

OBJECT	DESCRIPTION
Anchor	Constructed on occurrences of the <a> element. This is a child object of the document object.
Applet	Constructed on occurrences of the <applet> element. This is a child object of the document object.
Area	Constructed on occurrences of the <area> element. This is a child object of the document object.
Button	Constructed on occurrences of the <button> element, or <input type="button">. This is a child object of the Form object.
Checkbox	Constructed on occurrences of the <input type="checkbox"> element. This is a child object of the Form object.
document	Constructed on occurrences of the <html> element. This is a child object of the window object.
window	Constructed for each browser window that is open. This is a top-level object.
Frame	Constructed on occurrences of the <frameset> element. This is a child object of the window object.

continues

(Continued)

OBJECT	DESCRIPTION
Location	Constructed by the location box in which the URLs are typed. This is a child object of the window object.
History	Constructed on occurrences of a historical URL visited. This is a child object of the window object.
Layer	Constructed on occurrences of the <layer> element. This is a deprecated Netscape-only feature. This is a child object of the document object.
Style	Constructed on occurrences of document.ids, document.classes, document.tags, and document.contextual. This is a deprecated Netscape-only feature. This is a child object of the document object.
Link	Constructed on occurrences of the <link> element. This is a child object of the document object.
Image	Constructed on occurrences of the <img> element. This is a child object of the document object.
Plugin	Constructed on occurrences of a plug-in loaded by the browser. This is a child object of the document object and navigator object.
Form	Constructed on occurrences of the <form> element. This is a child object of the document object.
Textarea	Constructed on occurrences of the <textarea> element. This is a child object of the Form object.
Text	Constructed on occurrences of the <input type="text"> element.
FileUpload	Constructed on occurrences of the <input type="fileupload"> element. This is a child object of the Form object.
Password	Constructed on occurrences of the <input type="password"> element. This is a child object of the Form object.
Hidden	Constructed on occurrences of the <input type="hidden"> element. This is a child object of the Form object.
Submit	Constructed on occurrences of the <input type="submit"> element. This is a child object of the Form object.
Reset	Constructed on occurrences of the <input type="reset"> element. This is a child object of the Form object.
Radio	Constructed on occurrences of the <input type="radio"> element. This is a child object of the Form object.
Select	Constructed on occurrences of the <select> element. This is a child object of the Form object.
Option	Constructed on occurrences of the <option> element. This is a child object of the Select object.

(Continued)

OBJECT	DESCRIPTION
navigator	Constructed by the browser. This is a top-level object.
MimeType	Constructed on occurrences of a supported mime-type by a plug-in loaded by the browser.

NOTE Because many of the objects will become obsolete with the widespread adoption of the Document Object Model (DOM), which we will discuss in the next chapter, we will only cover a few important objects in this chapter. Be sure to stay on top of DOM implementation that is currently within Netscape 6 and Internet Explorer 5+ browsers. You can find more information on DOM in Appendix B, including some reference Web sites.

navigator

The navigator object is constructed and represents the browser software in use. Using this object, you can retrieve information about the name, version, and other aspects of the user agent. This object is often used to *sniff* the client so that you can perform certain tasks for a particular browser. We will use this technique in the next chapter when deciding how to create DHTML in the browser rendering the document. Table 9.18 contains a list of methods and properties in this object.

Table 9.18 Navigator Object Methods and Properties

TYPE	ITEM	DESCRIPTION
Method	javaEnabled( )	Tests to see if Java is supported in the browser.
	plugins.refresh( )	Checks for any newly installed plug-ins.
	preference( )	Allows reading and setting of various user preferences in the browser.
	taintEnabled( )	Tests to see if data-tainting is enabled.
Property	appCodeName	Represents the code name of the browser.
	appName	Refers to the official browser name.
	appVersion	Refers to the version information of the browser.
	language	Refers to the language of the browser.
	mimeTypes	Refers to an array of mimetype object that contains all the MIME types that the browser supports.

continues

(Continued)

TYPE	ITEM	DESCRIPTION
	platform	A string representing the platform on which the browser is running.
	plugins	Refers to an array of plug-in objects that contains all the plug-ins installed on the browser.
	userAgent	A string that represents the user-agent header.

The following is an example that will write out several of the properties of the navigator object:

```
<!DOCTYPE html PUBLIC "-//W3C//DTD XHTML 1.0 Transitional//EN"
      "http://www.w3.org/TR/xhtml1/DTD/xhtml1-transitional.dtd">
<html xmlns="http://www.w3.org/1999/xhtml" lang="en" xml:lang="en">
<head>
 <title>XHTML Essentials</title>
</head>
<body>
<script type="text/javascript">
 document.write("navigator.appCodeName: " + navigator.appCodeName
         + '<br />');
 document.write("navigator.appName: " + navigator.appName
         + '<br />');
 document.write("navigator.appVersion: " + navigator.appVersion
         + '<br />');
 document.write("navigator.platform: " + navigator.platform
         + '<br />');
 document.write("navigator.userAgent: " + navigator.userAgent
         + '<br />');
</script>
</body>
</html>
```

Figure 9.12 shows the results of this code run in an Internet Explorer 5.5 browser on Windows 2000.

window

The window object is the top-level object for all XHTML documents. It is the parent object for the entire client-side JavaScript object hierarchy, and contains all other client-side objects (except the navigator object, which is not part of the document). This object is created when a new browser window is opened, and can be used to interact with the user agent application rendering the XHTML page.

For instance, if you wanted to open a new window, you could call the window.open( ) method, passing it the URI, name, and any windowing options. Or, you could change the text of the status bar of the window, with this code:

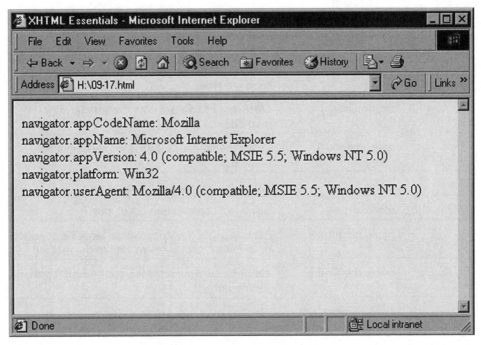

Figure 9.12 Running an example of the navigator object in an Internet Explorer 5.5 browser.

```
window.status = 'Here is the new text'
```

Like the other objects, the window object has many properties and methods, which are listed in Table 9.19. Because it is the top-level object, some of these can be called without having the preceding window reference. The alert( ) method, as we discussed earlier, is an example of this.

Table 9.19 Window Object Properties and Methods

TYPE	ITEM	DESCRIPTION
Method	alert( )	Displays an alert dialog box with the text string passed.
	atob( )	Decodes a string that has been encoded using base-64 encoding.
	back( )	Loads the previous page in place of the window instance.
	blur()	Removes the focus from a window.
	btoa()	Encodes a string using base-64 encoding.

continues

(Continued)

TYPE	ITEM	DESCRIPTION
	captureEvents( )	Sets the window to capture all events of a specified type.
	clearInterval( )	Clears the interval set with the setInterval( ) method.
	clearTimeout( )	Clears the timeout set with the setTimeout( ) method.
	close( )	Closes the instance of the window.
	confirm( )	Displays a confirmation dialog box.
	crypto.random( )	Returns a random string whose length is specified by the number of bytes passed to the method.
	crypto.signText( )	Returns a string of encoded data, which represents a signed object.
	disableExternal-Capture( )	Disables external event capturing.
	enableExternal-Capture( )	Enables external event capturing for the pages loaded from other servers.
	find( )	Displays a Find dialog box where the user can enter text to search the current page.
	focus( )	Assigns the focus to the specified window instance.
	forward( )	Loads the next page in place of the window instance.
	handleEvent( )	Invokes the handler for the event passed.
	home()	Loads the user's specified home page in place of the window instance.
	moveBy( )	Moves the window by the amounts specified.
	moveTo( )	Moves the window to the specified location.
	open()	Opens a new instance of a window.
	print( )	Invokes the Print dialog box so the user can print the current window.
	prompt( )	Displays a prompt dialog box.
	releaseEvents( )	Releases the captured events of a specified type.
	resizeBy( )	Resizes the window by the specified amount.
	resizeTo( )	Resizes the window to the specified size.

(Continued)

TYPE	ITEM	DESCRIPTION
	routeEvent( )	Passes the events of a specified type to be handled natively.
	scroll( )	Scrolls the document in the window to a specified location.
	scrollBy( )	Scrolls the document in the window by a specified amount.
	scrollTo( )	Scrolls the document, both width and height, in the window to a specified location.
	setHotKeys( )	Enables or disables hot keys in a window that does not have menus.
	setInterval( )	Invokes a function or evaluates an expression every time the number of milliseconds has passed.
	setResizeable( )	Specifies whether a user can resize a window.
	setTimeout( )	Invokes a function or evaluates an expression when the number of milliseconds has passed.
	setZOptions( )	Specifies the z-order stacking behavior of the window.
	stop( )	Stops the current window from loading other items within it.
	unwatch( )	Used to turn off the watch on a particular property.
	watch( )	Used to turn on the watch on a particular property
Property	closed	Specifies if the window instance has been closed.
	crypto	Actually a subobject of the window object, which allows access to the browser's encryption features.
	defaultStatus	Is the default message in the window's status bar.
	document	References all the information about the document within this window. See the document object for more information.
	frames	References all the information about the frames within this window. See the Frame object for more information.
	history	References the URLs the user has visited.
	innerHeight	Contains the height of the display area of the current window in pixels.

continues

(Continued)

TYPE	ITEM	DESCRIPTION
	innerWidth	Contains the width of the display area of the current window in pixels.
	length	Represents the number of frames in the current window.
	location	Contains the current URL loaded into the window.
	locationbar	References the browser's location bar.
	menubar	References the browser's menu bar.
	name	Name of the window.
	offScreenBuffering	Specifies whether updates to a windows are performed in an off-screen buffer.
	opener	Contains the name of the window from which a second window was opened.
	outerHeight	Contains the height of the outer area of the current window in pixels.
	outerWidth	Contains the width of the outer area of the current window in pixels.
	pageXOffset	Contains the x-coordinate of the current window.
	pageYOffset	Contains the y-coordinate of the current window.
	parent	References the uppermost window that is displaying the current frame.
	personalbar	References the browser's personal bar.
	screenX	Specifies the x-coordinate of the left edge of the window.
	screenY	Specifies the y-coordinate of the top edge of the window.
	scrollbars	References the browser's scroll bars.
	self	References the current window.
	status	References the message in the window's status bar.
	statusbar	References the browser's status bar.
	toolbar	References the browser's toolbar.
	top	References the uppermost window that is displaying the current frame.
	window	References the current window.

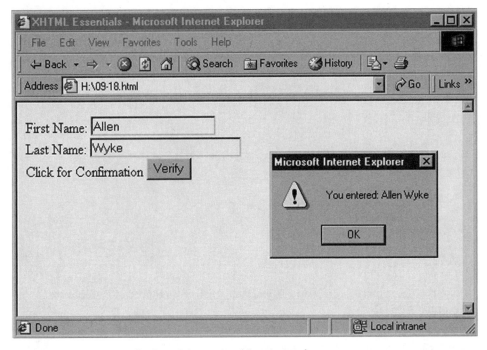

Figure 9.13 Browser display of the Form object example.

Form

Forms give life to static pages by providing an interface for users to submit data to servers, as well as a method to pass data to internal scripts within a document. They allow you to place buttons, text, or other interface objects within a document. The Form object within JavaScript provides a means to access this data, and therefore use it in any processing that you may have. Let's take a look at a quick example to help you understand how this object can be used.

Here we have included a form within the <body> of our XHTML document. That form contains two text fields and a button. The button, when pressed, will call the verify( ) function that we defined in the <head> of the document. Through the Form object, this function accesses the form, then the input instances to retrieve the values entered, which will be displayed in an alert box. Figure 9.13 shows how this will look when used within a browser.

```
<!DOCTYPE html PUBLIC "-//W3C//DTD XHTML 1.0 Transitional//EN"
     "http://www.w3.org/TR/xhtml1/DTD/xhtml1-transitional.dtd">
<html xmlns="http://www.w3.org/1999/xhtml" lang="en" xml:lang="en">
<head>
 <title>XHTML Essentials</title>
 <script "type="text/javascript">
  function verify(){
   var firstName = document.myForm.first.value;
   var lastName = document.myForm.last.value;
```

```
    alert("You entered: " + firstName + " " + lastName);
  }
</script>
</head>
<body>
<form name="myForm" action="null">
 First Name:
 <input type="text" name="first" size="20" />
 <br/>
 Last Name:
 <input type="text" name="last" size="25" />
 <br/>
 Click for Confirmation
 <input type="button" value="Verify" name="check"
    onclick='verify()' />
</form>
</body>
</html>
```

Like the other objects, the Form object has a list of methods and properties. Table 9.20 contains this list.

Table 9.20   Form Object Methods and Properties

TYPE	ITEM	DESCRIPTION
Property	action	Contains the action attribute value of Form instance.
	elements	Contains the array reflecting elements within Form.
	elements.length	Specifies length of elements array.
	encoding	Contains the enctype attribute value of Form instance.
	length	Gives the number of elements within form.
	method	Accesses the method attribute value of Form instance.
	name	Represents the Form instance's unique name.
	target	Contains the target attribute value of Form instance.
Method	handleEvent( )	Handles specific event.
	reset()	Resets Form elements.
	unwatch( )	Removes a watchpoint on a Form property.
	watch( )	Sets a watchpoint on a Form property.

Summary

With this introduction to JavaScript under your belt, it is time to put some of that knowledge to work. And what better way to do it than through the application of scripting XHTML documents—also known as DHTML.

XHTML Essentials

CHAPTER 10

Scripting XHTML Documents

We begin here with a discussion of what that phrase "scripting XHTML documents" means, because many might interpret it as a synonym for Dynamic HTML, or DHTML, as it is more commonly referred. Though that interpretation is somewhat correct, it is not really an accurate method of describing how content is changed dynamically within the current browser environment.

A little background is in order here, because before we can dive into the topic of what "scripting XHTML documents" means in today's world, we must review how content was dynamically controlled and manipulated in DHTML. Dynamic HTML, when implemented in version 4 browsers, was one of the hottest things going. Everyone wanted to add some kind of interactivity to their site, whether it was truly functional features such as expanding and collapsing menus (as shown in Figure 10.1), or simply for fun or "cool" purposes (see Figure 10.2). But as time went on, things changed. DHTML came to be used in the complex user interfaces of a variety of Web-based applications, and more recently to create the entire interface of Netscape's newest browser, Netscape 6.

Defining Dynamic HTML

DHTML was made possible primarily as a result of the implementation of layers within HTML, JavaScript, and cascading style sheets (CSS). Netscape Communicator 4 was the first to support this *scripting of HTML tags*; but soon after its release, Internet

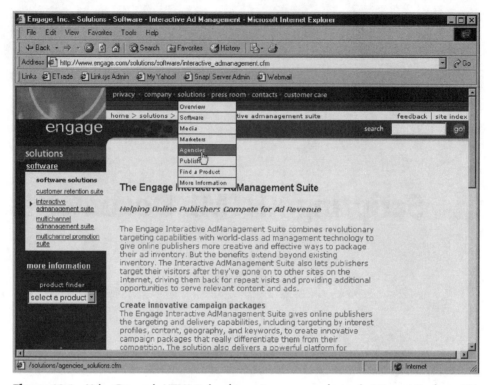

Figure 10.1 Using Dynamic HTML to implement menus, as shown in Internet Explorer 5.5.

Explorer 4 came out with a similar, but slightly different method of accessing and managing dynamic content within the browser. In this section, we are going to talk about the purpose of this effort, provide a little history, and discuss the three main technologies involved in creating DHTML content.

History

Over the years within the Web publishing world, the term *Dynamic HTML* has meant more than one thing. To understand the purpose of DHTML and why it is important going forward, it is necessary to talk a little about its multifaceted history.

CGI Scripts

The first references to DHTML specifically referred to the capability of Web servers to generate content dynamically depending on the browser's request. This most commonly occurred when users responded to form queries in Common Gateway Interface (CGI) scripts. A browser would load a page with form fields on it, the user would then fill out the fields, the data would be submitted back to the server, and the server would dynamically build the resulting page based on the data passed to it. For instance, it might return a summary page of the information sent.

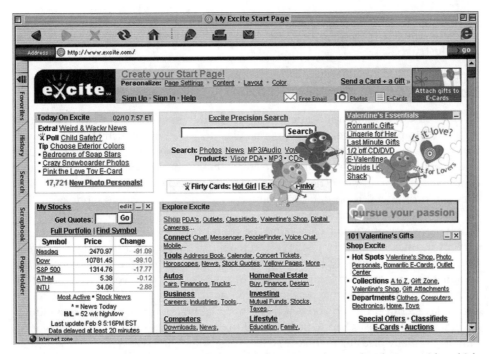

Figure 10.2 Dynamic HTML was used on this page to animate the three cupids, which flew around the page, as shown in Internet Explorer 5 for the Mac.

As more people began building Web sites, and more companies made their Web presence known, it became a cumbersome task to manage and update all the pages a given site may have had. A simple color or date change could take all day, even with the help of some automated scripts. Enter *server-side includes* (SSI).

Server-Parsed Pages

To help cope with these problems, servers started supporting server-parsed pages, which allowed site developers to do things like "include" (hence the previous reference to SSI) commands, files, and other items within their pages. When a request for the page occurred, the server would parse the page looking for these SSI directives. When found, they would execute them and send the final constructed page to the browser for rendering. This allowed people to store common page items, such as headers or footers, in a single, separate file, which would be included on all pages. If a change had to be made, they only had to do this on one page—the included file. This was a huge step toward being able to manage one's content for Web distribution. But things did not stop here.

Around the same time CGI scripts began getting more complex, as did the languages they were created in. People started using them to connect to databases, not just the file system. They would store the content, such as retail items or news, in the database, and then use the CGI script to pull it out, format it, and send it to the browser. So, if a person wanted to obtain more information on a product, for example, the script might pull out a detailed description, price, availability, and even a picture from the database. The term *database-driven Web sites* started to become commonly used across the industry.

Database-Driven Content

Over the next few years, applications that provided this sort of server-side functionality started to pop up. Their claim to fame was the ease with which Web developers could store and retrieve information from a database. They no longer had to be programmers or database administrators to create these complex scripts, but rather know how to use the application. The application would provide a simple interface in which they could drag and drop database connection components, values, and so on. The interface did the rest. Sounds nice, huh?

But there was one major complaint: the round trip between the browser and the server was often too slow, or just involved too much backing and forthing. If a person typed in a value incorrectly, he or she would not know it until the server checked the information and responded with the error. In a perfect world, it would have been nice if this information could have been verified and validated *before* being sent to the server. JavaScript provided some of this functionality; but often, secondary windows or annoying alert boxes had to be launched to display this information. There was no way, in a visually pleasing manner, to tell the user something was wrong. This is where DHTML came to life.

Client-Side DHTML

Driven primarily by the desire to be able to preprocess information within the browser before submitting it, DHTML was born. Another major force behind the desire for DHTML was interactivity. Simply, users and developers were getting tired of the plain, static pages they had become familiar with—look, click, look, click, and that was pretty much it. Java applets provided a means to embed games, spreadsheets, and other items. This was great, but learning Java proved to be a little too much for many HTML developers.

These developers want to apply knowledge they already had in HTML and JavaScript and the newfound CSS languages. They did not want to have to learn some completely new approach just to make a ball bounce or a menu expand. These requests became another requirement for DHTML to fulfill. People wanted not only to be able to validate data, but to be able to add interactivity to their pages. Most developers could not wait for the release of the newest browsers so they could begin their coding. However, this is where DHTML took a hit—the browsers.

During the so-called browser wars, it simply was not possible for both Netscape and Microsoft to agree on a common way of doing things. Traditionally, Netscape was first out with features; hence, it became a driving force behind standardization. Microsoft lagged a little behind, but often had a more complete browser in terms of standardization support. They battled between being first to include features, then for best implementation. These wars are the reason we have to discuss DHTML in terms of both Netscape and Microsoft browsers.

Navigator 4

Navigator 4, which was the browser component of the Communicator suite, added several items to allow for DHTML. First, it included two new tags: <layer> and <ilayer> ("i" stands for *inflow*). Unlike the similar tags in the official HTML 4 Recommendation, the <layer> and <ilayer> tags had attributes that allowed you to "style" the layers. For instance, you could specify within the tag the absolute or relative positioning of a layer.

It was also possible to load external HTML files right into the layer itself. By using the src attribute, you could reference another file that would be displayed within the dimensions of the layer. For instance, you could create a Weather layer on your page and have the content displayed there, but pulled from a completely different source.

The attributes of the <layer> and <ilayer> tags are included in Table 10.1. It is worth noting that these tags, although implemented in Navigator 4, were not and

Table 10.1   Attributes of <layer> and <ilayer>

ATTRIBUTE	DESCRIPTION
above	A layer higher in z-order of all other layers in the document.
background	The URL of a background image that can be used for the layer.
below	A layer lower in z-order of all other layers in the document.
bgcolor	The background color for the layer.
clip	Defines the clipping area (visible region for the layer. Anything outside of this area is "clipped" from view.
height	The height, in pixels, of the layer.
left	The x-axis position in, pixels, of the layer, relative to the origin of its parent layer.
name	The name of the layer.
src	The URL for the layer's content source, if not included between the beginning and ending <layer> or <ilayer> tags.
top	The y-axis position, in pixels, of the layer, relative to the origin of its parent layer.
visibility	Used to define the layer's visibility attributes. Can be any of the following: *show:* Displays the layer. *hide:* Hides the layer. *inherit:* Causes the layer to inherit the visibility of its parent layer.
width	The width in pixels of the layer.
z-index	The relative (to its siblings and parent) z-order of the layer.

will not be part of any HTML or XHTML standard. In fact, Netscape has announced that it has deprecated these tags in favor of elements defined in HTML 4 and XHTML 1.0. But if you are creating content for Navigator 4 browsers, this table should be beneficial.

The inclusion of layers was the first step in creating support for DHTML in the Navigator browser. The next item was support for CSS. Netscape's support for this recommendation, which was at Level 1 at the time, was not complete, but it did provide a baseline for what was needed in DHTML. Additionally, the W3C Note CSS Positioning, or CSS-P for short, was finalized; it allowed for the positioning of elements.

NOTE When Level 2 was released, the CSS-P Note was combined with the official recommendation.

The introduction of CSS gave developers a powerful way to express style, enhance presentation, and define a more consistent design in documents. One of the major disadvantages of publishing information to the Web was the fact that it was nearly impossible to have the control of the traditional desktop publishing world. Developers had to use all kinds of workarounds to place items in the right locations, or use fonts of the right type and size; they were forced to use tables to position elements.

The final enhancement added by Netscape came within the JavaScript language. Netscape added objects, properties, and methods to access, create, manipulate, and delete the dynamic elements on a page. It was this final component that provided a means to coordinate the presentational efforts of layers and CSS, with the functionally for the scripting language to build interactive elements. Table 10.2 contains a list of the particular JavaScript arrays that provided access to these items, while Table 10.3 contains the properties to which developers had access. These arrays are considered instances of the Style object, which is a subobject of the document object in Netscape's client-side JavaScript implementation.

Table 10.4 contains the properties and methods of the Layer object, which was also a subobject of the document object, within Netscape's client-side JavaScript implementation. It was through this object that layers were accessed from a programmatic standpoint.

NOTE To learn more about Layers in Navigator 4, go to http://developer.netscape.com/docs/technote/index.html?content=dynhtml .html. In addition to some Navigator-specific information, you will also see links to some cross-browser examples and information.

Internet Explorer 4 DHTML Object Model

As mentioned, Internet Explorer, until recently, usually trailed the Netscape line of browsers in the adoption of new standards. This "laggard" approach often made it possible for Microsoft to release a more complete and bug-free result. When DHTML was first implemented in Navigator 4, it did not confirm to the standards, such as HTML 4 and the Document Object Model (DOM) that were in progress. Internet Explorer 4, in contrast, adopted some of these works, which gave it a more complete approach to dynamic client-side pages. (Note: This was not full DOM Level 1 support; within the Microsoft implementation, it is called the DHTML Object Module.)

Table 10.2 JavaScript Arrays for Accessing DHTML Properties

ARRAY	EXAMPLE	DESCRIPTION
document.tags	document.tags.p.fontSize = "20pt";	A reference to HTML tags. After the element is referenced, the style property, which does not necessarily have the same name as defined in CSS, is then referenced.
	Specifies that all <p> tags should have a font size of 20.	
document.classes	document.classes.fontclass. blockquote.fontSize = "20pt";	Contains access to all tags with the class attribute specified. Following the object reference is the name of the class, then the element, if applicable, for which the class is defined.
	States that the font size for all <blockquote> elements should be 20.	
	document.classes.fontclass.all .fontsize = "20pt";	
	States that the font size for all elements should be 20.	
document.contextual	document.contextual (document.tags.P.document.tags DEL).colors="red";	Allows you to slectively apply a style to an HTML element that appears in a very specific context.
	Says that all <del> tags that occur within an opening and closing <p> tag should be in red text.	
document.ids	document.id.myid.fontSize = "20pt"	Contains access to all tags with the id attribute specified. Following the object reference is the name of the id and property it wishes to set.
	States that the font size for all elements with the id attribute set to myid should be 20.	

In the non-Navigator 4 world, a layer was created using an HTML tag and applying several CSS properties to position, show, and control the "layering" (remember Navigator 4 used <ilayer> and <layer>). The HTML Recommendation defined the <div> tag, which represents a division of data and is the most logical choice for creating referenceable layers. HTML 4 also defined the <iframe> tag, which gave developers the ability to load external documents to an *inline* frame. Not only did these operate much like the functionality of the tags in Navigator 4, but they did so in a standardized way.

Internet Explorer 4 also provided the ability to script elements via its client-side scripting languages. Within JScript it provided access to all the HTML elements on the page through the document.all collection. If you wanted to access a particular tag's CSS properties, you would do it through this collection. The syntax—where *tagname* is the value of the name attribute of the tag, and the *CSSproperty* is the property you wish to access—is how you would access this information, as shown here:

Table 10.3 Properties Accessible Through the Arrays in Table 10.2

TYPE	PROPERTY NAME	APPLIES TO	POSSIBLE VALUES	VALUE DEFINITIONS
Font Properties	fontSize	All elements	Absolute sizes	x-small, small, medium, large, x-large, point size
			Relative sizes	smaller, larger
			Percentage	150 percent bigger
	fontStyle	All elements		normal, italic, oblique, small caps
Text Properties	lineHeight	Block-level elements	Number	Units to increase height by
			Length	Absolute value of line height
			Percentage	Percentage of parent
	verticalAlign	All elements		baseline, sub, sup, top, text-top middle, bottom, text-bottom
	textDecoration	All elements		none, underline, overline, line-through, blink
	textTransform	All elements		capitalize, uppercase, lowercase, none
	textAlign	Block-level elements		left, right, center, justify
	textIndent	Block-level elements	Length	Numerical units to indent
			Percentage	Percentage of parent
Block-Level Properties	paddings( )	All elements	Number	Number of units of padding

continues

(Continued)

TYPE	PROPERTY NAME	APPLIES TO	POSSIBLE VALUES	VALUE DEFINITIONS
			Percentage	Percentage of parent
	borderWidths( )	All elements	Number	Number of units for width of border
	margins( )	All elements	Length	Margins in number of units
			Percentage	Percentage of parent
			Auto	Document autosizes margins
	borderStyle	All elements		none, solid, 3D
	width	Block-level elements	Length	Width in units
			Percentage	Percentage of parent
			Auto	Document autosizes width
	length	Block-level elements	Length	Length in units
			Auto	Document autosizes length
	align	All elements		left, right, none
Color Properties	color	All elements	Color	color names, RGB colors
	background-Image	All elements		URL
	background-Color	All elements	Color	color names, RGB colors
Classification Properties	display	All elements		block, inline, list-item, none
	listStyleType	Elements with display property		disc, circle, square, decimal, lower and upper-roman, lower and upper-alpha, none

continues

(Continued)

TYPE	PROPERTY NAME	APPLIES TO	POSSIBLE VALUES	VALUE DEFINITIONS
	whiteSpace	Block-level elements		Normal and pre

Table 10.4   Layer JavaScript Object Properties and Methods

TYPE	ITEM	DESCRIPTION
Method	captureEvents( )	Specifies the event types to capture.
	handleEvent( )	Invokes handler for specified event.
	load( )	Loads a new URL.
	moveAbove( )	Moves the layer above another layer.
	moveBelow( )	Moves the layer below another layer.
	moveBy( )	Moves the layer to a specified position.
	moveTo( )	Moves the top-left corner of the window to the specified screen coordinates.
	moveToAbsolute( )	Changes the layer position to the specified pixel coordinates within the page.
	releaseEvents( )	Sets the layer to release captured events of the specified type.
	resizeBy( )	Resizes the layer by the specified height and width values.
	resizeTo( )	Resizes the layer to have the specified height and width values.
	routeEvent( )	Passes a captured event along the normal event hierarchy.
Property	above	Specifies the layer above.
	background	Refers to the background image of the layer.
	below	Specifies the layer below.
	bgColor	Refers to the background color of the layer.
	clip.bottom	Refers to the bottom of the layer's clipping area.

continues

(Continued)

TYPE	ITEM	DESCRIPTION
	clip.height	Refers to the height of the layer's clipping area.
	clip.left	Refers to the left of the layer's clipping area.
	clip.right	Refers to the right of the layer's clipping area.
	clip.top	Refers to the top of the layer's clipping area.
	clip.width	Refers to the width of the layer's clipping area.
	document	Refers to the document object that contains the layer.
	left	Refers to the x-coordinate of the layer.
	name	Refers to the name of the layer.
	pageX	Refers to the x-coordinate relative to the document.
	pageY	Refers to the y-coordinate relative to the document.
	parentLayer	Refers to the containing layer.
	siblingAbove	Refers to the layer above in the zIndex.
	siblingBelow	Refers to the layer below in the zIndex.
	src	Refers to the source URL for the layer.
	top	Refers to the y-coordinate of the layer.
	visibility	Refers to the visibility state of the layer.
	window	Refers to the window or frame object that contains the layer.
	x	Refers to the x-coordinate of the layer.
	y	Refers to the y-coordinate of the layer.
	zIndex	Refers to the relative z-order of this layer with respect to its siblings.

```
document.all["tagname"].CSSproperty
```

Let's say, for instance, you wanted to hide a layer that you named mylayer. You could do this by executing:

```
document.all["mylayer"].visibility = hidden;
```

This collection also has two methods at its disposal. These are shown in Table 10.5.

Table 10.5   Methods Accessible from the document.all Collection

METHOD	DESCRIPTION
document.all.item( )	Provides a means by which you can retrieve a particular HTML tag from the document.all collection without having to know its position.
document.all.tags( )	Provides a means by which you can retrieve all instances of a particular HTML tag from the document.all collection.

Because Internet Explorer 4 allowed for greater access to the various HTML elements on the page by imposing no restrictions on what could be scripted, and because its implementation was more along the lines of the DOM efforts, it is referred to as the DHTML Object Model. That may be just some fancy "marketing speak" on Microsoft's part, but it actually is a pretty accurate way to describe what it has implemented. It's not Netscape's DHTML, and it's not DOM, but something in between.

TIP   Want more information on the DHTML Object Module? Microsoft has included a complete reference at http://msdn.microsoft.com/workshop/ author/dhtml/reference/dhtmlrefs.asp.

Defining the Document Object Model

So far we've talked about the DOM without really defining what it is. The DOM is a standard application programmer interface (API) to the structure of a document that aims to make it easy for programmers to access, delete, add, or edit elements, contents, attributes, and style.

The DOM is a robust evolution from the object model in the early version 3 browsers and the DHTML Object Model (its predecessor), which first appeared in Internet Explorer 4, because it provides a structured model and logical interface for programmers.

NOTE   If you are familiar with either of the previous object models, you should find the DOM implementation fairly straightforward to learn.

An object model is a mechanism for accessing and programming a document or program. As described, the DHTML Object Model in Internet Explorer 4 provides access to almost all elements and attributes in an HTML document. In the newest versions of Internet Explorer, every element is exposed to the DHTML Object Model. The DOM is consistent with the DHTML Object Model in that every element and every attribute is accessible in script.

History

There are various modules of the DOM, including XML and HTML. The DOM XML module relies on an internal treelike representation of the document, and allows programs to traverse the hierarchy accordingly. As with XHTML, the standard model of viewing an XML document is as a hierarchy of elements. DOM is a manner by which the computer can/should build an internal model of the document, based on this tree structure, and then make it accessible.

The second module, HTML DOM, provides a set of methods to manipulate HTML and, now, XHTML documents. The first-generation HTML DOM merely described methods of access—for instance, methods for accessing a tag by name as defined by the name attribute. This is the generation implemented in Netscape Navigator 3 and Internet Explorer 3, and is sometimes referred to as DOM Level 0, but was never an official standard. Its concepts and ideas were imported into DOM Level 1, the first real standard.

After DOM Level 1 was released, work on Level 2 was started; it was completed except for the HTML module, which is currently a Working Draft. Level 2 included features such as an events and style sheet model, as well as support for XML namespaces. Level 2 was blessed as a final Recommendation in November 2000.

The DOM Working Group is now hard at work on DOM Level 3. When released, it will provide:

- A means for users and applications to access keyboard events.

- An object model for accessing and modifying a content model for a document.

- An interface for loading XML source documents into a DOM representation and for saving a DOM representation as an XML document.

- An embedded object model to allow different vocabularies to work together.

A lot is going on around the DOM and that working group. The group is essentially defining a way to represent documents, which in turn will provide a standardized way for browsers to make the various elements, attributes, and content pieces available for scripting, styling, and other manipulation. In short, the group is working to establish a new way to perform DHTML. The question is, when will all of this be available in browsers and ready for Web developers to take advantage of?

NOTE For more information on the DOM, read about the W3C DOM Working Group's activities and the Level 1, 2, and 3 efforts at www.w3.org/DOM.

The Newest Browsers

Even from this short description of the DOM, you can begin to see its importance to the Web developer—the ability to access, delete, add or edit elements, contents, attributes, and style in a common manner across any language and any XML-based document. And although it has taken some time, we are starting to see implementations of the DOM in today's browsers.

As we discussed earlier, Internet Explorer 3 and Netscape Navigator 3 implemented an object model many call DOM Level 0, while one could argue that Internet Explorer 4's DHTML Object Model was the driving force behind the DOM Level 1 efforts. Netscape Navigator 4, part of the Communicator 4 suite, landed somewhere in between Level 0 and Level 1. It really wasn't until the next browser versions that we saw a true DOM implementation.

Internet Explorer 5 was the first to come out with DOM Level 1 support, adding features specific to the DOM HTML Level 1 module. However, this support has been considered spotty and buggy. Shortly after 5.0 was released on the Windows platform, the Mac OS version was released; it enhanced this support to include portions of the DOM Core Level 1 module as well as portions from Level 2—both of which are present in the 5.5 version that has since been released for Windows. Internet Explorer 6 will be out at about the time this book is published, and from what we can tell, support for these standards have greatly increased.

On the Netscape side of the market, Netscape 6 is the first version to truly support DOM. It not only fully supports the HTML Level 1 module, but also the Level 1 Core—except for a couple of minor features, Level 2 Events, and the Level 2 CSS Interface. With this release, Netscape has jumped back into the lead for standards support. The big issue for Netscape 6 is, of course, that because it is based primarily on actual standards, it has limited backward compatibility for many of its DHTML features in version 4—such as the <layer> and <ilayer> tags.

Scripting XHTML

With that basic—and admittedly somewhat confusing—history of DHTML out of the way, we can proceed to the real meat of the chapter: learning how to script these documents. Our objective is simple: to ensure that, by the end of this chapter, you have an understanding not only of how to script XHTML documents, but also how to write code that will execute in older browsers and how to handle other issues. In the process, we will of course address such issues as cross-browser implementations.

Addressing Implementation Issues

Before we jump into actual code, we need to first categorize and explain some of the differences in implementation. This will help you better understand the examples later in the chapter, and will provide a baseline on how to create cross-browser document scripts.

Old versus New

The first topic we are going to cover is how nonstandard and standard ways of doing things compete against each other. Essentially, we are going to look at the old DHTML implementations within Internet Explorer 4 and 5 and Netscape 4, and how they differ from the W3C standards. Table 10.6, which lists browser, DHTML method, and standards method of accomplishing a particular task, itemizes this information.

Transition to Netscape 6

Normally, we would not single out a browser and explain how to create scripts and content that span both the old and new way of doing things, but because Netscape 6 does not provide backward compatibility with some of its previous DHTML tags, it is necessary to do so. If you do not have to support Navigator 4 and Netscape 6 within the same document, we recommend the following steps:

Table 10.6   DHTML versus W3C Standards

BROWSER	DHTML	STANDARD
Internet Explorer 4 and 5	document.all	document.getElementById( ) ECMAScript binding defined in DOM Level 1.
	document.*elementName*	document.getElementById( ) ECMAScript binding defined in DOM Level 1.
	element.style.visibility = *value*	*element*.style.visibility = *value* defined in DOM Level 2.
	element.style.pixelLeft	parseInt(*element*.style.left) defined in DOM Level 2.
	element.style.pixelTop	parseInt(*element*.style.top) defined in DOM Level 2.
	element.style.pixelLeft = *x*; *element*.style.pixelTop = *y*;	*element*.style.left = *value* + "px" defined in DOM Level 2
	document.styleSheets[ ] .addRule (*selector*, *declaration*)	DOM Level 2's CSS interface for adding rule to a style sheet in the <head>
	element.innerHTML	DOM methods can be used to set the contents of the element.
Navigator 4	<layer>	<div> element defined in HTML 4.0
	<ilayer>	<iframe> element defined in HTML 4.0.
	<layer src=...>, <ilayer src=...>, <div src=...>	<iframe src=...> element defined in HTML 4.0.
	document.layers[]	document.getElementById( ) ECMAScript binding defined in DOM Level 1.
	document.*elementName*	document.getElementById( ) ECMAScript binding defined in DOM Level 1.
	element.visibility = *value*	DOM level 2 *element*.style.visibility = value;
	element.left	parseInt(*element*.style.left) defined in DOM Level 2.
	element.top	parseInt(*element*.style.top) defined in DOM Level 2.

continued

(Continued)

BROWSER	DHTML	STANDARD
	element.moveTo(x,y)	*element*.style.left = *value* + "px" defined in DOM Level 2.
	document.tags, document.ids, document.classes, document.contextual( )	DOM Level 2's CSS interface for adding rule to a style sheet in the <head>.
	handleEvent( )	dispatchEvent( ) defined in DOM Level 2.

1. Create one page for Navigator 4 with the specific version 4 features necessary to perform the needed tasks.

2. Create a second page for Netscape 6 with the specific W3C standards items necessary to perform the needed tasks.

3. On the server-side, sniff the HTTP USER_AGENT HTTP request header directive to return the appropriate page for either Navigator 4 or Netscape 6.

Many times, the needed server-side functionally may not be present, or you may simply not wish to maintain two separate sets of document code. For either of these reasons, you will want to create a single page that supports both browsers. Although this approach can become rather messy due to the level of client-side scripting needed, it is possible. The following steps provide the basic guidelines for doing so, and are complete for most all cases:

1. Position and set the id attribute on all <div> and <span> element instances.

2. Use document.write( ) statements to generate client-specific XHTML elements, such as named <iframe src=...> elements for Internet Explorer 3+ and Netscape 6+, and an identically named <ilayer src=...> tags for Navigator 4.

3. If you do not wish to use JavaScript, you can wrap data block elements (<iframe> or <div>) for Internet Explorer 4+ and Netscape 6+ in the appropriate Layer tag (<layer> or <ilayer>) of the same name/id for Navigator 4.

4. For JavaScript code, sniff the browser then include conditional blocks in your code that execute appropriately for the browser. Refer to Table 10.6 for what to use. Additionally, we will cover some of these items in the following pages.

> **NOTE** Want more information on sniffing browsers on the client-side? Check out Netscape's DevEdge site for its Ultimate Client Sniffer at http://developer.netscape.com/docs/examples/javascript/browser_type.html.

Defining Groups

The first step in scripting XHTML documents is to create the grouping of data you wish to script—the *layer* in old terms. Once defined correctly, we will be able position it with CSS and manipulate it with JavaScript.

In case you are not clear on what a block of data might be, think of a normal application, such as a browser: In this application, with the window being the first block, you might consider a menu, which is exposed when clicked on, the second block. This type of functionality does not have to be included only in full-blown applications, as we will see. Additionally, you may want to define blocks of data within a given element. For instance, within the body of a paragraph, you may wish to display the name of a book as underlined or italic.

Data Blocks

The best method of defining these blocks of data is through the use of the <div> element. This element creates a defined block-level structure in a document. When text is included between the beginning and ending element, it is often rendered similar to the <p> element, except <p> also dictates the start of a new paragraph.

Before we go any further, take a look at the attributes of this element and what they mean. These are contained in Table 10.7.

In addition to these core attributes, this element also has the following intrinsic events:

- onclick
- ondblclick
- onmousedown
- onmouseup
- onmouseover
- onmousemove
- onmouseout

Table 10.7   Attributes of the <div> Element

ATTRIBUTE	DESCRIPTION
align	Deprecated attribute that was originally used to align the data contained inside the element.
class	A comma-separated list of style classes that make the element an instance of those classes.
dir	Specifies the direction of any text contained in the element. A value of ltr means *left to right* and rtl means *right to left*.
id	Often used by style sheets to define the type of style that should be applied to the data in the element.
lang	Identifies the human language code of the data within the element.
style	Allows you to specify a style definition within the element, rather than within a style sheet.
title	Allows you to provide a more informative title for the element than the <title> element, which applies to the whole document.

- onkeypress
- onkeydown
- onkeyup

Using the <div> element is fairly easy. You simply place it around other elements and content that you wish to define as an entire block of data. The following code, which contains two <div> blocks, shows how this can be done. The first block contains the text "Hello, World!" while the second block simply states, "This is a data block."

```
<!DOCTYPE html PUBLIC "-//W3C//DTD XHTML 1.0 Transitional//EN"
      "http://www.w3.org/TR/xhtml1/DTD/xhtml1-transitional.dtd">
<html xmlns="http://www.w3.org/1999/xhtml" lang="en" xml:lang="en">
<head>
 <title>XHTML Essentials</title>
</head>
<body>
 <h1>First Block</h1>
 <div id="first">
  <p>Hello, World!</p>
 </div>
 <h1>Second Block</h1>
 <div id="second">
  <p>This is a data block</p>
 </div>
</body>
</html>
```

Inline Grouping

When you are within the body of an element already, but you wish to define a group inline, you will use the <span> element. In many ways, this element is like <div>, except that it exists within another element and is often used to change the formatting of the text. The attribute list for this element is the same as <div>, so refer to Table 10.7 for more information. The following code provides you with a simple example of what the use of this element may look like. Figure 10.3 shows how this is rendered.

```
<!DOCTYPE html PUBLIC "-//W3C//DTD XHTML 1.0 Transitional//EN"
      "http://www.w3.org/TR/xhtml1/DTD/xhtml1-transitional.dtd">
<html xmlns="http://www.w3.org/1999/xhtml" lang="en" xml:lang="en">
<head>
 <title>XHTML Essentials</title>
 <style type="text/css">
  #book{
    text-decoration: underline
   }
 </style>
</head>
<body>
 <p>I really like the <span id="book">XHTML Essentials</span> book.</p>
</body>
</html>
```

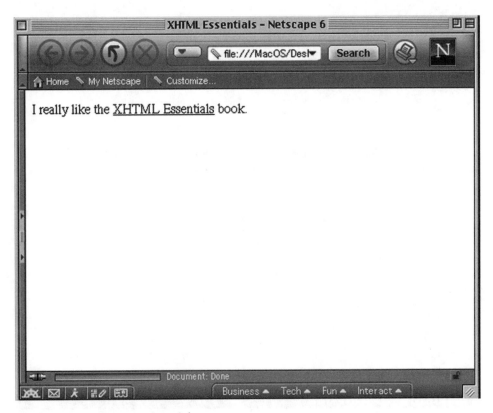

Figure 10.3   Inline grouping of data.

Including External Files

The <iframe> element allows you to pull in external files within the dimensions of this inline frame. This is often used as a mechanism to include content from a different location. A good example would be for a daily cartoon, which would change everyday. By using a single <iframe> element, you could reference a URL that contained the cartoon for each day. This would allow you to make the changes on the page at the end of that URL, which would affect all of pages loading it via an <iframe>. Table 10.8 contains the attributes of this element.

NOTE Before Netscape 6, Navigator 4 could accomplish this same task by using the src attribute within the <layer>, <ilayer>, and <div> tags.

Let's look at a quick example to demonstrate how this works. Because we will need to include a second file, two HTML files are needed in this example. The first file is as follows:

```
<!DOCTYPE html PUBLIC "-//W3C//DTD XHTML 1.0 Transitional//EN"
"http://www.w3.org/TR/xhtml1/DTD/xhtml1-Transitional.dtd">
<html xmlns="http://www.w3.org/1999/xhtml" lang="en" xml:lang="en">
<head>
```

```
  <title>XHTML Essentials</title>
</head>
<body>
 <iframe src="cartoon.html" scrolling="auto" frameborder="1">
  Your browser does not support inline frames.
 </iframe>
</body>
</html>
```

For the second file, which we referenced as cartoon.html in the first file, we will just include some text to signify where the cartoon file should load:

```
<!DOCTYPE html PUBLIC "-//W3C//DTD XHTML 1.0 Transitional//EN"
      "http://www.w3.org/TR/xhtml1/DTD/xhtml1-transitional.dtd">
<html xmlns="http://www.w3.org/1999/xhtml" lang="en" xml:lang="en">
<head>
 <title>XHTML Essentials</title>
</head>
<body>
<p>The cartoon would appear here</p>
</body>
</html>
```

Table 10.8   Attributes of the <iframe> Element

ATTRIBUTE	DESCRIPTION
align	Deprecated in favor of CSS, this attribute was originally used to align the data inside the <iframe> element. It took values of left, right, top, middle, and bottom.
class	A comma-separated list of style classes that instantiate the element as an instance of the defined classes.
frameborder	Takes a value of 0 or 1 to determine if a border should be drawn around the frame.
height	Specifies the height of the <iframe>.
id	Often used by style sheets to define the style that should be applied to the data in the element.
longdesc	Links to a longer description of the element contents.
marginheight	The number of pixels between the content of the frame and the top and bottom borders.
marginwidth	The number of pixels between the content of the frame and the right and left borders.
name	Used to give the block a name. This can be used by JavaScript to manipulate the layers.
scrolling	Takes the value of auto, yes, or no to determine if scrollbars are to be shown.

(Continued)

ATTRIBUTE	DESCRIPTION
src	Specifies the URL containing the content of the <iframe>.
style	Allows you to specify a style definition within the element, rather than outside in a style sheet.
title	Allows you to provide a more informative title for the <iframe> than the <title> element, which applies to the whole document.
width	Specifies the width of the <iframe>.

Take a look at Figures 10.4 and 10.5 to see how implementations of this code differ across browsers. Specifically notice the height of the inline frame.

Positioning Elements

As we mentioned earlier in the chapter, the proper and standardized way of positioning elements on a page is through the use of style sheets. We covered most of the necessary properties needed for this positioning in Chapter 8, "Formatting with Style Sheets," but there are two additional properties that we need to cover for the subject of

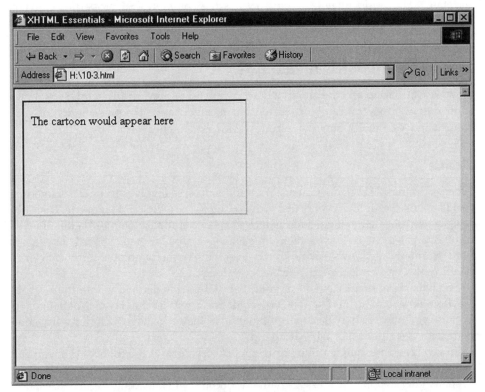

Figure 10.4 The <iframe> element rendered in Internet Explorer 5.5 on Windows 2000

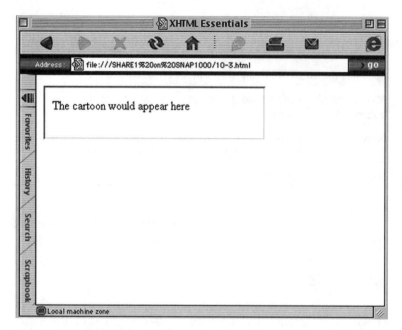

Figure 10.5 The <iframe> element rendered in Internet Explorer 5.0 on Mac OS 9.

scripting XHTML documents. Table 10.9 has the common CSS properties that you should understand for this purpose.

Manipulating with JavaScript

Now we can start to add the real dynamics by including JavaScript. In this section, we explain how JavaScript can be used to dynamically change the presentation of your content and, essentially, how you script XHTML documents.

Events

When scripting XHTML documents, part of the process involves fully understanding and knowing the various events that are exposed to the JavaScript language. Basically, when a user does something, such as moves his or her mouse pointer on top of, over, or off of an element, or maybe clicks an element or type on the keyboard, an event is fired. Normally, the browser handles that event, but at the same time the event can be handled, through JavaScript, by the Web developer.

You have more than 20 events at your disposal—some defined within the XHTML 1.0 Recommendation, and a few others defined within the JavaScript language. Because you may wish to use any combination of these, we have included a list, complete with descriptions, in Table 10.10.

To give you an example of how this might work, look at the following document. Within this document we have included a single image, and have used the onerror event handler to pop up a message if an error occurs when loading. Figure 10.6 shows what happens when this is loaded into a Netscape browser.

Table 10.9 CSS Properties Commonly Used while Scripting XHTML Documents

PROPERTY	POSSIBLE VALUES	DESCRIPTION
position	static, relative, absolute, or fixed	Tells the browser how and where to place elements.
left, right, top, and bottom	length (em = font-size, ex = x-height, or px = pixels), percentage (relative to other elements or the window), auto, or inherit (inherits parent element's value)	Allow you to specify the exact location of an element.
height and width	length (em = font-size, ex = x-height, or px = pixels), percentage (relative to other elements or the window), auto, or inherit (inherits parent element's value)	Allow you to specify the exact dimensions of an element.
visibility	collapse (same as hidden except when used on tables), hidden, visible, or inherit (inherits parent element's value)	Used to hide or show an element.
z-index	auto, integer (numerical value like 0, 1, or 2), or inherit (inherits parents elements value)	Specifies the stacking context of the element; 0 represents the same level as the document; 1 would be "on top" of 0; 2 would be on top of that; and so on.

NOTE The onerror event is not part of the XHTML 1.0 Recommendation, but rather the JavaScript language, so if you run this document through a validation application or service, it will complain about the existence of the attribute. This was done to demonstrate how scripting XHTML documents could in fact have items specific to the host executing them.

```
<!DOCTYPE html PUBLIC "-//W3C//DTD XHTML 1.0 Transitional//EN"
     "http://www.w3.org/TR/xhtml1/DTD/xhtml1-transitional.dtd">
<html xmlns="http://www.w3.org/1999/xhtml" lang="en" xml:lang="en">
<head>
 <title>XHTML Essentials</title>
</head>
<body>

<img src="sample.gif" alt="Sample Image"
    onerror="alert('400: File Not Found')" />

</body>
</html>
```

Table 10.10 Useful Event Handlers

EVENT	SUPPORT ELEMENTS	DESCRIPTION
onabort	<img>	Fired when the user agent Stop button has been hit while in progress of loading an image. This event is not defined within XHTML 1.0, but rather the JavaScript language.
onblur	<a>, <area>, <label>, <input>, <select>, <textarea>, and <button>	Fired when an element loses focus either by clicking the mouse to change selection or by tabbing navigation.
onchange	<input>, <select>, and <textarea>	Fired when a control loses the input focus, and its value has been modified since gaining focus.
onclick	Most elements	Fired when the mouse button is clicked over an element.
ondblclick	Most elements	Fired when the mouse button is double-clicked over an element.
ondragdrop	<body> and <frameset>	Fired when the user drops an object on the user agent window. This event is not defined within XHTML 1.0, but in the JavaScript language.
onerror	<img>, <body>, and <frameset>	Fired when an error has occurred while retrieving data for images and documents in framesets or the given window. This event is not defined within XHTML 1.0, but in the JavaScript language.
onfocus	<a>, <area>, <label>, <input>, <select>, <textarea>, and <button>	Fired when an element receives focus either by clicking the mouse or by tabbing navigation.
onkeydown	Most elements	Fired when a key is pressed over an element.
onkeypress	Most elements	Fired when a key is pressed and released over an element.
onkeyup	Most elements	Fired when a key is released over an element.
onload	<body> and <frameset>	Fired when the user agent finishes loading a window or all frames within a <frameset>.
onmousedown	Most elements	Fired when mouse button is pressed over an element.

(Continued)

EVENT	SUPPORT ELEMENTS	DESCRIPTION
onmousemove	Most elements	Fired when the mouse is moved while over an element.
onmouseout	Most elements	Fired when the mouse is moved away from an element.
onmouseover	Most elements	Fired when the mouse is moved onto an element.
onmouseup	Most elements	Fired when the mouse button is released over an element.
onmove	<body>, <frameset>, and internal "layers" as defined by the developer.	Fired when the user attempts to move a window, frame, or internal data block. This event is not defined within XHTML 1.0, but in the JavaScript language.
onreset	<form>	Fired when a form is reset.
onresize	<body> and <frameset>	Fired when the user attempts to resize a window or frame. This event is not defined within XHTML 1.0, but in the JavaScript language.
onselect	<input> and <textarea>	Fired when a user selects some or all of the text in a text field.
onsubmit	<form>	Fired when a form is submitted.
onunload	<body> and <frameset>	Fired when the user agent removes a document from a window or frame.

Cross-Browser Coding

Without a doubt, even with all the standards out there today, the most difficult task of scripting XHTML documents is being able to make them readable in all browsers (or at least as many as you can). This not only means coding for different implementations of functionality, such with Internet Explorer 4 and Netscape 4 DHTML, but also for browsers that either do not support scripting or have it disabled. You have to make the difficult decision of whether you want to support those not executing scripts or do a lot of extra XHTML coding to accommodate them.

Overall, even though it will take more time, it is best to code for all browsers. Just as you should use <noframes> for your framed sites, you should use <noscript> sections for your scripts. Users should still be able to navigate your site even if they do not have JavaScript at their disposal or they do not wish to enable it. For coding purposes, however, we do recommend that you keep it simple; that means replace expandable and collapsible menus with clicks to a new page that offers the same choices as the menus.

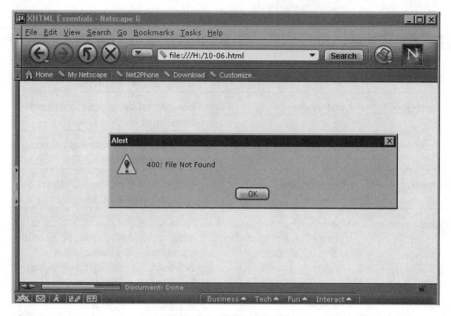

Figure 10.6 Firing the onerror event within the <img> element.

The Basics

When creating cross-browser code, the first guideline is to use *only* standardized XHTML elements, syntax, and semantics. In the past, tags such as <blink> or <marquee> were used by developers, but these are specific to particular browsers, so they should be avoided.

Tags or elements specific to a particular browser are not the only thing you should avoid; also avoid depreciated features. For instance, the <center> and <font> elements have been depreciated in favor of CSS, so stay away from them. One good reason is that XHTML 1.1 no longer supports these elements; they have been removed completely.

Next, we recommend that you avoid using items that, though standardized, are not supported universally across platforms or browsers. For instance, Internet Explorer 5 for the Mac OS does not support the same CSS properties as its Windows counterpart. Moreover, Internet Explorer in general does not support the same properties that Netscape's or even Opera's browsers support. Though items are much more universally supported now, you should continue to avoid any that are controversial until all browsers and platforms that you plan to support have adopted them.

Finally, avoid using any buggy elements, including buggy XHTML elements, JavaScript items, and CSS properties. And by buggy, we do not just mean wrong implementations, but also different implementations. For instance, you may find that Netscape 6 on Linux renders a particular CSS property different from Opera 3.62 on BeOS.

JavaScript Coding

The first point we need to cover regarding accessing data blocks from JavaScript is the syntax to use to access the data. Because of the differences in implementation between Internet Explorer 4/5 and Navigator 4, you will have to access this information using different methods. And don't forget about the newer, more standardized browsers that support the DOM methods: they will have to be addressed as well. We'll address the older browsers first, move into the newer versions, and then talk about how to handle them all.

In the Navigator 4 browsers, data blocks are accessed via the document.layers array. Even though it is not defined in the XHTML 1.0 Recommendation, you must have a name attribute set in the <div> tag for this to work. The syntax is rather simple for accessing data blocks in this manner. All you have to do is reference the name of the <div> tag through the array. For instance, if you want to access datablock1, you could accomplish this through the following syntax:

```
document.layers['datablock1']
```

Internet Explorer 4 and 5, on the other hand, access data blocks through the document.all collection. Unlike the document.layers method, it does not rely on the nonstandard name attribute of the <div> tag, but rather the standardized id attribute. Again using the datablock1 as our example, you would access this data block in Internet Explorer 4 or 5 using the following syntax:

```
document.all['datablock1']
```

NOTE This is not the only way to access data blocks with JavaScript; however, for cross-browser coding, it is the recommended method because it reduces the amount of coding needed.

Now that you have access to the data block, you will want to access its properties. Within Navigator, this is accomplished by including the property you wish to access immediately after the document.layers['*layerName*'].*property* declaration. For Internet Explorer, however, you access it through the additional style collection, so your syntax will be something like document.all['*layerName*'].style.*property*.

At first glance, this really seems to pose a problem. It appears that we will have to write two different sets of code for each browser. This is somewhat true, but fortunately, there is a shortcut. Within the JavaScript language there is a top-level function called eval( ) that takes a string passed to it, and evaluates it as JavaScript code. So, for instance, it allows us to dynamically build a piece of JavaScript code, such as a data block reference based on the browser accessing the page, and then pass it to the eval( ) function to be executed. Let's take a look at a simple example that accesses and modifies the visibility property to demonstrate this approach.

The first step is to determine the browser rendering the page. For our simple test, we will simply check the user-agent string for the existence of MSIE or Nav to determine the browser type. (Note: If you are deploying real-world code, then we recommend the client sniffer from Netscape mentioned earlier. You can grab that at http://developer .netscape.com/docs/examples/javascript/browser_type.html.) We are going to store this browser-checking code in a function and call it via the onload event handler we will include within the <body> tag. The function will look like this:

```
function checkBrowser(){
  if(navigator.userAgent.indexOf("MSIE") != -1){
  block = ".all";
```

```
  style = ".style";
 }else if(navigator.userAgent.indexOf("Nav") != -1){
  block = ".layers";
  style = "";
 }
}
```

Notice that after we determined which browser was rendering the page, we assigned values to two variables (block and style). Remember our syntactical differences for Internet Explorer and Navigator? Well, we are going to use these values to build the correct syntax for each browser in conjunction with the eval( ) function.

We must now create the data block and position it. We will do this using an instance of the <div> element and position it using CSS properties. Above the block we will have two buttons, one for hiding the block and one for showing it. The result will be a page with two buttons and a yellow box that reads "Data block."

In the following code we pull this all together. As you will see, we have created a single data block and positioned it under two form buttons. After the page loads, the checkBrowser( ) function we just went over is called and processed. Once complete, we are able to show and hide the data block by clicking the buttons, which makes a call to the changeState( ) function. It is within this function that we build the data block reference and execute the eval( ) function. The visibility property, when hiding, needs to be set to "hidden"; it should be set to "visible" when exposing.

We have even included an alert box that will pop up when the buttons are pushed to display what the eval( ) function returns. As mentioned, this script will execute correctly in Navigator 4 and Internet Explorer 4 and 5 browsers.

```
<!DOCTYPE html PUBLIC "-//W3C//DTD XHTML 1.0 Transitional//EN"
       "http://www.w3.org/TR/xhtml1/DTD/xhtml1-transitional.dtd">
<html xmlns="http://www.w3.org/1999/xhtml" lang="en" xml:lang="en">
<head>
 <title>XHTML Essentials</title>
 <style type="text/css">
 <!--
  #datablock1{
  background-color: yellow;
  height: 100px;
  left: 10px;
  position: absolute;
  top: 50px;
  width: 100px
  }
 -->
 </style>
 <script type="text/javascript" language="JavaScript1.2">
 <!--
 // global variables for browser
 var block = new String();
 var style = new String();

 // set appropriate variables depending on document scripting method
 function checkBrowser(){
```

```
      if(navigator.userAgent.indexOf("MSIE") != -1){
       block = ".all";
       style = ".style";
      }else if(navigator.userAgent.indexOf("Nav") != -1){
       block = ".layers";
       style = "";
      }
     }

     // Take the state passed in, and change it.
     function changeState(dblock, state){
      eval("document" + block + "['" + dblock + "']" + style +
         ".visibility = '" + state + "'");
      alert("document" + block + "['" + dblock + "']" + style +
         ".visibility = '" + state + "'");
     }
    //-->
    </script>
   </head>
   <body onload="checkBrowser()">
    <form name="form1" action="null">
     <input type="button" value="Hide"
         onclick="changeState('datablock1','hidden')" />
     <input type="button" value="Show"
         onclick="changeState('datablock1','visible')" />
    </form>
    <div name="datablock1" id="datablock1">
     <p>Data block</p>
    </div>
   </body>
   </html>
```

Now that we have briefly covered the old DHTML way of scripting documents, we must now cover the newer way that is present in Netscape 6, somewhat in Internet Explorer 5, and in Internet Explorer 6. The creation and positioning of the data blocks stay the same, but as listed in Table 10.6, the JavaScript used to access and manipulate them changes.

The first thing we must add to our script is a couple of new variables. In these variables we will store a Boolean true or false value depending on the browser's support for the new way of scripting XHTML documents, or the old DHTML way. For the Netscape line of browsers, which are actually built with the Gecko rendering engine maintained by Mozilla.org, we will look for the existence of the string "Gecko." For Internet Explorer 5+, we will check to make sure the version is greater than 5, which we will have stored in a variable. To include this functionally, we are going to extend our checkBrowser( ) function to the following:

```
function checkBrowser(){
 if((ieVerLoc < 5) && (ieVerLoc > 0)){
  block = ".all";
  style = ".style";
  isOldDHTML = "true";
 }else if(navigator.userAgent.indexOf("Nav") != -1){
```

```
  block = ".layers";
  style = "";
  isOldDHTML = "true";
  }else if((navigator.userAgent.indexOf("Gecko") != -1)
      || (ieVerLoc >= 5)){
  isNewDHTML = "true";
 }
}
```

The next thing we need to add is how the data block is accessed and changed. We will need to modify the changeState( ) function to account for these differences. The first thing we need to do is add in an if...else statement. In the first part, we will account for the older browsers using DHTML. In the second part of the statement, we will account for the newer browsers that use the DOM to access and modify elements. But this statement is not the only thing that we will add.

We must also add the code to hide and expose the data block. This we accomplish by using the document.getElementById( ) method to return a pointer to the data block, and then use the style.visibility property that is now accessible through the pointer to set the value to hidden or visible depending on which button is pushed.

And that does it—our code is complete and works in Internet Explorer 4+ and Navigator 4+ (including Netscape 6) browsers. Here is the complete code:

```
<!DOCTYPE html PUBLIC "-//W3C//DTD XHTML 1.0 Transitional//EN"
     "http://www.w3.org/TR/xhtml1/DTD/xhtml1-transitional.dtd">
<html xmlns="http://www.w3.org/1999/xhtml" lang="en" xml:lang="en">
<head>
 <title>XHTML Essentials</title>
 <style type="text/css">
 <!--
  #datablock1{
  background-color: yellow;
  height: 100px;
  left: 10px;
  position: absolute;
  top: 50px;
  width: 100px
  }
 -->
 </style>
 <script type="text/javascript" language="JavaScript1.2">
 <!--
 // global variables for browser
 var block = new String();
 var style = new String();
 var isOldDHTML = new Boolean(false);
 var isNewDHTML = new Boolean(false);

 // determine IE version
 var ieVerLoc = navigator.userAgent.indexOf("MSIE");
 var ieVer = parseInt(navigator.userAgent.charAt(ieVerLoc + 5));
```

```
   // set appropriate variables depending on document scripting method
   function checkBrowser(){
    if((ieVerLoc < 5) && (ieVerLoc > 0)){
     block = ".all";
     style = ".style";
     isOldDHTML = "true";
    }else if(navigator.userAgent.indexOf("Nav") != -1){
     block = ".layers";
     style = "";
     isOldDHTML = "true";
    }else if((navigator.userAgent.indexOf("Gecko") != -1)
        || (ieVerLoc >= 5)){
     isNewDHTML = "true";
    }
   }


   // Take the state passed in, and change it.
   function changeState(dblock, state){
    if(isOldDHTML == "true"){
     eval("document" + block + "['" + dblock + "']" + style +
       ".visibility = '" + state + "'");
    }else if(isNewDHTML == "true"){
     var blockElement = document.getElementById(dblock);
     blockElement.style.visibility = state;
    }
   }
 //-->
 </script>
</head>
<body onload="checkBrowser()">
 <form name="form1" action="null">
  <input type="button" value="Hide"
      onclick="changeState('datablock1','hidden')" />
  <input type="button" value="Show"
      onclick="changeState('datablock1','visible')" />
 </form>
 <div name="datablock1" id="datablock1">
  <p>Data block</p>
 </div>
</body>
</html>
```

Introducing the Rollover Effect

There are many different effects you can achieve with DHTML and through the scripting of XHTML documents; hiding and showing data blocks or layers is only one. Another common effect often used is called *rollovers*. Many times, the rollover effect is used to signify, visually, to users that they have in fact placed their mouse over a particular item. Rollovers are not just limited to images, which we cover here, but can be applied to regular text as well.

Not only are rollovers very helpful, they are not too hard to learn. But the learning process does incorporate several different lessons, so we will not limit the examples here to just one method. We will cover image rollovers (swapping) as well as style rollovers (hovering).

Implementing Image Rollovers

There are several methods of implementing image rollovers, but the easiest is to use two arrays. The first array will contain the images you want to preload, while the second array will contain the original images by referencing their indexed location within the document through the document.images array.

The first thing we do is store all of the images into two arrays of Image objects. Next we set the src attribute of the Image objects to point to the appropriate images. These arrays can be created with the following code:

```
// Create arrays to hold images
var overImg = new Array();
overImg[0] = new Image(24,24);
overImg[1] = new Image(24,24);

var defaultImg = new Array();
defaultImg[0] = new Image(24,24);
defaultImg[1] = new Image(24,24);

// Preload images in the array
overImg[0].src = "back-over.gif";
overImg[1].src = "forward-over.gif";

defaultImg[0].src = "back.gif";
defaultImg[1].src = "forward.gif";
```

Now we need to write a function to swap them when users roll their mouse over them. The function we are going to write will take two parameters. The first is the indexed location of the image that needs to be swapped; the second is the type of swap ("over" or "out") that needs to occur. Once these parameters are passed, we will use a switch statement to determine from which array to pull the replacement image, and then perform the swap. We will use the following function for this task:

```
function rollImage(img, type){
  switch(type){
   case "over":
    document.images[img].src = overImg[img].src;
    break;
   case "out":
    document.images[img].src = defaultImg[img].src;
    break;
  }
}
```

The only other things we need to do at this point is complete the XHTML document, and make sure the proper event handlers are used within the <img> element. Because we want to create a rollover effect, we will be using the onmouseout and onmouseover handlers. The following is the completed code; Figure 10.7 shows one of the images rolled over.

```
<!DOCTYPE html PUBLIC "-//W3C//DTD XHTML 1.0 Transitional//EN"
      "http://www.w3.org/TR/xhtml1/DTD/xhtml1-transitional.dtd">
<html xmlns="http://www.w3.org/1999/xhtml" lang="en" xml:lang="en">
<head>
 <title>XHTML Essentials</title>
 <script type="text/javascript" language="JavaScript1.2">
 <!--

  // Create arrays to hold images
  var overImg = new Array();
  overImg[0] = new Image(24,24);
  overImg[1] = new Image(24,24);

  var defaultImg = new Array();
  defaultImg[0] = new Image(24,24);
  defaultImg[1] = new Image(24,24);

  // Preload images in the array
  overImg[0].src = "back-over.gif";
  overImg[1].src = "forward-over.gif";

  defaultImg[0].src = "back.gif";
  defaultImg[1].src = "forward.gif";

  // Change the state of image
  function rollImage(img,type){
   switch(type){
    case "over":
     document.images[img].src = overImg[img].src;
     break;
    case "out":
     document.images[img].src = defaultImg[img].src;
     break;
   }
  }
 //-->
 </script>
</head>
<body>
 <table border="1" cellpadding="5" cellspacing="0">
  <tr>
   <td align="center">
    <a href="javascript:void(0)"
       onmouseout="rollImage('0','out')"
       onmouseover="rollImage('0','over')">
      <img border="0" src="back.gif" width="24" height="24"
```

```
          alt="Back" />
    </a>
    </td>
    <td align="center">
     <a href="javascript:void(0)"
        onmouseout="rollImage('1','out')"
        onmouseover="rollImage('1','over')">
      <img border="0" src="forward.gif" width="24" height="24"
         alt="Forward" />
     </a>
    </td>
   </tr>
  </table>
 </body>
 </html>
```

Creating CSS Rollovers

To this point, we have focused completely on JavaScript to provide the interactivity for any dynamics. We want to include one last type of dynamic technique before we called it quits. In this section we are going to show you how to use CSS to create rollovers.

NOTE The functionality we are using for these rollovers was defined in CSS Level 2, so you must use Internet Explorer 5+ or Netscape 6+.

The functionality that we will be using revolves around a concept of pseudo-classes. As stated in the CSS Level 2 Recommendation, Section 5.10, "Pseudo-Elements and Pseudo-Classes" (www.w3.org/TR/REC-CSS2/selector.html#pseudo-elements), "Pseudo-classes classify elements on characteristics other than their name, attributes, or content; in principle, characteristics that cannot be deduced from the document tree. Pseudo-classes may be dynamic, in the sense that an element may acquire or lose a pseudo-class while a user interacts with the document."

The item we are most interested in is the hover class, which applies when a user designates an element without activating it. When applied to an <a> tag, for instance, you

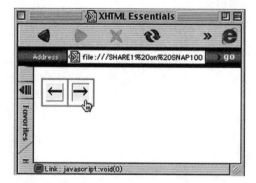

Figure 10.7 Rolling over an image.

can perform tasks such as change a link from being underlined or not. Applying this style is actually very simple. Here is a sample page with a single link:

```
<!DOCTYPE html PUBLIC "-//W3C//DTD XHTML 1.0 Transitional//EN"
    "http://www.w3.org/TR/xhtml1/DTD/xhtml1-transitional.dtd">
<html xmlns="http://www.w3.org/1999/xhtml" lang="en" xml:lang="en">
<head>
 <title>XHTML Essentials</title>
 <style type="text/css">
  a:hover{
   background-color: red;
   text-decoration: none;
   color: blue;
  }
 </style>
</head>
<body>
 <a href="http://www.wiley.com">Wiley!</a>
</body>
</html>
```

By including the style sheet in this document, the link will, when rolled over, change its background to red. In addition, the line under the link will be removed, and the color of the link will change to blue.

Summary

This chapter covered some of the most fun and complex topics in the Webmastering world; it also addressed many of the advanced uses of technology surrounding XHTML: tables, forms, and frames, style sheets, JavaScript, and, finally scripting XHTML documents. By now you should feel very comfortable using XHTML in the real world.

The final chapters in this book cover additional topics in the world of Web publishing. In the next chapter, we discuss metadata (data about data), followed by events, XHTML Basic (a slimmed down version of XHTML), and what to expect next from the HTML Working Group at the W3C.

Metadata

Metadata is defined as "data about data." When you write documents to be displayed on an electronic device, it is helpful to supply information about the document as a whole. This information can include details about how the document should be indexed and how the device should display the document.

In this chapter, we explain the proper use of metadata in the context of XHTML documents and their handling in today's browsers and search engines.

Defining the meta Element

Metadata is commonly referred to as meta tags, because the element used to place metadata into an XHTML document is <meta />.

NOTE As you work with the meta element, keep in mind the following three rules for its use: (1) It is an empty element, so, as you know by now, it must have the ending slash to properly close it. (2) It may not include any other elements. (3) Meta elements must be placed within the <head>...</head> of the document. If they are placed outside of that area, the browser will ignore them.

By itself, the meta element does not do anything. To impart any actual data, you must use a combination of its three available elements: name, http-equiv, and content.

In all cases, you must use one of the first two attributes followed by the content attribute. Which of the first two you use, name or http-equiv, depends on what you want the metadata to do for you: enable better indexing of your document or assert some control over the browser that is viewing the document. (Note that values for name and http-equiv may not contain spaces.)

Indexing Documents

Currently, the most common use for metadata is to supply information to search engines for indexing purposes. Today, when any Web document is indexed by an Internet-based search engine, such as HotBot or AltaVista, the search engine's indexing program, known as a spider, will access that document and index the source code—in our case, the XHTML code, not what the user sees in the browser. By using metadata, you, as a Web author, can choose the information in your document that will be indexed by the spider.

NOTE   Actually, users *can* see the information you identify for indexing if they use the view|source feature of the browser.

For this purpose, the two meta element attributes you need to use are name (which specifies the type of information being represented) and content (which contains the information described in the name attribute). Here is a one simple example:

```
<meta name="keywords" content="bond, movies, spies, spy, on her
majesty's secret service" />
```

Here, we are assigning a value of keywords to the name attribute. The content for the keyword metadata needs to be a comma-delimited list of keywords or key phrases that you would like the spider to index.
Here is another simple example:

```
<meta name="description" content="This page pays homage to the best
actor to ever play James Bond in the movies, George Lazenby" />
```

In this example, we have set a value of description to the name field. The content for the description metadata needs to be a narrative description of the document.
If we put these two meta elements together in a document, and place them in the appropriate location in the document code, we will have:

```
<head>
<title>The George Lazenby Fan Page</title>
<meta name="keywords" content="bond, movies, spies, spy, on her
majesty's secret service" />
<meta name="description" content="This page pays homage to the best
actor to ever play James Bond in the movies, George Lazenby" />
</head>
```

When a search engine's spider indexes this document, it will find this information and process it according to its own rules. That means that, though not all search engines will deal with this data in the same way, if at all, general standards have been established for indexing. Here is what will commonly happen:

1. The spider will index the words in the keyword metadata as if they were part of the document and give them a higher importance than words in the body of the document. This will occur regardless of whether these words actually appear in the body of the document. This is why, when you do a search on a word in an Internet-based search engine, you sometimes find a result in which your search word does not appear on the screen. If, however, you check the metadata, it is probably there.

2. When the spider finds the description metadata, it will set aside the narrative description to present to the user when the result is retrieved from a search.

Here is an example of the metadata from the home page or the Bibliographical Center for Research (BCR):

```
<head>
<title>BCR - Home Page</title>
<meta name="description" content="The Bibliographical Center for
Research (BCR) is organized as a nonprofit corporation to assist in the
effective and economical delivery of high-quality library and informa-
tion services."> <meta name="keywords" content="BCR, library services,
OCLC, FirstSearch, SilverPlatter, reference, database, cataloging,
Internet, Web, CD-ROM">
<meta name="author" content="Sharon Hoffhines">
</head>
```

NOTE Note in the preceding code the absence of trailing slashes on the meta elements. In this example (taken from a live document), I am using an HTML document not an XHTML document. To make this example XHTML-compliant, all you would need to do is add the trailing slash to appropriately close the element.

When a user conducts a search in, say, AltaVista for the keywords *oclc silverplatter*, that search engine will return the page shown in Figure 11.1. As you can see, because at least one of the search terms does not appear on the user's screen, AltaVista has found this document based on the metadata keywords. AltaVista has also used the metadata description field to describe the page to the searcher as part of the displayed result.

This example also demonstrates that some search engines have a set a limit on how much information they will allow—typically either a maximum word or character count. Here the description has been cut off after 22 words. To find out a search engine's limit, check the documentation.

Though, today, most Internet-based search engines pay attention only to keywords and description metadata, in the BCR example you can see one other metadata field, author:

```
<meta name="author" content="Sharon Hoffhines">
```

Why? In this case, it was included for an internal business purpose, not for indexing purposes. When the site was recently redesigned (fall 2000), the design committee decided that the organization wanted a way to track which employees had worked on which pages. Clearly, this information did not need to be displayed to users, so the designers decided to use metadata. They used a value of author for the name attribute, then entered a comma-delimited list of the names of those authors into the content field. Whenever someone else works on the document, that person adds his or her name to the metadata, so that the committee has an accurate trail of update procedures.

This use demonstrates that any value of the name attribute is valid. For example, we can create the following metadata on a document:

```
<meta name="author-education" content="MLS, University at Albany, 1995" />
<meta name="author-city" content="Aurora, CO" />
<meta name="copyright" content="2001" />
```

This example will be ignored by any search engine, but the information will be in the source code of the document, for reference purposes.

The Dublin Core

Another use for this type of metadata is for indexing by local, site-specific search engines. If you use a search engine that indexes and searches only your site, you may be able to program it to look for and index specific types of metadata for your site—the possibilities are endless. The potential downside of this capability is, of course, that

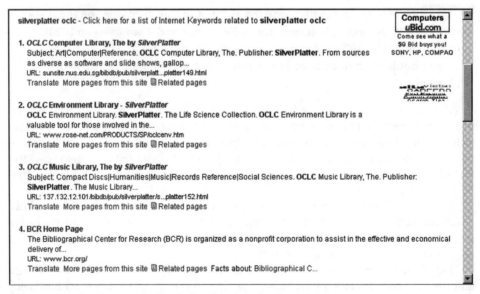

Figure 11.1 AltaVista results for the keywords *oclc silverplatter*.

indexing site may get worse instead of better—too many cooks spoiling the broth, as it were. However, at least one solution to this problem has been suggested.

The World Wide Web Consortium (W3C), along with Online Computer Library Center, Inc. (OCLC) and other organizations, has created a set of 15 choices for the name attribute, dubbed the "Dublin Core" (the Dublin here is in Ohio, the location of OCLC). The objective for establishing this set, which is currently under consideration as a standard, is to discourage users from making up their own values and use only those in this element set.

The Dublin Core was designed by librarians to address the needs for fully describing a document. The 15 values in the set are title, creator, subject, description, publisher, contributor, date, type, format, identifier, source, language, relation, coverage, and rights. According to the Dublin Core Web site (http://purl.org/DC/documents/rec-dces-19990702.htm) this is how each of them should be used:

Title
Definition: A name given to the resource.
Comment: Typically, a Title will be a name by which the resource is formally known.

Creator
Definition: An entity primarily responsible for making the content of the resource.
Comment: Examples of a Creator include a person, an organization, or a service. Typically, the name of a Creator should be used to indicate the entity.

Subject
Definition: The topic of the content of the resource.
Comment: Typically, a Subject will be expressed as keywords, key phrases, or classification codes that describe a topic of the resource. Recommended best practice is to select a value from a controlled vocabulary or formal classification scheme.

Description
Definition: An account of the content of the resource.
Comment: Description may include, but is not limited to: an abstract, table of contents, reference to a graphical representation of content, or a free-text account of the content.

Publisher
Definition: An entity responsible for making the resource available.
Comment: Examples of a Publisher include a person, an organization, or a service. Typically, the name of a Publisher should be used to indicate the entity.

Contributor
Definition: An entity responsible for making contributions to the content of the resource.
Comment: Examples of a Contributor include a person, an organization, or a service. Typically, the name of a Contributor should be used to indicate the entity.

Date
Definition: A date associated with an event in the life cycle of the resource.

Comment: Typically, Date will be associated with the creation or availability of the resource. Recommended best practice for encoding the date value is defined in a profile of ISO 8601 and follows the yyyy-mm-dd format.

Type
Definition: The nature or genre of the content of the resource.
Comment: Type includes terms describing general categories, functions, genres, or aggregation levels for content. Recommended best practice is to select a value from a controlled vocabulary (for example, the working draft list of Dublin Core Types. To describe the physical or digital manifestation of the resource, use the FORMAT element.

Format
Definition: The physical or digital manifestation of the resource.
Comment: Typically, Format may include the media-type or dimensions of the resource. Format may be used to determine the software, hardware, or other equipment needed to display or operate the resource. Examples of dimensions include size and duration. Recommended best practice is to select a value from a controlled vocabulary (for example, the list of Internet Media Types (MIME) defining computer media formats).

Identifier
Definition: An unambiguous reference to the resource within a given context
Comment: Recommended best practice is to identify the resource by means of a string or number conforming to a formal identification system. Example formal identification systems include the Uniform Resource Identifier (URI) (including the Uniform Resource Locator (URL)), the Digital Object Identifier (DOI), and the International Standard Book Number (ISBN).

Source
Definition: A Reference to a resource from which the present resource is derived.
Comment: The present resource may be derived from the Source resource in whole or in part. Recommended best practice is to reference the resource by means of a string or number conforming to a formal identification system.

Language
Definition: A language of the intellectual content of the resource.
Comment: Recommended best practice for the values of the Language element is defined by RFC 1766 [RFC1766] which includes a two-letter Language Code (taken from the ISO 639 standard [ISO639]), followed, optionally, by a two-letter Country Code (taken from the ISO 3166 standard [ISO3166]). For example, en for English, fr for French, or en-uk for English used in the United Kingdom.

Relation
Definition: A reference to a related resource.
Comment: Recommended best practice is to reference the resource by means of a string or number conforming to a formal identification system.

Coverage
Definition: The extent or scope of the content of the resource.

Comment: Coverage will typically include spatial location (a place name or geographic coordinates), temporal period (a period label, date, or date range), or jurisdiction (such as a named administrative entity). Recommended best practice is to select a value from a controlled vocabulary (for example, the Thesaurus of Geographic Names [TGN]) and that, where appropriate, named places or time periods be used in preference to numeric identifiers such as sets of coordinates or date ranges.

Rights
Definition: Information about rights held in and over the resource.
Comment: Typically, a Rights element will contain a rights management statement for the resource, or reference a service providing such information. Rights information often encompasses Intellectual Property Rights (IPR), Copyright, and various Property Rights. If the Rights element is absent, no assumptions can be made about the status of these and other rights with respect to the resource.

DCdot: The Dublin Core Metadata Editor

The U.K. Office for Library and Information Networking (UKOLN) has made available on the Web an automatic metadata generator known as DCdot. Since this is a library-related organization, which was involved in the creation of the Dublin Core, its metadata generator creates Dublin Core metadata. DCdot can be found at www.ukoln.ac.uk/metadata/dcdot/.

Let's give it a try on a Web site dedicated to L. E. Modesitt, Jr., the science fiction and fantasy author. We'll go to the site and enter the following URL into the available field:

```
www.webpan.com/msauers/modesitt/
```

After confirming that the "Attempt to determine DC.Publisher automatically" option is checked (why we do this is explained later), we click Submit.

By default, the results are generated in HTML, but because we are working in XHTML, let's translate to that. We can do this on the results page, via the "Display format" drop-down list. After choosing XHTML, we see the results shown in Figure 11.2.

Except for the line numbers, added to more easily identify the specific items, the code appears as shown here:

```
1. <link rel="schema.DC" href="http://purl.org/dc" />
2. <meta name="DC.Title" content="Recluce, The Unofficial L.E.
      Modesitt, Jr. Web Site" />
3. <meta name="DC.Subject" content="Frequently Asked Questions;
      Appearances; Recluce; Chronology; Reviews; Ephemera; Biography &
      Bibliography; Contacting; Publications; Advertisements; Buy the
      Books; Science Fiction; Maps; The Spellsong Cycle; Site News -
      11/29/00; The Octagonal Raven; Michael's Home; Pulp Fiction; The
      Works; Credits/Disclaimer; The Resources; Mailing List; Outside
      Links" />
4. <meta name="DC.Publisher" content="UUNET Technologies, Inc." />
5. <meta name="DC.Date" scheme="W3CDTF" content="2001-02-08" />
```

```
6. <meta name="DC.Type" scheme="DCMIType" content="Text" />
7. <meta name="DC.Format" content="text/html" />
8. <meta name="DC.Format" content="8413 bytes" />
9. <meta name="DC.Identifier" content="http://www.webpan.com/msauers/
   modesitt/" />
```

Let's take a look at each line the program has generated:

Line 1. A link statement allowing the browser to find the document describing the Dublin Core scheme.

Line 2. Extracts the content of the document's title element and copies it into the title metadata.

Line 3. Extracts keywords from the document and places them into the subject metadata field. This is the line that will need the most editing, as the program extracts keywords without regard to context. If, for example, you have a home link on the screen, one of the keyword may end up being "home," which, unless your document is about your home, is probably not relevant.

Line 4. The "publisher" of the document. Providing you checked this option, as specified earlier, this line will generate automatically. In this case, it picked UUNet as the publisher because somewhere in the larger picture of the Internet, the connection is from UUNet. Clearly, UUNet is not the publisher of this information, so this is an item that usually needs editing.

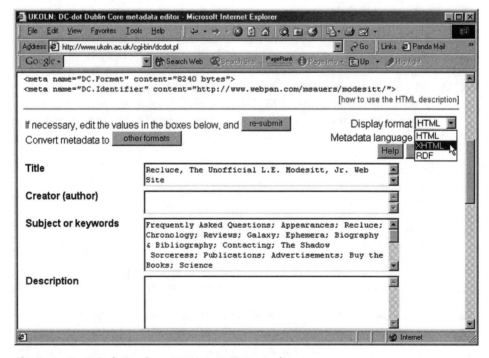

Figure 11.2 Translating from HTML to XHTML results.

CONTROLLING DESCRIPTIVE METADATA

An important issue to address is the lack of authority control or a controlled vocabulary in the use of meta elements. In short, this means that authors can use any words they want for indexing purposes. Therefore, some authors choose keywords that are not actually related to their document for the express purpose of getting more visitors. Though technically not allowed, and certainly unethical, without established controls, little can be done to stop it.

Another problem that can arise with the use of metadata is what is known as *keyword spamming*. This refers to the practice of repeating a particular keyword or set of keywords in an attempt to trick the search engine into regarding that word or words as important enough to give the page a higher ranking. (This can be done in either the metadata or in the body of the document.) In an effort to forestall this practice, many search engines have established an anti-keyword spamming policy, whereby words that appear more than a certain number of times will be ignored. Check the documentation of the search engine you're using for its policy.

Line 5. The date. In this case, DCdot has found the date on the page and used it as the date for this field. If the document has been updated since then, you will need to edit in the more recent date.

Line 6. The content type, in this case, text. Had the URL been for an Adobe Acrobat file, the result would have been different.

Lines 7 and 8. Identify the format of the document's data. This information is pulled from the HTTP headers sent with the document when it is requested. The data is the MIME content type (see Chapter 14 for more details on MIME types) and the length of the document in bytes.

Line 9. The identifier of the document. In non-Dublin Core parlance, the document's URL.

In most instances, this system is generally good for quick generation of metadata for your documents. With the few exceptions mentioned, little editing on your part will be required.

If, however, you find that you need to do more extensive editing of the generated code, you have two options for doing so. The first is to copy the existing code into your XHTML document from the Web page and then edit it by hand. The other option is to use the editing boxes further down the screen, as shown in Figure 11.3.

These fields contain the data as automatically generated in an editable format. You can edit the existing data and/or add more data to the fields. Once you have finished, all you need to do is click the Re-submit button. This will regenerate the code at the top of the page to include your changes. You can then copy the code and paste it into your document.

NOTE DCdot can also generate XML-based Resource Description Format (RDF) metadata through the "Display format" drop-down list. We discuss RDF at the end of the chapter. All told, DCdot can generate 11 different metadata formats. For more details on all of the possibilities, click on the Other formats button.

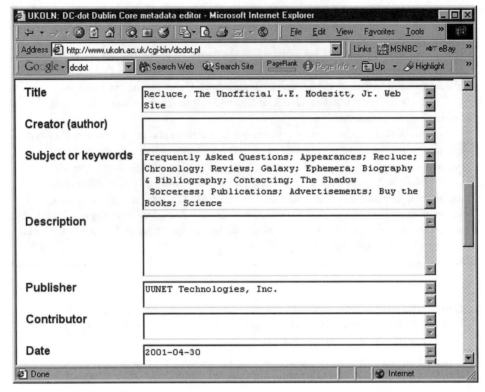

Figure 11.3 Using the DCdot editing fields.

Instituting Browser Control

This section introduces the second attribute available for the meta element, http-equiv, which can be used in place of name.

When documents are transferred using the Hypertext Transport Protocol (HTTP) method, certain additional information about what is being transferred is also sent. By using the HTTP-Equiv attribute we can simulate some of that information and cause the browser to act accordingly. Through the manipulation of these headers we can control for how long the document will be displayed and how the document will be cached; we can also control document content types, indexing, and relationships to other documents.

Refreshing the Document

During your travels on the Web you have most likely run across a page that looks like the one shown in Figure 11.4. After a few seconds, you automatically move to the next document, usually the new location of the Web site you were attempting to access. Have you even wondered how Web site authors do that? Here's how:

```
<meta http-equiv="Refresh" content="10; URL=http://www.foo.bar/file-
name.html" />
```

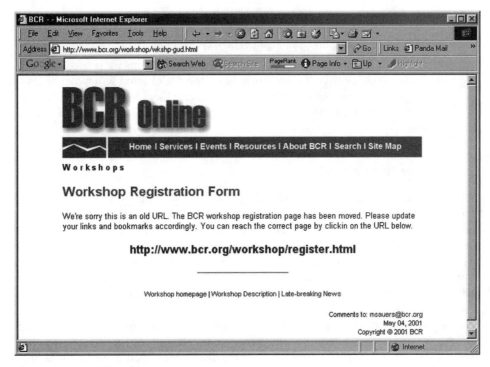

Figure 11.4   Redirecting users to a new screen.

This metadata, when included in the head of the document will cause the browser to wait 10 seconds and then load the document specified. This is commonly referred to as a *client-side redirect* since it is the browser requesting a new document of the server, not the server doing a forced send to the browser. It is mainly used when a page has moved and the author wants to send the user to the new location automatically.

Proper Use of a Redirect

When using a redirect, there are three important points to keep in mind:

- In the previous example, the number 10, representing the number of seconds the browser is to wait before performing the redirect, is followed by a semicolon, a space, URL=, and the address of the file the browser is to retrieve. Notice that this line of code contains two pairs of quotation marks. A common mistake is to insert an extra quotation mark after URL=; doing so will cause an odd number of quotation marks to exist, thus breaking the instruction. This is the only time in XHTML where an equal sign is not followed by a quotation mark.

- Some older browsers do not support this method of redirection, therefore it is always a good idea to supply a hyperlink on the current screen so that users can still get to the new address if the browser does not perform the redirect.

■ It is considered poor form to set a time limit of zero seconds, also known as an instantaneous redirect. The theory behind setting a zero wait is to automatically send the user to the new document, thus making the redirection nearly transparent. Unfortunately, this can cause serious problems for novice users. If they want to back out of the site, clicking on the Back button will return them to the page with the redirect, which will only send them forward again. To the users, it will seem as if they are trapped at the site. This is a sure way to lose visitors.

Controlling the Cache

Whenever a document and all its related files are displayed by a browser, a copy of those files, called a *cookie*, is stored on the user's computer, usually on the hard drive but also temporarily in memory, to enable faster retrieval in the future. The length of time a cookie is stored in the cache of a user's computer is based upon the size of that user's hard drive. The larger the hard drive, the larger the cache, hence the longer a copy of your document will remain on the user's computer. The browser stores newer cookie files in the "front" of the cache and deletes the oldest files from the "back" when it needs the space.

Though users can set their browser to check for updated versions of your document, many don't or don't know how or why they should. This can cause problems for you, especially if the content of your document changes often or on a specific schedule. Obviously, some users may be looking at an old copy of your document stored in their cache instead of the most recent updated version. Fortunately, through use of the http-equiv attribute on the meta element, you can instruct the user's browser on how to cache your document.

Setting an Expiration Date

Let's say that you have a document you update every Sunday night, and you want to be sure that your users see the latest version of the document come Monday morning. Here's the code for instructing your users' browser to get a fresh copy of your document:

```
<meta http-equiv="expires" content="Mon, 15 Jan 2001 00:00:01 GMT" />
```

By including this line of code in the head of your document you set an expiration date on the copy of the document in the users' cache. After the specified date and time, the cache copy will be rendered invalid and the browser will be forced to go back to the originating server and retrieve a fresh copy of the document.

To set the date and time, you must follow the format that you see in the example: a three-letter abbreviation of the day, followed by a comma and a space; then a two-digit date, another space: a three-letter abbreviation of the month, a space; a four-digit year; two-digit hour, a colon; two-digit minute, a colon; two-digit second, a space; and, finally, a three-letter time zone.

The example here uses Greenwich Mean Time, but the other standard three-letter time zones are also valid. So, if you live in Colorado, you can use the Mountain Standard Time (MST) time zone. The user's browser will adjust the time accordingly for his or her local time.

Preventing Caching of the Document

You can also prevent the browser from caching the document. There are two ways to do this, one indirect but reliable, the other direct but not as reliable. Which you choose depends on your situation.

The indirect route, though reliable, actually only simulates noncaching, by setting the expiration date to a date in the past. What you are really doing is allowing the browser to cache the document, but never use it. Since the page will always be considered expired, a fresh copy will be retrieved every time.

The direct method is to use the following metadata:

```
<meta http-equiv="Pragma" content="no-cache">
```

This method actually does prevent the document from being cached. Because there is no cached copy, a new copy will be retrieved each time. The problem with this method is that it is not as reliable as the indirect method. If there are any proxies or gateways between your server and the user, they may not be set up to accept this metadata, in which case, the command will be ignored. Furthermore, this only prevents the caching of the XHTML code. Any associated files, including images, will be cached.

Controlling Indexing

The http-equiv attribute can also be used to control whether or not to you want your document indexed at all. By setting http-equiv to a value of robot, you instruct the search engine's spider (also known as a robot) either to index or not index the current page and/or any pages to which it links. The available values for content in this case are as follows:

all. Allows all of the files to be indexed (this is the default value).

none. Does not index the current page or any linked pages.

index. Allows the page to be indexed.

noindex. Prevents the page from being indexed.

follow. Allows the spider to proceed to linked pages for indexing.

nofollow. Prevents the spider from proceeding to linked pages for indexing.

Let's say you want a page to be indexed but don't want the spider to follow any links on that page in order to index them. To achieve this, you would write the following code:

```
<meta http-equiv="robots" content="index, nofollow" />
```

If, on the other hand, you would like to prevent the current page and all linked pages from being indexed, you could write either of the following codes:

```
<meta http-equiv="robots" content="none" />
<meta http-equiv="robots" content="noindex, nofollow" />
```

STYLE TYPES

As described in Chapter 8, when using the <style> element it is good practice to include the type attribute so the browser knows which style language you are using. It is possible to specify the type of style code being used through metadata. The following code specifies that we are using CSS for our style sheet language.

```
<meta http-equiv="content-style-type" content="text/css" />
```

Unfortunately, most current browsers will ignore this metadata.

Introducing the Resource Description Framework

The Resource Description Framework (RDF) is the next stage in metadata presentation in XML documents. RDF was created as a way to describe a document through metadata in a more robust manner than provided for in previous specifications. For example, RDF makes it easier for computers to index and retrieve your documents.

NOTE Because most current Internet-based search engines do not support RDF, this section is intended only as an introduction. For more information, pick up a book on XML or visit one of the many excellent online resources including the RDF page on the W3C site (www.w3.org/RDF/) and Dave Beckett's RDF Resource Guide (www.ilrt.bris.ac.uk/discovery/rdf/resources/).

RDF enables you to represent your data in any scheme you choose, thereby giving you greater flexibility. The following is an example of an RDF file representing The World Wide Web Library Directory:

```
<?xml version="1.0"?>
<!DOCTYPE rdf:RDF SYSTEM "http://purl.org/dc/schemas/dcmes-xml-
20000714.dtd">
<rdf:RDF  xmlns:rdf="http://www.w3.org/1999/02/22-rdf-syntax-ns#"
          xmlns:dc="http://purl.org/dc/elements/1.1/">
<rdf:Description about="http://www.webpan.com/msauers/libdir/">
   <dc:title>
     The World Wide Web Library Directory
   </dc:title>
   <dc:subject>
     Web sites of libraries from around the world
   </dc:subject>
```

```
      <dc:date>
        2001-02-11
      </dc:date>
      <dc:type>
        Text
      </dc:type>
      <dc:format>
        text/html
      </dc:format>
      <dc:format>
        15226 bytes
      </dc:format>
    </rdf:Description>
</rdf:RDF>
```

NOTE This code was originally generated using the DCdot service described earlier, and then modified for use here.

Notice the differences between the XHTML <meta /> and the RDF format. In RDF, each value for name has become its own element. Also note that each element is preceded by "dc:" to indicate that we are using the Dublin Core metadata scheme.

Although this is a much more complex method of representing a document, it is much more robust, as a computer processing this data can focus on particular pieces of descriptive data.

Summary

This chapter demonstrated that, through the use of the <meta> element in your code, you can improve the odds that search engines will retrieve and index your documents. You also learned that metadata can give you some control over how a user's browser displays and caches your documents.

Events

In the early days of the Internet, HTML documents were static, offering little or no interactivity; and the presentation process was simple: the browser requested a document from a server, the server delivered, and the browser rendered. At that point, the user could either type in a new URL or click on a link to request another document. But as time went on, and document interactivity became more complex, Web developers began to demand greater control over user actions. They wanted to know, for example, when a user "rolled over" an image, or entered text into a form field. As we discussed in Chapter 9, JavaScript was the programming language that gave Web developers the capability to accomplish these tasks. But we didn't explain how.

In this chapter, therefore, we are going to discuss XHTML events, which reference the actions that users take while viewing an XHTML document. For instance, when a user clicks on a link, the action "fires" an event within the browser. Typically, the browser handles this event by requesting the linked page. But browsers with scripting language support also expose that event for scripting, enabling the developer to process the event, or even to override the default behavior of the browser.

Defining an Event

Perhaps the most basic way to define an event is as an action. In the case of Web documents, actions—events—may be initiated by the users or the developers of those documents. For the purpose of this chapter, we're more interested in events initiated by developers. The introduction of markup languages gave developers the ability to control events, by giving them the ability to add interactivity to their pages, to set events to occur at certain times, to handle errors, and even to conduct some preprocessing of data before submitting to a server.

Understanding Event Handlers

In this section we talk about the events that were defined for the first time in HTML 4 and that exist today in XHTML 1.0, and we are going to touch on how they can be used with scripting languages. In Chapters 9 and 10 we went over some of these, but here we will discuss them in more detail as they pertain to XHTML.

As just stated, HTML 4 was the first version of the hypertext markup language to support the exposure of events within a document. In HTML 4 were defined a group of *intrinsic events* that exposed certain elements within a document. These events were supported by attributes known as *event handlers* placed within the elements.

Event-Handling Attributes and the Example Template

Event handlers allowed the Web developer to set a string of scripting code as the value of the attribute to be executed when an event was invoked. So, for instance, if the Web developer, using JavaScript as the scripting language, wanted an alert box to pop up when a user clicked on an image, he or she might have written something like the following:

```
<img src="http://www.w3.org/Icons/valid-xhtml10"
    alt="Valid XHTML 1.0!" height="31" width="88"
    onclick="alert('You clicked!')" />
```

Focus on the onclick attribute and its value. In human terminology, this basically says, "If the user clicks on this element (remember, it is an image), then call the alert( ) method of the JavaScript language, passing it the phrase 'You clicked!' When this example is run in a supporting browser, it displays as shown in Figure 12.1, with an alert box that pops up when the user clicks on the image.

The general syntax for these event handlers is as given in the following code sample, where *eventhandler* is the name of the event handler, and *code* is the code that should be executed when the event is invoked.

```
eventhandler="code"
```

For all of the examples in this section we will use the same XHTML document template. Other than the event handler name, very little else will change from one example to the next, so there is no need to write each one out fully. The template is as follows:

```
<!DOCTYPE html PUBLIC "-//W3C//DTD XHTML 1.0 Transitional//EN"
        "http://www.w3.org/TR/xhtml1/DTD/xhtml1-transitional.dtd">
```

```
<html xmlns="http://www.w3.org/1999/xhtml" lang="en" xml:lang="en">
<head>
  <title>XHTML Essentials</title>
  <script type="text/javascript">
    function myEventFunction(type){
       alert('You just invoked the ' + type + ' event!');
     }
  </script>
</head>
<body>
 <!--
     place event handler examples here unless told otherwise
  -->
</body>
</html>
```

Document Handlers

The first group of event handlers we are going to discuss impact the entire XHTML document. These are events that you use when you need to perform a task that is applicable to the entire document.

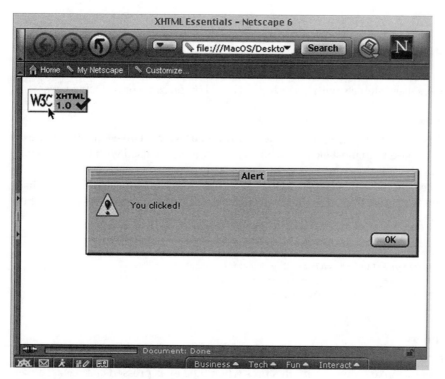

Figure 12.1 Handling an onclick event.

onload

The onload event is fired when the user agent finishes loading a window or all the frames within a <frameset>. The corresponding event handler can be used with both <body> and <frameset> elements, and often is responsible for calling functions that initialize variables for scripts. Here's the syntax:

```
<body onload="myEventFunction('onload')">
```

onunload

The onunload event is fired when the user agent finishes unloading a window or all the frames within a <frameset>. The corresponding event handler can be used with both <body> and <frameset> elements, and often is responsible for calling functions that clear, or pass, variables within scripts.

In this example code, because we need a method of unloading a document from the browser, we have included a link. After clicking on the link, the current document is cleared from memory to make way for a newly requested document. Here, as you can see, at the Wiley Web site, the event is fired and an alert box pops up.

```
<body onunload="myEventFunction('onunload')">
<p>
  <a href="http://www.wiley.com">Wiley!</a>
</p>
</body>
```

Keyboard

The event handlers in this section are those invoked from the keyboard—that is, they fire when a user interacts with his or her keyboard by pressing or releasing keys.

onkeydown

The onkeydown event occurs when a key is pressed down over an element. This attribute may be used with most elements, but is most commonly used with form elements, specifically buttons.

In our example for this event, we have taken our form and attached the event handler to the text field. If the user clicks inside the field and then presses a keyboard button, the event is fired and the function is called.

```
<form action="null">
  <input type="text" value="Try to type here"
         onkeydown="myEventFunction('onkeydown')" />
  <input type="submit" value="Submit" />
</form>
```

onkeypress

The onkeypress event occurs when a key is pressed and released over an element. Similar to the onkeydown event, this fires when the key is pressed *and* released over an element.

```
<form action="null">
  <input type="text" value="Try to type here"
         onkeypress="myEventFunction('onkeypress')" />
  <input type="submit" value="Submit" />
</form>
```

onkeyup

The onkeyup event occurs when a key is released over an element. This is the inverse of the onkeydown event, but functions in a similar manner.

```
<form action="null">
  <input type="text" value="Try to type here"
         onkeyup="myEventFunction('onkeyup')" />
  <input type="submit" value="Submit" />
</form>
```

Pointing Devices

The next type of event is fired by the actions of the user's pointing device, today still commonly a mouse, although the advent of wireless technologies will certainly introduce new methods of input. These are some of the most common events you will find captured and used within today's Web pages.

onclick

The onclick event, which may be captured with most elements, occurs when a mouse button is clicked over an element. Some of the more common elements on which you may use this handler are <img>, <input type="submit" />, <input type="reset" />, <input type="button" />, <button>, and <a>. Refer back to the code sample for this event given at the beginning of the chapter.

ondblclick

The ondblclick event is much like the onclick event, except that it occurs when the mouse button is double-clicked over an element. Currently, you do not see this event handler used very much, although you may find it useful if you are building a Web-based application, and want the look and feel to be similar to Windows or Mac operating systems.

```
<form action="null">
  <input type="button" value="Double Click Me!"
         ondblclick="myEventFunction('ondblclick')" />
</form>
```

onmousedown

The onmousedown event occurs when a mouse button is pressed over an element. You see this used often when developers are trying to simulate buttons within major applications, such as Microsoft Word. When the user clicks on a button, it is shown in a depressed state. This state is triggered by the onmousedown event.

```
<p>
  <a href="http://www.wiley.com" onmousedown="myEventFunction('onmouse-
down')">
    Wiley!</a>
</p>
```

onmousemove

The onmousemove event occurs when a mouse is moved while it is over an element. This is commonly used in creating dynamic XHTML. For instance, if you create a dragable layer, you want the layer to move when the mouse does. Using this event handler within the element you used to create the layer, you could accomplish this task.

In this example, we capture this event within the <body> element. This means that as soon as the user move his or her mouse over the document loaded in the browser, the alert dialog with pop up.

```
<body onmousemove="myEventFunction('onmousemove')">
```

But note, because the alert box is called every time the mouse is moved, the user cannot click the OK button to stop the script from running. As soon he or she does, the box pops up again. The solution is to move the mouse outside of the document-rendering part of the browser, and then hit the Return or Enter key to close the alert box.

onmouseout

The onmouseout event occurs when a mouse is moved away from an element. This happens after the onmouseover event is fired. In our example, notice that the event does not fire when the user rolls "into" the area of the link, rather, when he or she rolls out of it. This may have to be done slowly, but it should be obvious how it works.

```
<p>
  <a href="http://www.wiley.com"
     onmouseout="myEventFunction('onmouseout')">
     Wiley!</a>
</p>
```

onmouseover

The onmouseover event occurs when a mouse is moved onto an element. This event is fired as soon as the mouse pointer enters into the area created by the element. It is the inverse of the onmouseout event that we just discussed.

```
<p>
  <a href="http://www.wiley.com"
     onmouseover="myEventFunction('onmouseover')">
     Wiley!</a>
</p>
```

onmouseup

The onmouseup event occurs when a mouse button is released over an element. Developers use this to simulate buttons within major applications, such as Microsoft Word.

When the user releases a click, the event returns to its default state, triggered by the onmouseup event.

```
<p>
  <a href="http://www.wiley.com"
  onmouseup="myEventFunction('onmouseup')">
  Wiley!</a>
</p>
```

Form

Event handlers and forms go together like peanut butter and jelly. Whether you are validating information entered by the user or verifying that all fields have been successfully addressed, using event handlers with your forms can mean less processing on the server-side.

onreset

The onreset event occurs when a form is reset; it can only be used within the <form> element. Although this event is rarely captured, it can be used to prompt the user to verify that he or she wants to reset the form data. This is especially useful when the form is long, containing numerous fields that must be filled out.

```
<form action="null" onreset="myEventFunction('onreset')">
  <input type="text" value="Try to type here" />
  <input type="submit" value="Submit" />
  <input type="reset" />
</form>
```

onselect

The onselect event occurs when a user selects some text in a text field. This event handler can be used only within the <input> and <textarea> elements. Note that, in the past, this event had some browser implementation issues, though these seem to be solved now.

```
<form action="null">
  <input type="text" value="Select some text"
  onselect="myEventFunction('onselect')" />
</form>
```

onsubmit

The onsubmit event occurs when a form is submitted to the server. This event handler can be used only within the <form> element.

```
<form action="null" onsubmit="myEventFunction('onsubmit')">
  <input type="text" value="Try to type here" />
  <input type="submit" value="Submit" />
  <input type="reset" />
</form>
```

Other Events

These are the elements that do not fall into any one category; they may be used in many different contexts.

onblur

The onblur event is a bit unusual. It occurs when an element loses focus, caused by mouse clicking or keyboard tabbing away. Its counterpart is the onfocus event, which fires when focus is securely on an element.

One of the most common uses of this event is within form elements. Let's say you want to verify that a user has entered a correctly formatted phone number before moving to the next field. Using the onblur event handler, you could call a function that processed the data in the field and then alerted the user to any errors. This attribute may be used with the <a>, <area>, <label>, <input>, <select>, <textarea>, and <button> elements.

Here is a simple form with a single text field and a submit button. By clicking in the text field and then pressing the Tab key, the focus changes to the Submit button. An alert box appears as soon this operation is performed.

```
<form action="null">
  <input type="text" value="" onblur="myEventFunction('onblur')" />
  <input type="submit" value="Submit" />
</form>
```

onchange

The onchange event is somewhat similar to the onblur event. It is invoked when an element loses the input focus *and* its value has been modified since gaining focus. This attribute, which applies only to <input>, <select>, and <textarea>, is often used to reset values that are not supposed to change within these elements.

We'll use the same example as for onblur, but add some text in the text field and, of course, change the event handler. This results in:

```
<form action="null">
  <input type="text" value="Change This!"
         onchange="myEventFunction('onchange')" />
  <input type="submit" value="Submit" />
</form>
```

onfocus

Remember from the description of onblur, the onfocus event occurs when an element receives focus either by clicking the mouse or tapping on the keyboard. This attribute may be used with the <a>, <area>, <label>, <input>, <select>, <textarea>, and <button> elements. As you can see, the example of this handler is very similar to that of onblur as well:

```
<form action="null">
  <input type="text" value="Click in here!"
         onfocus="myEventFunction('onfocus')" />
```

```
    <input type="submit" value="Submit" />
</form>
```

The onfocus event completes our coverage of the intrinsic events within XHTML. At this point, you now understand the scripting languages, the concepts of scripting documents, and the events that you can use to call your scripts and perform tasks.

But we want to also keep you apprised of ongoing work being done to improve XHTML capabilities, so the focus of the rest of this chapter is on the effort under way at the W3C to define next-generation events. This effort is geared toward defining and finalizing the XHTML Events Recommendation.

Introducing the XHTML Events Module

As you now recognize, events are powerful features that you, the Web developer, can include in your documents. However, the current implementation only allows for certain types of events to be captured and acted upon. And with the adoption of the Document Object Model (DOM), the model for accessing document elements slightly steers from the idea of having a common object model API. This is where the XHTML Events module comes into the picture.

Briefly, XHTML is going through a modularization process, whereby the language is being broken into several modules, such as Tables and Forms (described more fully in Chapters 13 and 14). The XHTML Events module will provide XHTML *host languages* with the capability to integrate events and other behaviors with the DOM Level 2 Events interface. And because different host languages will support different modules, a common event module is needed to interact and expose the documents to the DOM. The XHTML Events module will fill this need. This interface has many advantages, including the following:

- Generic event system
- Capability to register event handlers
- Capability to route events through a tree structure
- Context information about events
- System of processing, through capture, bubbling, and canceling of events

NOTE Check out www.w3.org/TR/DOM-Level-2-Events for more information on the DOM Level 2 Events Recommendation.

Because the XHTML Events module is currently in a public Working Draft state—meaning that the details of its implementation are sure to change—in this section, we focus on the core theories of this effort, and try to steer clear of those aspects most likely to change. We begin by taking a look at this module and the elements and attributes that comprise it.

NOTE Be sure to read the final Recommendation when it becomes available, at www.w3.org/TR/xhtml-events.

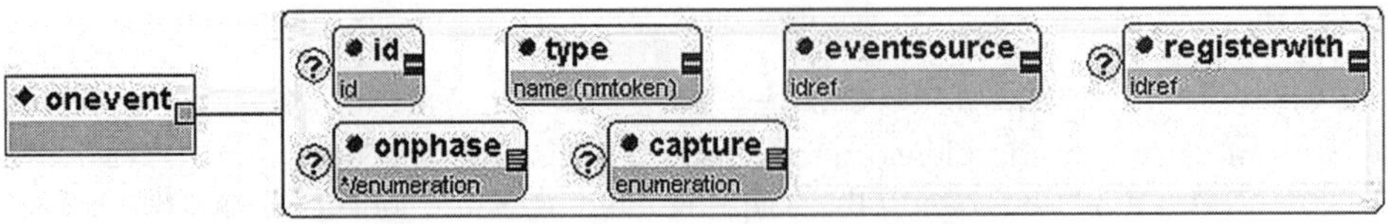

Figure 12.2 Visualizing the <onevent> element and its attributes.

Examining the Events Module

In this section, we cover the elements currently defined as of this writing, along with the naming of events.

Elements

There are three elements within the current XHTML Events module. The first is the <onevent> element. It provides the ability to register an event listener with the element's parent or the element specified in the registerwith attribute. Figure 12.2 provides a visual representation of the element and its attributes, and Table 12.1 contains a list of its current attributes and their descriptions.

The second element currently defined in the XHTML Events module is the action element. This element provides a mechanism for binding an event handler to an event listener. As a child of the <onevent> element, the action defined in this element is invoked when the event defined in <onevent> is seen. Table 12.2 contains the current attributes for the <action> element.

The final element currently defined is <stopevent>. As its name implies, this element is used to stop the propagation of an event after it has been handled. It is equivalent to the stopPropagation method in DOM Level 2. For those of you familiar with programming languages, this is your break statement. This element only has one attribute, id, which like the other elements, holds a document-unique identifier.

Table 12.1 Attributes of the <onevent> Element

ATTRIBUTE	DESCRIPTION
capture	Boolean attribute that specifies whether the specified element is to be captured.
eventsource	Specifies the node within the document that dispatched the event. If specified, only events that match this value and that of the type attribute will be considered.
id	Document-unique identifier.
onphase	Specifies when the event listener can see the event.
registerwith	Registers an event listener with the element, located through its id value, specified by this attribute.
type	Specifies the DOM Level 2 event type.

Table 12.2 Attributes of the <action> Element

ATTRIBUTE	DESCRIPTION
id	Document-unique identifier.
href	Links to an external or internal associated behavior.
type	Used as a hint to the content-type of the object pointed to by the href attribute.

NOTE **Want to know the namespace for the XHTML Events module? It uses www.w3.org/1999/xhtml.**

Event Naming

The naming of events, which is stored in the type attribute of the <onevent> element, is left entirely up to you, the Web developer. However, the XHTML Events module does recommend that to avoid confusion and collision between qualified names and event names you use the following syntax:

```
event_prefix-event_type_name
```

The hyphen between the prefix and the name is inserted to prevent confusion when namespaces are used to include other attributes and elements within your document.

The XHTML Events module also specifies event names as they correspond to their DOM equivalent. These are listed in Table 12.3, and are current at the time of this writ-

Table 12.3 Comparison of XHTML Event Type Names with DOM Level 2 Event Names

XHTML EVENT NAME	DOM EVENT NAME
dom-click	click
dom-mousedown	click
dom-mousemove	click
dom-mouseout	click
dom-mouseover	click
dom-mouseup	click
html-abort	abort
html-blur	blur
html-change	change
html-dblclick	not specified
html-error	error

continues

(Continued)

XHTML EVENT NAME	DOM EVENT NAME
html-focus	focus
html-keydown	not specified
html-keypress	not specified
html-keyup	not specified
html-load	load
html-reset	reset
html-scroll	scroll
html-select	select
html-submit	submit
html-resize	resize
html-unload	unload

ing. No doubt you will immediately notice the similarity of the names defined here to those of the intrinsic events discussed at the beginning of the chapter.

Using Events

As a reminder, before we delve into the examples for using XHTML Events, keep in mind that the status of this effort is still in the Working Draft state, and things will change, most likely syntactically or semantically. And because there will be changes, the examples here demonstrate the syntactical theories, rather than the absolute syntax. For example, we will include comments where event handlers will be placed, rather than placing event handlers explicitly.

Registering Listeners

Registering an event listener is basically like assigning a value for one of the intrinsic event attributes, described at the beginning of the chapter. You are telling the user agent that you want it to pass the specified event to the specified handler for process, thereby putting it in your control.

XHTML Events allow for two different approaches to accomplish this. The first is to define the listener as a child element of the element to which you want to apply the listener. For instance, if you want to "listen in" on a specific pull-down menu option when it is selected (receives focus), you could do the following:

```
<option value="comp" id="comp-option">Computer
  <onevent id="my-event" type="html-focus">
    <!-- define desired event handler here -->
  </onevent>
</option>
```

The second approach is to use the registerwith attribute of the <onevent> element, as follows:

```
<onevent id="my-event" registerwith="comp-option" type="html-focus">
  <!-- define desired event handler here -->
</onevent>
<option value="comp" id="comp-option">Computer</option>
```

Bubbling Events

The concept of *bubbling* may be new to you, but it is not a new concept. Here's how it works: If, for instance, you want to expose an event after it has been processed, it is best to define your <onevent> element as a child of the targeted element's parent. This will allow you to apply the same <onevent> for multiple child elements of the parent.

In the following example, we have defined my-event as a child of the *newscontent* paragraph. By setting the onphase attribute of the <onevent> element to bubbling, we can apply the event to both images, which are descendants of the original *newscontent* paragraph:

```
<p id="newscontent">
  <onevent id="my-event" type="dom-click" onphase="bubbling">
    <!-- define desired event handler here -->
  </onevent>
  <img id="firstimg" src="/images/one.gif" alt="One" />
  <p id="sportsnews">
    <img id="secondimg" src="/images/two.gif" alt="Two" />
  </p>
</p>
```

In this example, if the user clicks on one.gif, the event will be propagated from *newscontent* to *firstimg*, and then back to *newscontent*. If two.gif is clicked on, the event will be propagated from *newscontent* to *sportsnews*, and then to *secondimg* before reversing and going back up the same path. Remember that two.gif is actually a child of the *sportsnews* paragraph, which is why we must go through it on the way down and back.

Overriding Events

Once you start bubbling events, you are sure to come across a situation where you do not want all child elements within a parent to be exposed to the event. In this case, you will need to override the event using the <stopevent> element. Take a look at how we would do this, building on our previous example:

```
<p id="newscontent">
  <onevent id="my-event" type="dom-click" onphase="bubbling">
    <!-- define desired event handler here -->
  </onevent>
  <img id="firstimg" src="/images/one.gif" alt="One" />
  <p id="sportsnews">
    <img id="secondimg" src="/images/two.gif" alt="Two" />
  </p>
```

```
        <img id="thirdimg" src="/images/three.gif" alt="Three">
          <onevent id="my-secondevent" type="dom-mouseover">
            <!-- define desired event handler here -->
            <stopevent />
          </onevent>
        </img>
      </p>
```

Here, we added a third image. As a child of that element, we defined a new event, *my-secondevent*, and gave it a different type. However, this time we included the <stopevent> element as a child of the <onevent> element, which prevents the bubbling up of events for this instance. Since the events do not bubble up, the *my-event* event will not have access, nor will it be able to execute its handler.

Interfacing with DOM Level 2 Events Using the XHTML Basic Events Module

The XHTML Events module will contain a lot of interfaces to the DOM Level 2 Events, which may be overkill for some simple applications and devices. For this reason, the Working Group has also defined a Basic Events module as part of their work. In this final section, we touch briefly on this module, so you are aware of what you may expect from it when it is complete.

Uses for the Basic Events Module

As wireless devices and other Web-accessing appliances begin to proliferate, a need for simpler languages and functionality emerges. Simply, these devices do not require all the bells and whistles that Web browsers running on today's powerful computers need; in contrast, they require only a small functionality set.

One prime example of this is the wireless phone. Due to limited screen size and memory, only so much content can appear on these devices. As a content provider, you do not want to adversely impact your user's experience by including, say, animations and interactivity. The XHTML Basic Events module is the answer.

Available Attributes

The XHTML Basic Events module supports a subset of the attributes described for the larger module. Additionally, the binding they represent is simplified by the fact the event listeners appear as child elements of the targeted node. This precludes the need to resolve element bindings for elements that have not been loaded into the DOM tree. The supported attributes are:

- id
- type
- onphase
- capture

Summary

We've said it before, but it bears repeating: Events are a very powerful and useful feature for Web developers; their implementation has been one of the greatest enhancements developed for this type of markup language. Without them, we would be restricted to plain vanilla static documents with about as much interest as a brick wall.

In the next chapter we are going to talk about one of the newest standards from the W3C to make it to a full Recommendation—XHTML Basic. We conclude the book with a short chapter on what else is happening and what you can expect next in the XHTML arena.

XHTML Basic

In the late 1990s, Web developers and Webmasters had to build content for only one type of user agent—Web browsers. To do this, they used the HTML markup language to tag and format their content. Since then, many aspects of this process have changed: in particular, HTML has evolved into XHTML, and abstract formatting has given way to the use of cascading style sheets (CSS). There has also been a major shift in the user agents—the devices to which Web developers deliver their content.

Until recently, based on the limitations of the various Web browsers in use, developers typically took one of two approaches for providing content: They either used the older, more widely adopted HTML 3.2 version, which did not contain many enhancements such as frames and scripting support, or they worked with the user agent and device manufacturers to define their own language to mark up their content. The latter approach, as can be imagined, caused increased difficulty for the Web developer. A number of new markup languages emerged, among them the Wireless Markup Language (WML) and Compact HTML; then, with the widespread emergence and adoption of the wireless Web, mobile phones, interactive TV, and a variety of other devices based on Internet-style content delivery, developers faced not just multiple markup languages, but multiple user agents.

Clearly, the Web developers were facing a major challenge. And though some tools and servers became available to help meet the challenge, such as the Apache Cocoon (http://xml.apache.org/cocoon) and Enhydra (http://enhydra.enhydra.org), these products did not always solve the task at hand, and could often be overkill for the smaller or medium-sized sites. A more overarching solution was needed. The W3C calls that solution XHTML Basic, the focus of this chapter.

Defining XHTML Basic

XHTML Basic is a recent W3C Recommendation produced by the HTML Working Group. The objective of the group in this effort was to take the requirements of other languages such as Compact HTML and WML, and create a new language with a common core set of elements—as opposed to defining still more new languages for specific devices. Specifically, this effort applied the concepts of XHTML modularization, a topic we introduced in the previous chapter, and which we go into more fully in Chapter 14. The basic idea of modularization is to break up the XHTML 1.0 language into modules that address certain types of functionality, such as tables, forms, or scripting.

NOTE To read more about the Modularization of XHTML Recommendation, go to www.w3.org/MarkUp.

The approach was actually quite simple. Link certain of the core modules from the XHTML modularization effort to form what is, essentially, a subset of XHTML. This new language—XHTML Basic—will serve as the foundation, a minimum requirements set of elements for publishing Web-related content.

Meeting the Needs of Web Devices

Although XHTML Basic can be used to accomplish a variety of different tasks, its most relevant use currently is to produce content for delivery to Internet appliances and other wireless devices. Like computers, these devices are becoming more advanced and powerful every day, but because they are very small, hence have more strict limitations as to the amount and complexity of data they can process and render, they present some specific challenges to the Web developer.

It is to address the inherent limitations of these devices that XHTML Basic was developed. One goal of the HTML Working Group was to create an XHTML document type that offered a rich tagging scheme for defining content and could be shared across technologies, including TV, mobile phones, and kiosks. And because these various devices support different functionality (for example, as what happens after a menu item is selected), this language had to be flexible and extensible.

Establishing Requirements

As part of the recommendation, the Working Group has listed a number of the devices to which this effort is geared. You can think of these as the test cases for the language. The list, as published at www.w3.org/TR/2000/REC-xhtml-basic-20001219, is as follows:

- Mobile phones
- Televisions
- PDAs
- Vending machines
- Pagers
- Car navigation systems

- Mobile game machines
- Digital book readers
- Smart watches

In addition, to cover all the needs of previously defined languages, as well as to lay a foundation for extensibility, the group also examined the WML from the WAP Forum (www.wapforum.org), and Compact HTML for Small Information Appliances (www.w3.org/TR/1998/NOTE-compactHTML-19980209). In analyzing these languages, the group found some overlapping areas. These include:

- Meta information, which is often used to provide additional descriptors about the content.
- Basic text, including headings, paragraphs, and lists.
- Hyperlinks and links to other documents and objects.
- Images that could be contained in the content.
- Basic forms for data collection and submission.
- Basic tables for describing information in a tabular format.

The group had its work cut out for it: XHTML Basic would have to fill a lot of gaps and meet divergent needs. It had to be flexible enough for implementation across a wide range of platforms, and at the same time be able to support a core set of functionality.

Acknowledging Limitations

As you will see, though XHTML Basic goes a long way to filling the gaps and meeting the needs, it does have some limitations you, as a developer need to be aware of. First, as a subset of the XHTML 1.0 Recommendation, XHTML Basic excludes certain items. Some have been left out for obvious reasons, while others have been removed in favor of other methods for accomplishing the same thing. Table 13.1 outlines what has been left out, and why.

Table 13.1   XHTML 1.0 Exclusions from XHTML Basic

EXCLUSION	DESCRIPTION
Event handlers	Event handlers, such as onclick, onmouseover, and onload are not supported because the corresponding scripting languages necessary to process events have been excluded.
Forms	Basic forms, as defined by the Modularization of XHTML Recommendation, are supported, but some of the more complex aspects, such as file uploading, are not.
Presentation	Many of the deprecated presentation elements, such as <center>, <font>, and <b> are not supported, in favor of the use of style sheets.

continues

(Continued)

EXCLUSION	DESCRIPTION
`<script>` and `<noscript>`	Due to processing power and memory limitations, the embedding of scripting languages is not supported.
`<style>`	Due to bandwidth and caching limitations, the `<style>` element is not supported. It is still possible, however, to use external style sheets using the `<link>` element.
Tables	Basic tables, as defined by the Modularization of XHTML Recommendation, are supported, but some of the more complex aspects, such as nesting, are not.

Keep in mind that these limitations are necessary if XHTML is to serve as the foundation for markup language implementations across a wide variety of platforms and devices.

Following XHTML Basic Guidelines

Like XHTML, Basic requires that you follow some general rules and guidelines. These focus primarily on ensuring the conformance of documents and the supporting user agents. By adhering to these guidelines when creating your documents, you will be able to support more clients.

Conforming Documents

The material in this section will really be a review for you after having read the book to this point. First and foremost, as we've said repeatedly, your documents must conform with the XHTML DTDs, with the included entity references and modules contained in the XHTML Basic schema. When you open the schema and look at the XML code, you will notice that it is nothing more than a list of modules previously defined in the Modularization of XHTML Recommendation.

Second, there must be a `<!DOCTYPE>` declaration in the document before the root element. The public identifier included in this declaration must reference the xhtml-basic10.dtd DTD found using its Formal Public Identifier (FPI). The following shows how this should look:

```
<!DOCTYPE html PUBLIC "-//W3C//DTD XHTML Basic 1.0//EN"
          "http://www.w3.org/TR/xhtml-basic/xhtml-basic10.dtd">
```

The root element of the document must be `<html>`. This, of course, is the same as with XHTML 1.0. Along with this, the name of the default namespace on this root element must be the XHTML namespace name (www.w3.org/1999/xhtml), as follows:

```
<html xmlns="http://www.w3.org/1999/xhtml" xml:lang="en">
```

Finally, the DTD subset must not be used to override any parameter entities in the DTD.

Supporting User Agents

This information is actually targeted toward companies or individuals building user agents to support XHTML Basic, but it can be of value to Web developers as well, as it can point out where implementations are different, and how currently unsupported features may be made to work.

User agent conformance for XHTML Basic is the same as for XHTML 1.0, so rather than restate those rules here, we'll just highlight the most relevant ones.

- User agents must parse XHTML documents to be well formed according to the XML 1.0 Recommendation.
- If an unrecognized element is encountered, the text contained within this element must be rendered.
- If an unrecognized attribute is encountered, the attribute should be ignored.
- If an unrecognized attribute value is encountered, the attribute should be rendered with the default value.

NOTE For more information on XHTML 1.0 conformance, see www.w3.org/TR/2000/REC-xhtml1-20000126#uaconf.

Using the Basic Modules

Now it is time to get to the good stuff—the modules included with the XHTML Basic language. There are eleven of them, each containing elements we have already covered in detail in previous chapters.The purpose of this section is to demonstrate how they might be used.

Building a Structure

The first module we are going to look at is the Structure module. As you might imagine, it contains the four basic elements that all documents should have at a minimum. A representation of this module can be seen in Figure 13.1.

As you can see, this module consists of the top level <html> element, with <head> and <body> as children elements. Additionally, there is a <title> element, which is a child of the <head> element. The following is an example that contains only these elements with the corresponding <!DOCTYPE>:

```
<!DOCTYPE html PUBLIC "-//W3C//DTD XHTML Basic 1.0//EN"
          "http://www.w3.org/TR/xhtml-basic/xhtml-basic10.dtd">
<html xmlns="http://www.w3.org/1999/xhtml" xml:lang="en">
<head>
  <title>XHTML Essentials</title>
```

```
  </head>
  <body>
  </body>
  </html>
```

Adding Metainformation

Next we are going to look at the Metainformation module. It contains only the <meta> element, which is a child of the <head> element. This element is used to include metainformation, such as an author's name, document keywords, or HTTP header directives, in the document. The following builds upon our first example by including the author's name:

```
<!DOCTYPE html PUBLIC "-//W3C//DTD XHTML Basic 1.0//EN"
          "http://www.w3.org/TR/xhtml-basic/xhtml-basic10.dtd">
<html xmlns="http://www.w3.org/1999/xhtml" xml:lang="en">
<head>
  <meta name="Author" content="R. Allen Wyke" />
  <title>XHTML Essentials</title>
</head>
<body>
</body>
</html>
```

Laying a Base

Like the Metainformation module, the Base module contains only one element, in this case (<base>), which is a child element of <head>. This element is used to set the base URI of relative URIs specified in the document. So, for instance, if you included a link to /mydocs/page2.html within your document, the browser would know that /mydocs/page2.html was actually located relative to the base URI, which could have been http://www.wiley.com. This information can be used by offline browsers and user agents in general to help find absolute paths for items that contain relative paths.

> **NOTE** For those of you who are not familiar, an *absolute path* is a complete URI that includes the host and full path name, such as http://www.wiley.com/index.html. A *relative path*, on the other hand, is a path relative to the resource requested. So, just saying index.html would mean that index.html file is in the same directory as the page you currently see, and /index.html would be the index.html file at the root of the server.

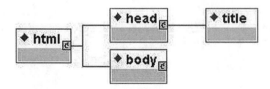

Figure 13.1 Structure module.

Still building on our example, here we include an instance of the <base> element to show that our base URI is located at http://www.wiley.com/books:

```
<!DOCTYPE html PUBLIC "-//W3C//DTD XHTML Basic 1.0//EN"
          "http://www.w3.org/TR/xhtml-basic/xhtml-basic10.dtd">
<html xmlns="http://www.w3.org/1999/xhtml" xml:lang="en">
<head>
  <meta name="Author" content="R. Allen Wyke" />
  <base href="http://www.wiley.com/books" />
  <title>XHTML Essentials</title>
</head>
<body>
</body>
</html>
```

Linking

The Link module is another with only one element: (<link>). It is a child of the <head> element. The <link> element is a very important element as we move forward in representing the relativity of documents through linking. It takes a *link type* as a value to its rel attribute. This type can define several things, such as the first page of a document, or the next or previous ones. But links are used for more.

NOTE Want more information on link types? Check out www.w3.org/TR/html4/types.html#type-links.

Links can also be used to reference external style sheets. As we mentioned earlier, many of the formatting elements present in XHTML 1.0 have been left out of XHTML Basic in favor of style sheets. After placing these style sheets in a separate file, you can use the <link> element to include them in your document.

Finally, this element can be used to reference and define additional information for search engines, such as related documents or versions written in another language. You can even specify a URL for a help document related to your document.

The sample code here illustrates each of these uses of the <link> element. The first points to the next page after our document; the second imports an external style sheet; and the third provides a pointer to the French version of our document.

```
<!DOCTYPE html PUBLIC "-//W3C//DTD XHTML Basic 1.0//EN"
          "http://www.w3.org/TR/xhtml-basic/xhtml-basic10.dtd">
<html xmlns="http://www.w3.org/1999/xhtml" xml:lang="en">
<head>
  <meta name="Author" content="R. Allen Wyke" />
  <base href="http://www.wiley.com/books" />
  <link rel="Next"  href="page2.html" />
  <link title="French" type="text/html" rel="Alternate" hreflang="fr"
        href="french.html" />
  <link href="xhtml-basic-styles.css" rel="Stylesheet"
        type="text/css" />
  <title>XHTML Essentials</title>
</head>
```

```
<body>
</body>
</html>
```

Adding Text

The Text module represents 24 elements all relevant to text description. The module includes everything from frequently occurring paragraph and heading elements to acronyms and abbreviations. Table 13.2 contains a list of these elements and a brief description of each.

For our example, we include <p>, <h1>, <h2>, <acronym>, <abbr>, <pre>, <em>, <strong>, and <address>:

```
<!DOCTYPE html PUBLIC "-//W3C//DTD XHTML Basic 1.0//EN"
          "http://www.w3.org/TR/xhtml-basic/xhtml-basic10.dtd">
<html xmlns="http://www.w3.org/1999/xhtml" xml:lang="en">
<head>
  <meta name="Author" content="R. Allen Wyke" />
  <base href="http://www.wiley.com/books" />
  <link rel="Next"  href="page2.html" />
  <link title="French" type="text/html" rel="Alternate" hreflang="fr"
        href="french.html" />
  <link href="xhtml-basic-styles.css" rel="Stylesheet"
        type="text/css" />
  <title>XHTML Essentials</title>
</head>
<body>
<h1>Company Name</h1>
<p>
  <acronym>XHTML</acronym> Developer's <abbr>Inc.</abbr>
</p>
<h2>Address</h2>
<pre>
  R. Allen Wyke
  100 Anywhere
  Sometown, NC 55555
</pre>
<p>
  <em>We <strong>love</strong> what we do!</em>
</p>
<p>
  <acronym>XHTML</acronym> Developer's <abbr>Inc.</abbr>
  is a new company focusing on XHTML development.
</p>
<address>
  Webmaster Joe
</address>
</body>
</html>
```

Figure 13.2 shows how this looks when rendered in the Netscape 6 browser.

Table 13.2   Text Module Elements

ELEMENT	DESCRIPTION
<abbr>	Abbreviated form of a word or phrase
<acronym>	Acronym for a given phrase
<address>	Information on author
<blockquote>	Long quotation
 	Forced line break
<cite>	Citation
<code>	Computer code fragment
<dfn>	Instance definition
<div>	Generic language/style container
<em>	Emphasis
<h1>	Level 1 heading
<h2>	Level 2 heading
<h3>	Level 3 heading
<h4>	Level 4 heading
<h5>	Level 5 heading
<h6>	Level 6 heading
<kbd>	Text entered by the user via a keyboard
<p>	Paragraph
<pre>	Preformatted text
<q>	Short inline quotation
<samp>	Sample program output, scripts, and so on
<span>	Generic language/style container
<strong>	Strong emphasis
<var>	Instance of a variable or program argument

Including Hypertext

The Hypertext module contains only the anchor, <a>, element. As you know by now, this element is used to link to other documents, as well as to signify linkable locations within the current document. In our example we will add a hyperlink to the Wiley Web site:

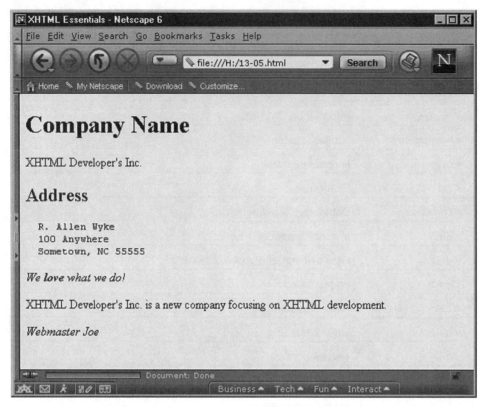

Figure 13.2 Rendering text elements in Netscape 6.

```
<p>
  Click <a href="http://www.wiley.com">here</a> if you wish to go to
  the Wiley site.
</p>
```

Making Lists

The List module, whose elements can be child elements of many other elements, has the primary purpose of describing lists: definition lists (<dl>), ordered lists (<ol>), and unordered lists (<ul>). The definition lists, whose data model is shown in Figure 13.3, can have term (<dt>) and description (<dd>) child elements, while the ordered and unordered lists can have repeating instances of list item (<li>) elements.

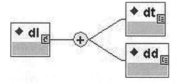

Figure 13.3 Data model of the List module.

Our code includes examples of each of these. The lists are "wrapped" with the <div> element, which can be a parent of each of these elements. The first, an ordered list, will be rendered by most user agents as numerical or alphabetical. The second, an unordered list, is commonly referred to as a bulleted list. The final list, a definition list, defines the term happy as it pertains to the context of our document.

```
<div>
  Our three step process is as follows:
  <ol>
    <li>Define the problem/issue</li>
    <li>Recommend a design</li>
    <li>Completely build the solution</li>
  </ol>
  Following these steps ensures us of the following....
  <ul>
    <li>Good understanding of the situation</li>
    <li>A mutual understanding of ownership and accountability</li>
    <li>A happy customer!</li>
  </ul>
  <dl>
    <dt>Happy</dt>
      <dd>Defines a customer is nothing short of 110% satisfied
          with our work</dd>
  </dl>
</div>
```

Developing an Image

The <img> element is the only element in the Image module. It is used to embed images within the document itself, and therefore requires a block-level parent element. The embedding action is accomplished using the href attribute to point to the URI of an image file.

In our example, the image appears at the bottom of the page within the <address> element. The image itself is the XHTML 1.0 compliance image from W3C. The complete code to do this, including the <address> block, is:

```
<address>
  Webmaster Joe
  <img src="http://www.w3.org/Icons/valid-xhtml10" height="31"
       width="88" alt="Valid XHTML 1.0!" />
</address>
```

Catching Up

Let's take a time-out, to catch up on the modules we've covered so far. Take a look at the entire example, as it currently stands:

```
<!DOCTYPE html PUBLIC "-//W3C//DTD XHTML Basic 1.0//EN"
         "http://www.w3.org/TR/xhtml-basic/xhtml-basic10.dtd">
```

```
<html xmlns="http://www.w3.org/1999/xhtml" xml:lang="en">
<head>
  <meta name="Author" content="R. Allen Wyke" />
  <base href="http://www.wiley.com/books" />
  <link rel="Next"  href="page2.html" />
  <link title="French" type="text/html" rel="Alternate" hreflang="fr"
        href="french.html" />
  <link href="xhtml-basic-styles.css" rel="Stylesheet"
        type="text/css" />
  <title>XHTML Essentials</title>
</head>
<body>
<p>
  Click <a href="http://www.wiley.com">here</a> if you wish to go
  to the Wiley site.
</p>
<h1>Company Name</h1>
<p>
  <acronym>XHTML</acronym> Developer's <abbr>Inc.</abbr>
</p>
<h2>Address</h2>
<pre>
  R. Allen Wyke
  100 Anywhere
  Sometown, NC 55555
</pre>
<p>
  <em>We <strong>love</strong> what we do!</em>
</p>
<div>Our three step process is as follows:
  <ol>
    <li>Define the problem/issue</li>
    <li>Recommend a design</li>
    <li>Completely build the solution</li>
  </ol>
  Following these steps ensure us of the following....
  <ul>
    <li>Good understanding of the situation</li>
    <li>A mutual understanding of ownership and accountability</li>
    <li>A happy customer!</li>
  </ul>
  <dl>
    <dt>Happy</dt>
      <dd>Defines a customer is nothing short of 110% satisfied
          with our work</dd>
  </dl>
</div>
<p>
  <acronym>XHTML</acronym> Developer's <abbr>Inc.</abbr>
  is a new company focusing on XHTML development.
</p>
<address>
```

```
   Webmaster Joe
   <img src="http://www.w3.org/Icons/valid-xhtml10" height="31"
        width="88" alt="Valid XHTML 1.0!" />
</address>
</body>
</html>
```

Embedding Objects

Due to device limitations, most current user agents on small Web appliances are unable to process external programs and objects. Perhaps in anticipation of future capabilities, XHTML Basic makes it possible to embed these objects in your document. Basic includes the <object> and <param> elements, which are used to embed, for example, ActiveX controls or Java applets within your documents. The <param> element is used to define parameters that these objects may need.

Because these objects can be very specific to the user agent and platform in which they are rendered, our example does not include these tags. However, you can see from the following code how they might be used. Here we have specified a Java applet, passing it a parameter named "color" with a value of "red":

```
<!DOCTYPE html PUBLIC "-//W3C//DTD XHTML Basic 1.0//EN"
          "http://www.w3.org/TR/xhtml-basic/xhtml-basic10.dtd">
<html xmlns="http://www.w3.org/1999/xhtml" xml:lang="en">
<head>
  <title>XHTML Essentials</title>
</head>
<body>
<p>
  <object codetype="application/java-archive"
          classid="java.program.start">
    <param name="color" value="red" />
  </object>
</p>
</body>
</html>
```

Setting Basic Tables

Including tables in documents has always required a more complex set of content descriptors. For this reason, in the Modularization of XHTML Recommendation, tables have been broken into two modules; XHTML Basic includes the Basic Tables module, whose data model can be seen in Figure 13.4. It is made up of the <table> parent element, which contains <caption> and <tr> (table row) child elements. The table row child element can contain instances of table headings (<th>) and table data (<td>).

In our example we create one of these basic tables, with a caption that states that the table contains our hours of operation. In the first row, we use table headings, which are often rendered in bold text in Web browsers, to name our two columns. Next is a Monday-Friday row, followed by a Saturday-Sunday row. The complete code looks like this:

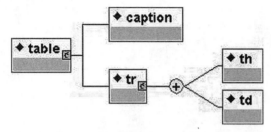

Figure 13.4 Basic Tables module data model.

```
<table>
  <caption>Hours of operation</caption>
  <tr>
    <th>Day</th>
    <th>Hours</th>
  </tr>
  <tr>
    <td>Monday - Friday</td>
    <td>8:00am - 5:00pm</td>
  </tr>
  <tr>
    <td>Saturday - Sunday</td>
    <td>9:00am - 1:00pm</td>
  </tr>
</table>
```

Designing Basic Forms

The Basic Forms module completes the definition of XHTML Basic. Forms, like tables, can be very complex within XHTML documents; for this reason, XHTML Basic only imports the Basic Forms module. Like the Basic Table module, it contains a reduced number of child elements and functionality, all of which are described in Table 13.3.

Table 13.3 Basic Forms Module Elements

ELEMENT	DESCRIPTION
<form>	Interactive form
<input>	Form control used to create a variety of form elements, through the use of the type attribute
<label>	Form field label text
<option>	Selectable choice
<select>	Option selector
<textarea>	Multiline text field

In our form example, we include a pull-down menu using a combination of <select> and <option> elements, a text area, and an input button for submitting the form. The final, completed code looks like the following:

```
<!DOCTYPE html PUBLIC "-//W3C//DTD XHTML Basic 1.0//EN"
         "http://www.w3.org/TR/xhtml-basic/xhtml-basic10.dtd">
<html xmlns="http://www.w3.org/1999/xhtml" xml:lang="en">
<head>
  <meta name="Author" content="R. Allen Wyke" />
  <base href="http://www.wiley.com/books" />
  <link rel="Next"  href="page2.html" />
  <link title="French" type="text/html" rel="Alternate" hreflang="fr"
        href="french.html" />
  <link href="xhtml-basic-styles.css" rel="Stylesheet"
        type="text/css" />
  <title>XHTML Essentials</title>
</head>
<body>
<p>
Click <a href="http://www.wiley.com">here</a> if you wish to go to the
Wiley site.
</p>
<h1>Company Name</h1>
<p>
  <acronym>XHTML</acronym> Developer's <abbr>Inc.</abbr>
</p>
<h2>Address</h2>
<pre>
  R. Allen Wyke
  100 Anywhere
  Sometown, NC 55555
</pre>
<p>
  <em>We <strong>love</strong> what we do!</em>
</p>
<div>Our three step process is as follows:
  <ol>
    <li>Define the problem/issue</li>
    <li>Recommend a design</li>
    <li>Completely build the solution</li>
  </ol>
  Following these steps ensure us of the following....
  <ul>
    <li>Good understanding of the situation</li>
    <li>A mutual understanding of ownership and accountability</li>
    <li>A happy customer!</li>
  </ul>
  <dl>
    <dt>Happy</dt>
      <dd>Defines a customer is nothing short of 110% satisfied
          with our work</dd>
```

```
      </dl>
    </div>
    <p>
      <acronym>XHTML</acronym> Developer's <abbr>Inc.</abbr>
      is a new company focusing on XHTML development.
    </p>
    <table>
      <caption>Hours of operation</caption>
      <tr>
        <th>Day</th>
        <th>Hours</th>
      </tr>
      <tr>
        <td>Monday - Friday</td>
        <td>8:00am - 5:00pm</td>
      </tr>
      <tr>
        <td>Saturday - Sunday</td>
        <td>9:00am - 1:00pm</td>
      </tr>
    </table>
    <form action="null">
      <p>What kind of service are you looking for?
        <select name="service">
          <option value="consult">Consulting</option>
          <option value="design">Design</option>
          <option value="build">Implementation</option>
        </select>
        <br />
        <br />
        Do you have any additional comments?
        <br />
        <textarea name="comments" cols="100" rows="8"></textarea>
        <br />
        <input type="submit" value="Send to Server" />
      </p>
    </form>
    <address>
      Webmaster Joe
      <img src="http://www.w3.org/Icons/valid-xhtml10" height="31"
          width="88" alt="Valid XHTML 1.0!" />
    </address>
    </body>
    </html>
```

Figure 13.5 shows what it looks like in Internet Explorer 5 for the Mac.

Summary

This chapter explained XHTML Basic, from its objectives and requirements to its modules and elements. Though simple, this subset of the XHTML language and host lan-

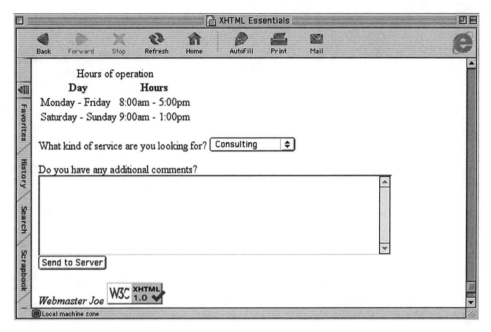

Figure 13.5   Viewing the completed XHTML Basic example in Internet Explorer 5 for the Mac.

guage of the Modularization of XHTML Recommendation is a powerful approach to defining a common language that can be "spoken" across various devices. When you create content using this limited set of elements, you almost guarantee that your users will be able to access and read your documents on most supporting devices.

In the next and last chapter, we take a peak at the future of XHTML to apprise you of some of the interesting developments you'll want to follow. We also go into greater detail on the Modularization of XHTML Recommendation.

Looking Ahead

Owing to its HTML roots, XHTML may be one of the easiest XML-based applications to learn and understand; nevertheless it presents certain challenges to Web authors:

- The syntax and overall semantics rules are stricter.
- Documents must conform more precisely to organizational structure.
- The task of migrating existing HTML content to XHTML can be time-consuming.

But the fact remains, XHTML is the way of the future, widely expanding the number of user agents and applications that can process your content. Thanks to XHTML, you can use the same document for your own as well as for other Web sites.

Exploring the Future of XHTML

A lot of interesting work is being done to improve the world of Web publishing, a great deal of which is focused on the enhancements brought by the Document Object Model (DOM), ECMAScript (aka JavaScript and JScript) and Cascading Style Sheets (CSS). But XHTML, too, is very much a part of that work. With all that XHTML offers already, we can't help but wonder what to expect from future XHTML developments. What other benefits are in the works, and how will we be able to apply them to meet our own objectives? That's a question we try to answer in this chapter. To do that, we will explore some of the ongoing efforts of the W3C HTML Working Group. Specifically, we will be looking at:

- Media Type Definition
- XHTML Modularization
- XHTML Profile Vocabulary
- Other Directions
- Next Versions

NOTE The HTML Working Group's activity statement can be found at www.w3.org/MarkUp/Activity; their road map can be found at www.w3.org/MarkUp/xhtml-roadmap. By going to both of these URLs, you will gain insight to the future of XHTML.

Standardizing a Media Type Definition

If you are not familiar with how browsers and Web servers communicate, you may not immediately understand the purpose of a Media Type Definition. Briefly, this is an effort whose goal is to create and standardize for XHTML a new MIME type, also referred to as content-type.

NOTE MIME is an acronym for Multipurpose Internet Mail Extensions. This standard was established to extend the Simple Mail Transfer Protocol (SMTP) to enable data, such as video, sound, and binary files, to be transmitted via Internet e-mail without having to be translated in ASCII format first.

A MIME type signifies the type of content being returned from the Web server to the browser. More simply, it is the information that instructs the browser how to display the data that has been returned to it. If you have ever wondered how your Windows Media, Real, or QuickTime player knows to launch when you click on an audio link, MIME is the answer. When the browser, the application that receives the initial response, "sees" in the HTTP header a content-type that it does not handle internally, it looks to match it up with a plug-in or "helper" application. At that time, the helper application or component is launched or loaded to process the data.

Or, if the browser is supposed to display the returned page in pure ASCII format, it "knows" this from the content-type header, which will indicate "text/plain." If it is supposed to render the page in HTML, then the content-type header will read "text/html."

NOTE For more information on the registration of text/html check out www.ietf.org/rfc/rfc2854.txt.

Defining a New Media Type

The release of XHTML 1.0 signaled the need for a new media type for the language. Meeting that need presented specific challenges, raised by the *modularization* of XHTML, a topic we touched on in the last chapter and which we will cover more fully in the next section. Moreover, because XHTML is an XML application, another issue was that the language must be able to process the DTDs, which may differ from page to page, referenced in the documents.

The first step in defining a new media type is to define the content-type. This is the easy part. The current proposed type is application/xhtml+xml. Complicating the matter is that, when the browser requests content from a server, it passes what's called an *Accept header directive*. This directive states the type of information that the browser is expecting. So, for example, if a form is submitted and the browser expects back an HTML page, it will send Accept: text/html. If it expects back plain text, it will pass Accept: text/plain. How does this translate in the XHTML world?

To answer that question, we must point out the various XHTML1.0 DTDs. In addition to Strict, Transitional, and Frameset, there is also XHTML Basic DTD, which we covered in the previous chapter. So what if your browser supports only the Basic DTD, and none of the others? It somehow has to alert the Web server to this limitation. According to the current Internet Draft for the XHTML Media Type Definition, this is accomplished through the use of an optional directive specified as *schema-location.*

The idea is that the browser or other user agent will pass this directive with the URL of the DTD to which it expects the response to conform. This would provide the needed mechanism for the agent to alert the server that it can process only a certain type of DTD.

> **NOTE** For more information or to check the status of the application/xhtml+xml Media Type definition, go to www.ietf.org/internet-drafts/draft-baker-xhtml-media-reg-01.txt.

Modularizing XHTML

As you learned in Chapter 13, a high-priority goal of the HTML Working Group is the modularization of the language. In short, this means breaking information into modules of logically related elements based on functionality. Theoretically, taking this approach will make it possible to extend content models to include a Web author's own tags.

> **NOTE** The importance and urgency of completing the modularization effort can be found, as we explained in the previous chapter, in the recent explosion of wireless devices in the marketplace, including cell phones, PDAs, in-vehicle navigation systems, interactive TV, kiosks, and many others. To date, we have seen a very fragmented set of methods for defining content for these devices: Some authors use their own language, others borrow from HTML, and still others support older versions of HTML, like 2.0 or 3.2.

XHTML Modularization puts an end to the confusion—and the incompatibilities. By logically dividing the XHTML language into usable groups, it will provide a means of sharing these language elements. Subsequently, it is hoped, wireless device manu-factures and user agent software companies will borrow entire modules from the language for their implementations. No longer will they have to define a table or form; the Modularization of XHTML Recommendation will have done it for them. All they'll have to do is literally select the modules they want to use and build a new DTD specific to their product, which could also include proprietary modules they built for their devices. A spreadsheet program, for instance, might only select to support the XHTML Tables and Text modules.

To give you a better idea of how XHTML modularization is being carried out, take a look at Table 14.1. It outlines the current modules and provides a brief description of what is included in them.

Table 14.1 XHTML Modularization Modules

MODULE	DESCRIPTION
Structure	Includes the main document tags: <html>, <head>, <body>, and <title>.
Text	Includes heading elements: <h1>, , <code>, <blockquote>, <pre>, and numerous others.
Hypertext	Contains only the <a> element currently. In the future, based on efforts around XLink, XPointer, and XML Base, other items may be added.
List	Contains elements relating to lists: <ol>, <ul>, and <dl>, as well as the item elements (<li>, <dd>, and <dt>) that appear within a list.
Applet	Contains the <applet> element.
Presentation	Includes <b>, <big>, <hr>, <sup>, and related elements.
Edit	Includes <ins> and <del> elements, to reflect insertions or deletions in documents.
Bidirectional	Contains the <bdo> element for use in documents that include languages that are not read left to right.
Basic Forms	Includes the <form>, <input>, <label>, <select>, <option>, and <textarea> elements.
Forms	Includes the same elements as the Basic Forms module, but adds <button>, <fieldset>, <legend>, and <optgroup>.
Basic Tables	Contains the <table>, <caption>, <tr>, <td>, and <th> elements.
Tables	Contains the same elements as the Basic Tables module, but adds <col>, <colgroup>, <tbody>, <thead>, and <tfoot>.
Image	Contains the <img> element.
Client-side Image Map	Contains the <map> and <area> elements that make it possible to implement image maps.

(Continued)

MODULE	DESCRIPTION
Server-side Image Map	Defines the ismap attribute in the <img> element that alerts the browser on the server-side to the inclusion of image maps.
Object	Defines the <object> and <param> elements, for use when embedding external components, such as a browser plug-in, in your documents.
Target	Contains the target attribute, which may appear in several elements such as <a>, <base>, and <form>.
Frame	Contains frame-related elements, such as <frame> and <frameset>.
Iframe	Contains the <iframe> inline frame element.
Intrinsic Events	Contains a list of attributes, such as onblur, onfocus, and onsubmit, that are common across many of the elements for scripting purposes.
Metainformation	Contains only the <meta> element.
Scripting	Includes the <script> and <noscript> elements, of particular use with XHTML Modularization-based languages that include support for a scripting language.
Stylesheet	Contains the <style> element, which is necessary for embedding a style sheet within a document.
Style Attribute	Contains the information that enables styles to be applied directly to an element. The properties are defined in the style attribute.
Link	Contains the <link> element, which enables the linking of, for example, external style sheets, to a document.
Base	Contains the <base> element, which makes it possible to specify base URLs for relative paths in a document.
Name	Contains the name attribute, which appears in many elements such as <a>, <img>, and <form>.
Legacy	Contains all the previous version elements and attributes, such as <center> and <font>, and the language attribute of the <script> tag.

With an eye always on the future, the HTML Working Group is also taking steps to ensure the extensibility of the XHTML Modularization effort. As part of the XML Schema support, they provide a means for creating and adding new elements new attributes as well.

> **NOTE** For more information on the Modularization of XHTML
> Recommendation, check out www.w3.org/TR/xhtml-modularization.

Learning the XHTML Profile Vocabulary

One of the major challenges of transmitting any kind of data is making sure that the recipient can handle the information. Even in today's browsers, one will support a specific tag or element, and another one may not. And of course, the older browsers, like Navigator 2 and Internet Explorer 3, have all kinds of differences.

To "clean up the language," as it were, another W3C HTML Working Group effort, the XHTML Profile Vocabulary, is to define a framework for content negotiation so that user agents and/or devices can, when a request for content is made, pass a *profile.* This profile would contain information about its capabilities. For instance, if the device is unable to handle tables, this information will be contained in its profile so that the server processing its request, if capable, can modify or transform the content being returned so that no tables are included. And now there is XSLT (Extensible Stylesheet Language Transformations), a Recommendation that provides functionality to transform content from one language, like XML, into another, like XHTML or WML (Wireless Markup Language).

Currently, the XHTML Profile Vocabulary is in a requirements-collection stage, so it will be a while before we can expect a full Recommendation. A sample of what it will include is, however, available in a related Note that has been released, which describes similar functionality and is geared to the wireless community. The Composite Capability/Preference Profiles (CC/PP) Note is intended to extend the existing RDF (Resource Description Format) to allow mobile phones and other devices to pass their capabilities back and forth during requests.

> **NOTE** For more information on the XHTML Profile Vocabulary, check out the
> current requirements document at www.w3.org/TR/xhtml-prof-req. For more
> information on CC/PP, go to www.w3.org/TR/NOTE-CCPP.

Going in Other Directions

In addition to the uses for the language we've described throughout this book, the XHTML 1.0 Recommendation, coupled with the Modularization and Document Profile efforts, emerges as a powerful platform for creating new languages. Case in point is the Wireless Markup Language, WML.

WML 2.0

The 1.x versions of the WML contained its own elements—was, essentially, a separate language. But beginning with version 2.0, WML will be implemented as a new module according to the rules governing XHTML Modularization. This means WML will inherit the core XHTML modules needed to define content and will define its own module extension specific to the WAP (Wireless Application Protocol) environment.

NOTE If you want more information on WAP and WML, visit the official WAP Forum site at www.wapforum.org.

New Versions

As you might imagine, the Working Group is also focusing on the next versions of XHTML, for which they are planning a variety of new features. Let's take a quick peak at what is in XHTML 1.1, and the next full version, XHTML 2.0.

XHTML 1.1

The primary focus of XHTML 1.1, which just became a formal Recommendation, removes all deprecated features of HTML 4.01 and XHTML 1.0. The idea is simple: to provide a markup language that is strong in structure, but completely relies on style sheets for presentation. Table 14.2 provides a complete list of how this shakes out.

Table 14.2 Early-Version Elements and Attributes Removed from XHTML 1.1

ELEMENT	CHANGE
ALL	The lang attribute has been removed from all elements.
a	The following attributes have been removed: accesskey, name, tabindex, and target.
area	The target attribute has been removed.
base	This element has been removed.
basefont	This element has been removed.
body	The following attributes have been removed: background, bgcolor, text, link, vlink, and alink.
br	The clear attribute has been removed.
caption	The align attribute has been removed.
center	This element has been removed.
div	The align attribute has been removed.
font	This element has been removed.
frame	This element has been removed.
frameset	This element has been removed.
h1	The align has been removed.
h2	The align has been removed.

continues

(Continued)

ELEMENT	CHANGE
h3	The align has been removed.
h4	The align has been removed.
h5	The align has been removed.
h6	The align has been removed.
hr	The following attributes have been removed: align, noshade, size, and width.
iframe	This element has been removed.
img	The following attributes have been removed: align, border, hspace, and vspace.
input	The align has been removed.
isindex	This element has been removed.
legend	The align has been removed.
li	The following attributes have been removed: type and value.
link	The target has been removed.
map	The name has been removed.
menu	This element has been removed.
noframes	This element has been removed.
object	This element has been removed.
ol	The following attributes have been removed: compact, start, and type.
p	The align has been removed.
pre	The width has been removed.
s	This element has been removed.
script	The language has been removed.
strike	This element has been removed.
table	The following attributes have been removed: align and bgcolor.
td	The following attributes have been removed: bgcolor, height, nowrap, and width.
th	The following attributes have been removed: bgcolor, height, nowrap, and width.

continues

(Continued)

ELEMENT	CHANGE
tr	The bgcolor has been removed.
u	This element has been removed.
ul	The following attributes have been removed: compact and type.

In addition to the changes listed here, we want to point out one other major difference in the way XHTML 1.1 efforts are implemented. They are defined in the Modularization of XHTML Recommendation. Within version 1.1, you will find the following abstract modules we defined in Table 14.1: Applet, Basic BDO, Edit, Forms, Hypertext, Image, Image Map, Intrinsic Events, Metainformation, Link, List, Presentation, Structure, Tables, Text, Scripting, and Stylesheet.

One additional module, the Ruby Annotation module, is contained in XHTML 1.1. "Ruby" refers to short runs of text alongside base text, typically found in East Asian documents, to indicate pronunciation or to provide a short annotation. The Ruby Annotation module is the result of the attempt to define a markup for this text. You can obtain more information on Ruby Annotation at www.w3.org/TR/ruby.

NOTE To access more information on XHTML 1.1, check out www.w3.org/TR/xhtml11.

XHTML 2.0

At the time of this writing there are no drafts for XHTML 2.0; to date, only a few comments on what it will contain have been posted to the HTML Working Group's Roadmap. Of course, this means things could—and probably will—change; nevertheless, it offers insight into what we can expect to see in the final Recommendation.

XHTML 2.0, whose functionality is expected to remain similar to, or be a superset of 1.1, may be altered semantically and syntactically primarily to conform with the requirements of other and related XML standards, such as XLink, XPointer, XML Base, XForms, and XML Schema. The objective of these changes is to ensure the new XHTML version can be supported by XML user agents and devices, without having to know previous HTML semantics. These semantics would include linking, image maps, and forms. Version 2.0 is expected to require new modules or revisions to existing modules.

By enforcing what some may regard as restrictions, the W3C HTML Working Group is actually freeing the XHTML language from its fragmented past. XHTML 2.0 will mark the convergence of the old and the new, honoring the old-school Web publishing world and at the same time accelerating the momentum of XML-related standards.

Conclusion

Together we've covered a lot of material in this book: We've explored XHTML, touched on some design issues, and delved into some related topics. We've talked about the fundamentals of creating XHTML documents—how to format and style them and how to script them—and we have gone into detail on such items as tables, forms, and events. To conclude, we have pointed you in the right direction for tracking future enhancements to the world of XHTML.

Now it's time for you to begin publishing XHTML documents, to apply the knowledge that you have learned in these pages, all the while following the recommended practices to which you've been exposed. While you work, remember that XHTML is more than just a markup language for Web browsing; it is in fact an XML application, and with that comes an extremely flexible and useful architecture for disseminating information to a variety of people and/or applications and in a variety of ways.

XHTML Element Quick Reference

Throughout this book, we have explored XHTML, a truly effective markup language; along the way, we taught you how to create documents and showed you some advanced scripting and styling techniques. But no XHTML book would be complete without a quick reference.

Our objective in this appendix is simple: to provide you with information that does the following:

- Provides the name of the XHTML elements.

- Provides information on the type of element (empty, or not).

- Gives you a description of the element's use.

As we mentioned in the last chapter, XHTML 1.1 no longer includes support for deprecated elements. For this reason, this appendix contains two tables: Table A.1 includes current and active elements; Table A.2 includes deprecated elements, which you can expect to go by the wayside.

Table A.1 Active Elements

ELEMENT	TYPE	DESCRIPTION
<a>	Nonempty	Anchor: Used to specify a link to another location, or location within the current content that can be linked to.
<abbr>	Nonempty	Abbreviated form of a word or phrase.
<acronym>	Nonempty	Acronym for a given phrase.
<address>	Nonempty	Information on author.
<area>	Empty	Client-side image map area.
<b>	Nonempty	Bold text style.
<base>	Empty	Document's base URI for relative paths.
<bdo>	Nonempty	I18N BiDi override.
<big>	Nonempty	Large text style.
<blockquote>	Nonempty	Lengthy quotation.
<body>	Nonempty	Document body.
 	Empty	Forced line break.
<button>	Nonempty	Pushbutton.
<caption>	Nonempty	Table caption.
<cite>	Nonempty	Citation.
<code>	Nonempty	Computer code fragment.
<col>	Empty	Table column.
<colgroup>	Nonempty	Table column group.
<dd>	Nonempty	Definition description.
<del>	Nonempty	Deleted text.
<dfn>	Nonempty	Instance definition.
<div>	Nonempty	Generic language/style container.
<dl>	Nonempty	Definition list.
<dt>	Nonempty	Definition term.
<em>	Nonempty	Emphasis.
<fieldset>	Nonempty	Form control group.
<form>	Nonempty	Interactive form.
<frame>	Empty	Subwindow.
<frameset>	Nonempty	Window subdivision.

(Continued)

ELEMENT	TYPE	DESCRIPTION
\<h1>	Nonempty	Level 1 heading.
\<h2>	Nonempty	Level 2 heading.
\<h3>	Nonempty	Level 3 heading.
\<h4>	Nonempty	Level 4 heading.
\<h5>	Nonempty	Level 5 heading.
\<h6>	Nonempty	Level 6 heading.
\<head>	Nonempty	Document head.
\<hr>	Empty	Horizontal rule.
\<html>	Nonempty	XHTML document root element.
\<i>	Nonempty	Italic text style.
\<iframe>	Nonempty	Inline frame.
\<img>	Empty	Embedded image
\<input>	Empty	Form control that can, through the use of the type attribute, be used to create a variety of form elements.
\<ins>	Nonempty	Inserted text.
\<kbd>	Nonempty	Text to be entered by the user via a keyboard.
\<label>	Nonempty	Form field label text.
\<legend>	Nonempty	Fieldset legend.
\<li>	Nonempty	List item.
\<link>	Empty	A media-independent link.
\<map>	Nonempty	Client-side image map.
\<meta>	Empty	Generic meta information.
\<noframes>	Nonempty	Alternate content for nonframe-supporting user agents.
\<noscript>	Nonempty	Alternate content for nonscript-supporting user agents.
\<object>	Nonempty	Generic embedded object.
\<ol>	Nonempty	Ordered list.
\<optgroup>	Nonempty	Option group.
\<option>	Nonempty	Selectable choice.

continues

(Continued)

ELEMENT	TYPE	DESCRIPTION
<p>	Nonempty	Paragraph.
<param>	Empty	Named property value.
<pre>	Nonempty	Preformatted text.
<q>	Nonempty	Short inline quotation.
<samp>	Nonempty	Sample program output, scripts, etc.
<script>	Nonempty	Script statements.
<select>	Nonempty	Option selector.
<small>	Nonempty	Small text style.
<span>	Nonempty	Generic language/style container.
<strong>	Nonempty	Strong emphasis.
<style>	Nonempty	Style info.
<sub>	Nonempty	Subscript.
<sup>	Nonempty	Superscript.
<table>	Nonempty	Table.
<tbody>	Nonempty	Table body.
<td>	Nonempty	Table data cell.
<textarea>	Nonempty	Multiline text field.
<tfoot>	Nonempty	Table footer.
<th>	Nonempty	Table header cell.
<thead>	Nonempty	Table header.
<title>	Nonempty	Document title.
<tr>	Nonempty	Table row.
<tt>	Nonempty	Teletype or monospaced text style.
<ul>	Nonempty	Unordered list.
<var>	Nonempty	Instance of a variable or program argument.

Table A.2 Deprecated Elements

ELEMENT	TYPE	DESCRIPTION
<applet>	Nonempty	Java applet.

(Continued)

ELEMENT	TYPE	DESCRIPTION
\<basefont\>	Empty	Base font size.
\<center\>	Nonempty	Shorthand for \<div align="center"\>.
\<dir\>	Nonempty	Directory list .
\<font\>	Nonempty	Local change to font.
\<menu\>	Nonempty	Menu list.
\<isindex\>	Empty	Single line prompt.
\<s\>	Nonempty	Strikethrough text style.
\<strike\>	Nonempty	Strikethrough text.
\<u\>	Nonempty	Underlined text style.

Resources

It is fitting that XHTML should serve as the markup language for its greatest resource—the Internet. Using this simple approach, we can be catapulted directly to the source of all our information needs. We no longer have to search through hundreds of magazines, books, newspapers, or other periodicals to find what we need to know; instead, using a few simple keywords and our favorite search engine or site, we can access anything we want—and much more.

In this appendix, we share with you several of our favorite resources. Table B.1 points to standards; Table B.2 lists helpful implementation and information sites; and Table B.3 includes a list of tools we often work with.

Table B.1 Standards

STANDARD	URL
CSS Level 1	www.w3.org/TR/REC-CSS1
CSS Level 2	www.w3.org/TR/REC-CSS2
DOM Level 1	www.w3.org/TR/REC-DOM-Level-1
DOM Level 2 Core	www.w3.org/TR/DOM-Level-2-Core
DOM Level 2 Style	www.w3.org/TR/DOM-Level-2-Style

continues

(Continued)

STANDARD	URL
DOM Level 2 Events	www.w3.org/TR/DOM-Level-2-Events
ECMA-262 (ECMAScript)	www.ecma.ch/ecma1/STAND/ECMA-262.HTM
Modularization of XHTML Proposed Recommendation	www.w3.org/TR/xhtml-modularization
XHTML 1.0	www.w3.org/TR/xhtml1
XHTML 1.1	www.w3.org/TR/xhtml11
XHTML Events Working Draft	www.w3.org/TR/xhtml-events
XForms Working Draft	www.w3.org/TR/xforms
XML 1.0 Second Edition	www.w3.org/TR/REC-xml

Table B.2 Implementation and Information Resources

URL	DESCRIPTION
www.w3.org/MarkUp	HTML Working Group at W3C.
www.w3.org/Style/CSS	Cascading Style Sheet Working Group at W3C.
www.w3.org/DOM	Document Object Model Working Group at W3C.
http://msdn.microsoft.com/workshop/author	MSDN Online Web Workshop.
http://sites.netscape.net/ekrockhome/standards.html	Transitioning from proprietary DOMs and markup to W3CRecommendations, which includes enhancing pages that use <layer>, <ilayer>, document.layers[], and document.all to real standards.
www.mozilla.org/newlayout/faq.html	A list of supported elements in the Gecko rendering engine, put out by Mozilla.org and contained in Netscape 6.

Table B.3 Tools

TOOL	URL	DESCRIPTION
CSS Validator	http://jigsaw.w3.org/css-validator	Validates documents against the CSS Recommendation.
HTML Tidy	www.w3.org/People/Raggett/tidy	Identifies errors in an HTML document, such as missing end tags.

(Continued)

TOOL	URL	DESCRIPTION
HTML Validator	http://validator.w3 .org	Validates documents against the XHTML Recommendation.
Internet Explorer	www.microsoft.com/ windows/ie www.microsoft.com/ unix/ie www.microsoft.com/ mac/products/ie	Microsoft's very popular browser.
Macromedia Dreamweaver	www.macromedia .com/software	Incredibly powerful Web development tool for simplifying tasks such as scripting XHTML documents.
Mozilla	www.mozilla.org	Open-source effort that built the rendering engine and other functionality for Netscape 6. Supports standards and a variety of platforms.
Netscape 6	http://home.netscape .com/download	The latest and greatest browser and supporting tools from Netscape, which produced the Navigator and Communicator suites.
Opera	www.opera.com	Well-known browser alternative to the Netscape and Microsoft offerings. Based heavily on standards.

Index